Bloom's Classic Critical Views

GEORGE ELIOT

Bloom's Classic Critical Views

Alfred, Lord Tennyson
Benjamin Franklin
The Brontës
Charles Dickens
Edgar Allan Poe
Geoffrey Chaucer
George Eliot
George Gordon, Lord Byron
Henry David Thoreau
Herman Melville
Jane Austen
John Donne and the Metaphysical Poets
John Milton
Jonathan Swift
Mark Twain
Mary Shelley
Nathaniel Hawthorne
Oscar Wilde
Percy Shelley
Ralph Waldo Emerson
Robert Browning
Samuel Taylor Coleridge
Stephen Crane
Walt Whitman
William Blake
William Shakespeare
William Wordsworth

Bloom's Classic Critical Views

GEORGE ELIOT

Edited and with an Introduction by
Harold Bloom
Sterling Professor of the Humanities
Yale University

Bloom's Classic Critical Views: George Eliot

Copyright © 2009 Infobase Publishing

Introduction © 2009 by Harold Bloom

All rights reserved. No part of this publication may be reproduced or utilized in any form or by any means, electronic or mechanical, including photocopying, recording, or by any information storage or retrieval systems, without permission in writing from the publisher. For more information contact:

Bloom's Literary Criticism
An imprint of Infobase Publishing
132 West 31st Street
New York NY 10001

Library of Congress Cataloging-in-Publication Data
George Eliot / edited and with an introduction by Harold Bloom ; Juliette Atkinson, volume editor.
    p. cm. — (Bloom's classic critical views)
   Includes bibliographical references and index.
   ISBN 978-1-60413-433-9 (hardcover)
  1. Eliot, George, 1819–1880—Criticism and interpretation. I. Bloom, Harold. II. Atkinson, Juliette. III. Title. IV. Series.
   PR4688.G372 2009
   823'.8—dc22   2009001607

Bloom's Literary Criticism books are available at special discounts when purchased in bulk quantities for businesses, associations, institutions, or sales promotions. Please call our Special Sales Department in New York at (212) 967-8800 or (800) 322-8755.

You can find Bloom's Literary Criticism on the World Wide Web at http://www.chelseahouse.com

Volume editor: Juliette Atkinson
Series design by Erika K. Arroyo
Cover designed by Takeshi Takahashi
Printed in the United States of America
IBT IBT 10 9 8 7 6 5 4 3 2 1

This book is printed on acid-free paper.

All links and Web addresses were checked and verified to be correct at the time of publication. Because of the dynamic nature of the Web, some addresses and links may have changed since publication and may no longer be valid.

Contents

Series Introduction	ix
Introduction by Harold Bloom	xi
Biography	1
Personal	5
Thomas Henry Huxley (1880)	7
C. Kegan Paul "George Eliot" (1881)	8
Edith Simcox "George Eliot" (1881)	10
F.W.H. Myers "George Eliot" (1881)	11
Emily Dickinson (1883)	12
J.W. Cross (1885)	13
Henry James "George Eliot's Life" (1885)	15
Margaret Oliphant "The Life and Letters of George Eliot" (1885)	16
Thomas Adolphus Trollope (1887)	17
Grant Allen (1895)	19
May Clarissa Gillington Byron (1912)	19
William Hale White "George Eliot as I Knew Her" (1915)	21
General	25
Mary Elizabeth Braddon (1863)	26
Edward Dowden "George Eliot" (1872)	27
Edmund Clarence Stedman (1875)	30
Leslie Stephen "George Eliot" (1881)	31
Anthony Trollope (1883)	50
George Willis Cooke "The Limitations of Her Thought" (1884)	51
Charlotte Yonge (1888)	60
Oscar Browning (1890)	61
William Ernest Henley (1890)	64

George Saintsbury "Three Mid-Century Novelists" (1895)	66
Vida D. Scudder "George Eliot and the Social Conscience" (1898)	69
W. C. Brownell "George Eliot" (1900)	72
Richard Burton "George Eliot" (1909)	77
Ford Madox Ford "English Literature of Today: I" (1911)	78
Virginia Woolf "George Eliot" (1919)	80

WORKS

Scenes of Clerical Life	95
George Eliot (1857)	95
Unsigned "Scenes of Clerical Life" (1858)	97
Richard Simpson "George Eliot's Novels" (1863)	100
Oscar Browning (1890)	101
May Tomlinson "The Beginning of George Eliot's Art: A Study of Scenes of Clerical Life" (1919)	106
Adam Bede	107
Jane Welsh Carlyle (1859)	107
Charles Dickens (1859)	108
E.S. Dallas "Adam Bede" (1859)	109
George Augustus Sala "The Cant of Modern Criticism" (1867)	112
James Kenyon "George Eliot" (1901)	112
Leslie Stephen (1902)	113
The Mill on the Floss	119
Unsigned "The Mill on the Floss" (1860)	119
E.S. Dallas "The Mill on the Floss" (1860)	123
Algernon Charles Swinburne (1877)	125
John Ruskin "Fiction—Fair and Foul" (1881)	128
Leslie Stephen (1902)	130
Silas Marner	134
Unsigned "Silas Marner" (1861)	134
Henry James "The Novels of George Eliot" (1866)	137
Frederic Harrison "George Eliot" (1895)	138
Romola	140
R.H. Hutton "Romola" (1863)	140
Mathilde Blind (1883)	144
Leslie Stephen (1902)	146

Contents

Felix Holt	147
John Morley "Felix Holt" (1866)	147
Arthur Sedgwick "Felix Holt, the Radical" (1866)	151
John Hutton Balfour Browne (1907)	153
Middlemarch	154
Edith Simcox "Middlemarch" (1873)	154
Sidney Colvin "Middlemarch" (1873)	155
Henry James "Current Literature" (1873)	159
George Parsons Lathrop "Growth of the Novel" (1874)	166
Vida D. Scudder "George Eliot and the Social Conscience" (1898)	167
Daniel Deronda	170
George Saintsbury "Daniel Deronda" (1876)	170
R.E. Francillon "George Eliot's First Romance" (1876)	175
Henry James "Daniel Deronda: A Conversation" (1876)	177
Joseph Jacobs "Mordecai: A Protest Against the Critics" (1877)	193
Oliver Elton "George Eliot and Anthony Trollope" (1920)	201
Chronology	205
Index	207

Series Introduction

Bloom's Classic Critical Views is a new series presenting a selection of the most important older literary criticism on the greatest authors commonly read in high school and college classes today. Unlike the Bloom's Modern Critical Views series, which for more than 20 years has provided the best contemporary criticism on great authors, Bloom's Classic Critical Views attempts to present the authors in the context of their time and to provide criticism that has proved over the years to be the most valuable to readers and writers. Selections range from contemporary reviews in popular magazines, which demonstrate how a work was received in its own era, to profound essays by some of the strongest critics in the British and American tradition, including Henry James, G.K. Chesterton, Matthew Arnold, and many more.

Some of the critical essays and extracts presented here have appeared previously in other titles edited by Harold Bloom, such as the New Moulton's Library of Literary Criticism. Other selections appear here for the first time in any book by this publisher. All were selected under Harold Bloom's guidance.

In addition, each volume in this series contains a series of essays by a contemporary expert, who comments on the most important critical selections, putting them in context and suggesting how they might be used by a student writer to influence his or her own writing. This series is intended above all for students, to help them think more deeply and write more powerfully about great writers and their works.

Introduction by Harold Bloom

Any informed and mature critical view will regard George Eliot (Mary Ann Evans) as one of the central novelists of the English language. Before her there came Samuel Richardson, Henry Fielding, and Jane Austen. She stands with her strongest contemporaries: Charles Dickens, W.M. Thackeray, the Brontë sisters, Anthony Trollope, Thomas Hardy. Later come Joseph Conrad, E.M. Forster, Virginia Woolf, James Joyce, D.H. Lawrence, and Samuel Beckett. Her American peers include Hawthorne, Melville, Mark Twain, Henry James, Edith Wharton, Willa Cather, and Faulkner. Of those two dozen masters of fiction, you can argue (as I would) that only Richardson, Austen, Dickens, Joyce, and Henry James could create persons on her levels of scale, depth, and complexity. With them, she made characters of almost Shakespearean tremors of reality. Of European rivals in the wake of Cervantes I could suggest that Stendahl, Balzac, Flaubert, Dostoevsky, Tolstoy, and Proust round out a dozen with the English language novelists I have specified. George Eliot can be read side by side with those other great Europeans without diminishment.

I recall writing that George Eliot's particular gift was to make ghostlier the demarcations between moral renunciation and aesthetic power. In a curious way, that renders her invulnerable to parody. Her deepest affinities as a moral psychologist were with Freud, though my comparison would have been rejected by the founder of psychoanalysis. Both sages—novelist and essayist—chronicled our discontent with civilization and its high costs. Eliot's masterpiece, *Middlemarch*, is the supreme instance of achieved moral authority in the history of the novel. Trollope, a friend, and admirer of Eliot's fiction, cautioned her against firing over the heads of her readers, but that was asking her not to be George Eliot.

A more serious critique was provided by the rich ambivalence of Henry James, whose anxiety of influence pervades his remarks on *Middlemarch*. He sees accurately that the conveyed reality of Dorothea's spiritual quality is "the great achievement of the book." One wants James to develop this critical truth, but he swerves aside too readily in complaining that no one else in the book is Dorothea's equal. Yet that will be the art of Henry James in his major phase; Isabel Archer, Millie Theale, Maggie Verver stand as towers in the landscapes of their books. When James praises *Middlemarch* most fully, he says it sets a limit to the old-fashioned English novel, and clearly he hints his intention of changing the fashion.

I would revise that only by remarking that *Middlemarch*, in 1873, marks the beginning of the end of the traditional novel of social morality. The comic visions of Joyce, the tragic ambitions of Lawrence, the fantasias of Woolf all enter the domain of Freudian perplexities. George Eliot tempered her imaginative sympathies with the critical thought of the Age of Darwin. It fascinates me to ponder what she would have done thirty years later on.

BIOGRAPHY

GEORGE ELIOT
(1819–1880)

George Eliot was born Mary Ann (later Marian) Evans in Arbury, Warwickshire, on November 22, 1819. The daughter of an agent for an estate in Warwickshire, she attended schools in Griff, Attleborough, Nuneaton, and Coventry between 1824 and 1835. While at school she converted to Evangelicalism, which she later renounced under the influence of Charles Bray, a freethinking manufacturer she first met in 1841. Still strongly attracted by religious concepts of love and duty, in 1844 she began a translation of Strauss's *Das Leben Jesu*, which appeared anonymously in 1846 as *The Life of Jesus, Critically Examined*.

In 1849, Evans made her first trip to continental Europe, accompanied by the Brays. After returning to England in 1850, she met John Chapman, who had published her translation of Strauss, and in 1851 she became a paying guest in the Chapmans' London home, where her intimate relationship with the married Chapman proved an embarrassment. In that same year, Chapman purchased the *Westminster Review*, which Evans helped edit and to which she contributed regularly. In 1854, Evans published a translation of Feuerbach's *The Essence of Christianity*. By this time she had entered into a relationship with George Henry Lewes, a married man, with whom she began living after they returned from a trip to Germany in 1854, the first of many trips to continental Europe they would make together over the next twenty years.

Having begun to write fiction only a year earlier, in 1857 Evans published "The Sad Fortunes of the Rev. Amos Barton," the first of the *Scenes of Clerical Life*. It appeared in *Blackwood's Edinburgh Magazine* under the pseudonym "George Eliot," as did two other pieces, "Mr. Gilfil's Love-Story" and "Janet's Repentance," published later that same year and reprinted in volume form in 1858. These works were well received, and there was much speculation as to the identity of the author, who was widely believed to be a clergyman or a clergyman's wife. In 1859, Evans published *Adam Bede*, which immediately established her as a leading novelist. It was followed by *The Mill on the Floss* in 1860 and *Silas Marner* in 1861. In 1860, Evans visited Florence, where she conceived the idea for *Romola* (1863), a novel that began to appear in serial form in *Cornhill Magazine* in 1862. *Felix Holt* was published in 1866 and was followed in 1868 by *The Spanish Gypsy*, a dramatic poem inspired by the works of Tintoretto. *Middlemarch* appeared in installments (1871–72), as did *Daniel Deronda*, her last great novel (1874–76). *The Legend of Jubal and Other Poems* was published in 1874 and *Impressions of Theophrastus Such* in 1879.

In November 1878, George Henry Lewes died of cancer. Almost two years later, in May 1880, Evans married John Walter Cross, a man twenty years her junior whom she had met in Rome and who had subsequently become her financial adviser. Shortly afterward, she became ill and died on December 22, 1880. At the time of her death, George Eliot was widely regarded as the greatest contemporary English novelist; soon after, however, her reputation began to decline only to be revived by subsequent generations of critics and readers once again attuned to her prodigious talent.

PERSONAL

❖

George Eliot wrote that "just my works and the order in which they appeared is what the part of the public which cares about me may most usefully know" (*GE Letters*, VI: 67–68). Eliot's contemporaries and later readers did not share her wariness of biographical speculation, as the following extracts show. Three dominant concerns emerge from the letters and essays included here: Eliot's religious convictions, her relationship with George Henry Lewes, and, as she became increasingly famous, the manner in which she was celebrated.

When George Eliot was revealed to be Marian (or Mary Ann) Evans, it became known that the author of *Scenes of Clerical Life* and *Adam Bede* was an agnostic. Critics were often surprised at the sympathy with which an author holding such views depicted religious faith. Before refusing to attend church in 1842, Eliot had adopted strict religious views, which included a suspicion of fiction. Eliot never categorically rejected the Church and even expressed a lingering sympathy for the Anglican faith that, as she wrote, had formed such a significant portion of her "earliest associations and most poetic memories" (*GE Letters*, IV: 214). Eliot's ambiguous stance toward religious faith perplexed many of her readers. In the following extracts, Thomas Huxley and Henry James demonstrate a particular interest in her faith or lack of it. The first reflects on her antagonism to "Christian theory in regard to dogma," while the second considers how Eliot's youthful views may have continued to influence her. Both writers provide a useful introduction to many of the essays included in this volume: a rapid glance at the biographies of her critics reveals that a startling number of the men of letters who responded to her works had experienced a similar crisis of faith.

Far more controversial than Eliot's agnosticism, however, was her relationship with George Henry Lewes (1817–78). The pair met in 1851, when Eliot was working, anonymously, as the editor of John Chapman's *Westminster Review*. Lewes, who was a frequent contributor to the *Review*, had already published his popular *Biographical History of Philosophy* (1846) and would later publish works of philosophy and natural science, often with Eliot's help. Lewes was married to Agnes, who was herself in a relationship with the artist Thorton Leigh Hunt (1810–73). Eliot and Lewes became intimate around 1853, and the scandalous news of their relationship gradually became public. Eliot did not set out to court controversy: she considered the relationship as a marriage in all but name and regularly signed documents and dedications as Marian Lewes. Lewes brought her some much-needed happiness and self-esteem: Eliot had often feared that she would never find a companion, in no small part due to a sense of her personal unattractiveness, which Thomas Trollope comments on in this section. Lewes also acted as a valuable intermediary between Eliot and her publishers, ensuring that the novelist received proper encouragement and reward for her work. The reaction of many of Eliot's friends and relations upon hearing of the relationship was to cut her off. Few men initially dared to visit the Leweses at home and even fewer women. It was not until Eliot was firmly established as one of the country's leading novelists that the public showed signs of relenting, and their London home began to fill with guests.

Biographers and critics could not ignore the key relationship in Eliot's life: the extracts are replete with allusions to Eliot's chosen lifestyle. Huxley echoes a common view that her life displayed an "antagonism to Christian practice in regard to marriage," though some, such as Edith Simcox, held a warm appreciation of the couple's loving intimacy. In between lies the more curious reaction of the novelist Margaret Oliphant, who contemplates the gradual public tolerance of Eliot's life with a mixture of disapproval and envy. In an intriguing shift of public opinion, later writers frequently complained that Eliot had been too timid in her attitude and should have flaunted her unmarried status for the feminist cause, as the extract by Grant Allen indicates. William Hale White responds to such accusations with a strong statement about Eliot's bold intellectual and personal choices.

It is hardly surprising, given the intensity of the personal attacks made against her, that Eliot did not advertise what was already a courageous choice. Eliot's partial retreat from society, however, gave birth to a public conception of her which is the third major theme running through the extracts in this section: the idea of her distant, sibyl-like nature. Hints of this surfaced during Eliot's lifetime, but the idea veritably took hold after her death. C. Kegan Paul paints a picture of a more relaxed George

Eliot than was frequently the case but nevertheless dwells on her "wise," "weighty," and "epigrammatic" conversational style. The extract by F.W.H. Myers—possibly the most famous description of Eliot—carries this to an almost ludicrous level. The passage was responsible for perpetuating the myth that the novelist was pompous and humorless and caused considerable damage to Eliot's reputation. Myer's influence is evident in May Clarissa Gillington Byron's conception of an overly intellectual Eliot further isolated from the realm of common mortals by the excessive hero worship of her admirers. The man who Eliot married only a few months before her death, John Walter Cross, shares with Myers the responsibility for consolidating this image. In his three-volume biography of his wife, Cross aimed to demonstrate that Eliot, despite her unconventional choices, was profoundly respectable. Cross's ruthless editorial decisions meant that Eliot, who was never the most sparkling of letter writers, emerged from the work as a dour figure indeed. This is the image that endured throughout the early twentieth century, when Eliot seemed an ideal target for iconoclastic modernist critics and biographers, a view that has been qualified only comparatively recently.

THOMAS HENRY HUXLEY (1880)

Thomas Henry Huxley (1825–95) was an English biologist who earned the nickname "Darwin's bulldog" for his strong support of evolutionary views. Huxley was introduced to the staff of the *Westminster Review* by the philosopher and sociologist Herbert Spencer (1820–1903), who Eliot fell in love with before her relationship with Lewes. Like Eliot, Huxley experienced strong religious doubts and, in 1869, he coined the word *agnostic* to describe his views. Though they remained on friendly terms, Huxley's relationship with Eliot became strained in 1854 after he published a negative review in the *Westminster Review* of Lewes's *Comte's Philosophy of the Sciences* (1853).

After George Eliot's death, efforts were made to secure a plot for her in Poets' Corner in Westminster Abbey, where she could join such luminaries as Charles Dickens and Alfred Tennyson. Herbert Spencer played a leading role in gathering signatures to petition the dean. However, Eliot's agnosticism, together with the life she had shared with Lewes, made such a burial deeply problematic. The arguments against this proposal expressed by Huxley in this extract were hard to counter and eventually prevailed. Instead, Eliot was buried in Highgate Cemetery, near Lewes; a century after her death, a memorial tablet was laid in Poets' Corner.

However much I may lament the circumstance, Westminster Abbey is a Christian Church and not a Pantheon, and the Dean thereof is officially a Christian priest, and we ask him to bestow exceptional Christian honours by this burial in the Abbey. George Eliot is known not only as a great writer, but as a person whose life and opinions were in notorious antagonism to Christian practice in regard to marriage, and Christian theory in regard to dogma. How am I to tell the Dean that I think he ought to read over the body of a person who did not repent of what the Church considers moral sin, a service not one solitary proposition in which she would have accepted for truth while she was alive? How am I to urge him to do that which, if I were in his place, I should most emphatically refuse to do?

You tell me that Mrs. Cross wished for the funeral in the Abbey. While I desire to entertain the greatest respect for her wishes, I am very sorry to hear it. I do not understand the feeling which could create such a desire on any personal grounds, save those of affection, and the natural yearning to be near even in death to those whom we have loved. And on public grounds the wish is still less intelligible to me. One cannot eat one's cake and have it too. Those who elect to be free in thought and deed must not hanker after the rewards, if they are to be so called, which the world offers to those who put up with its fetters.

Thus, however I look at the proposal it seems to me to be a profound mistake, and I can have nothing to do with it.

—Thomas Henry Huxley, letter to Herbert Spencer, December 27, 1880, cited in Leonard Huxley, *Life and Letters of Thomas Henry Huxley*, vol. 2, 1900, p. 19.

C. Kegan Paul "George Eliot" (1881)

Charles Kegan Paul (1828–1902) was an English publisher and writer. During his initial career in the Church, he used his association with the Christian socialist movement to carry out a variety of reforms. Theological disagreements led him to seek a new career in publishing. He founded the publishing house C. Kegan Paul & Co. in 1877 after taking over Henry Samuel King's business. Authors published by the firm include Thomas Hardy and Robert Louis Stevenson, though not Eliot. Paul shared with her a strong interest in Comtist positivism, a philosophy that asserts that knowledge is derived solely from sensory experience and the strictures of the scientific method. They also shared an interest in Mary Wollstonecraft: Paul edited her letters and wrote extensively about her, while Eliot felt a certain kinship with a woman who, like her, had made unconventional choices. Paul's interest in Wollstonecraft suggests that he looked on Eliot's lifestyle with an open mind.

Visitors to the Priory, the Lewes's home in St. John's Wood, included Charles Dickens, Anthony Trollope, and the artist Edward Burne-Jones. As the extract suggests, Eliot could talk and socialize freely there. Her awareness that many people disapproved of, or even condemned, her personal choices meant that she rarely returned the visits she received. It was partly this sensitivity to gossip and partly the anxiety she felt each time one of her novels appeared that prompted Eliot to regularly abandon London with Lewes. Germany was a favorite destination of the pair, who enjoyed the tolerance with which they were met there. The couple bought the home to which Paul refers, the Heights in Witley, in 1876, though they were only able to enjoy it together for two years before Lewes's death.

It is difficult for any one admitted to the great honor of friendship with either Mr. Lewes or George Eliot to speak of their home without seeming intrusive, in the same way that he would have been who, unauthorized, introduced visitors, yet something may be said to gratify a curiosity which surely is not now impertinent or ignoble. When London was full, the little drawing-room in St. John's Wood was now and then crowded to overflowing with those who were glad to give their best of conversation, of information, and sometimes of music, always to listen with eager attention to whatever their hostess might say, when all that she said was worth hearing. Without a trace of pedantry, she led the conversation to some great and lofty strain. Of herself and her works she never spoke; of the works and thoughts of others she spoke with reverence, and sometimes even too great tolerance. But those afternoons had the highest pleasure when London was empty or the day wet, and only a few friends were present, so that her conversation assumed a more sustained tone than was possible when the rooms were full of shifting groups. It was then that, without any premeditation, her sentences fell as fully formed, as wise, as weighty, as epigrammatic, as any to be found in her books. Always ready, but never rapid, her talk was not only good in itself, but it encouraged the same in others, since she was an excellent listener, and eager to hear. Yet interesting as seemed to her, as well as to those admitted to them, her afternoons in London, she was always glad to escape when summer came, either for one of the tours on the Continent in which she so delighted, or lately to the charming home she had made in Surrey. She never tired of the lovely scenery about Witley, and the great expanse of view obtainable from the tops of the many hills.

—C. Kegan Paul, "George Eliot," *Harper's New Monthly Magazine*, vol. 62, May 1881, p. 921

Edith Simcox "George Eliot" (1881)

Edith Simcox (1844–1901) was an English anthropologist, political activist, and feminist. Simcox helped to lead a cooperative shirt-manufacturing enterprise between 1875 and 1884, and she remained active in the trade union movement throughout her life. Simcox met George Eliot in 1872 and developed a strong passion for the novelist, then twenty-five years her elder, who she sometimes addressed as "mother." Though Eliot did not return her affection, the pair maintained a close friendship. Simcox's account of the relationship is given in her diary *Autobiography of a Shirt Maker*, which was published in 1998.

Edith Simcox was one of many writers who speculated on the role that Lewes had in shaping Eliot's literary career. Lewes supported her ambition to write fiction, encouraged her when depressive tendencies threatened her progress and output, and shielded her as much as possible from negative reviews. He also served as liaison to her publishers John Blackwood and George Smith. Simcox is right to stress the importance of Lewes in the development of Eliot's life as a novelist, though it is possible to question her assumption that Eliot would not have written fiction without him, as Henry James also suggested in his 1885 essay on the novelist. This extract, and Simcox's respectful use of the title "Mrs. Lewes," also shows that condemnation of Eliot's relationship with Lewes was by no means universal.

In 1854 Miss Evans found what had been wanting to her loving and generous nature since her father's death—some one "whose life would have been worse without her." In return we owe to Mr. Lewes the complete works of George Eliot, not one of which would have been written or even planned without the inspiriting influence of his constant encouragement, his obvious, unfeigned, unforced delight in her powers and success, his total freedom from we will not say jealousy—but the least inclination towards self-comparison: even more might be said, but to say more would be to quote words which were not written to be published. It is needless now to guard such statements against the misinterpretation satirised in *Middlemarch*, where we read, of Fred's and Mary's authorship, how Middlemarch satisfied itself "that there was no need to praise anybody for writing a book, because it was always done by somebody else." Mr. Lewes had written novels, and Miss Evans had translated German books; therefore when George Eliot published stories and Mr. Lewes a *Life of Goethe*, the critics of the day agreed, with the worthies of Middlemarch, that each was inspired by the other, and so the work of neither ought to count for much. But it will not be out of place to acknowledge a further obligation. It is the snare of versatile and sympathetic natures to feel almost as if they themselves were convinced by the opinions held by those with whom they sympathise for reasons they have taken pains to understand. Mrs. Lewes was conscious of a temptation to agree too readily under such circumstances, to identify herself as it were dramatically with the views she did not really share, and she acknowledged a debt of gratitude to Mr. Lewes for his scrupulous anxiety that she should not be biassed in that way by him. He was careful to guard her mental independence even against her own too great readiness to defer to another, even though that other might be himself.

—Edith Simcox, "George Eliot,"
Nineteenth Century, vol. 9, 1881, pp. 47–48

F.W.H. Myers "George Eliot" (1881)

Frederic William Henry Myers (1843–1901) was an English psychical researcher and essayist. An academic and an inspector of schools, Myers was a strong supporter of female education. Like so many of his generation, he experienced spiritual crises and fluctuated between phases of religious apathy and intense piety. Myers spent some time among Eliot's social circle but, unsettled by the agnosticism he found widely espoused there, he became increasingly interested in spiritualism and co-founded the Society for Psychical Research in 1882.

This account of Myers's encounter with George Eliot is perhaps the most famous description of the novelist. It was also one of the most damaging, setting the standard for the ways in which Eliot would be caricatured by so many early-twentieth-century writers. Myers's depiction is fair insofar as Eliot's writings confirm that she placed a strong importance on duty. Yet the overinflated language creates an image of the novelist as a humorless, self-important figure—the type of severe moralist that modernists loved to deflate. The image of the sibyl Myers invokes was also repeatedly picked up. Edmund Gosse, for example, described her as "a large, thick-set sybil, dreamy and immobile" ("George Eliot," reprinted in *Aspects and Impressions*, 1922), a phrase that Virginia Woolf went on to quote in her own 1919 evaluation of the novelist.

I remember how at Cambridge I walked with her once in the Fellows' Garden of Trinity, on an evening of rainy May; and she, stirred somewhat beyond her wont, and taking as her text the three words which had been used so often as the inspiring trumpet-call of men—the words God, Immortality, Duty—pronounced with terrible earnestness how inconceivable was the first, how unbelievable was the second, and yet how peremptory and absolute the third. Never, perhaps, have sterner accents confirmed the sovereignty of impersonal and unrecompensing Law. I listened, and night fell; her grave, majestic countenance turned towards me like a sybil's in the gloom; it was as though she withdrew from my grasp, one by one, the two scrolls of promise and left me the third scroll only, awful with inevitable fates. And when we stood at length and parted, amid that columnar circuit of forest trees, beneath the last twilight of starless skies, I seemed to be gazing, like Titus at Jerusalem, on vacant seats and empty halls—a sanctuary with no Presence to hallow it, and heaven left empty of God.

—F.W.H. Myers, "George Eliot," *The Century Magazine*, vol. 23, 1881, p. 62

Emily Dickinson (1883)

The American poet Emily Dickinson (1830–86) maintained a strong awareness of contemporary literary developments despite her reclusive lifestyle at her home in central Massachusetts. Dickinson, an avid reader of George Eliot, praised *Daniel Deronda* in particular as "that wise and tender Book I hope you have seen—It is full of sad (high) nourishment." Dickinson was greatly saddened by Eliot's death. Her depiction of Eliot here was made in response to the first full-length biography of George Eliot published by Mathilde Blind in 1883. With its emphasis on loss and emptiness, this passage is in many ways more revealing about Dickinson's ideas about herself and the place of the female artist than about Eliot. The portrayal also fed into popular notions about Eliot's gloominess.

The Life of Marian Evans had much I never knew—a doom of Fruit without the Bloom, like the Niger Fig:—

Her losses make our gains ashamed—
She bore life's empty pack

As gallantly as if the East
Were swinging at her back.
Life's empty pack is heaviest,
As every porter knows—
In vain to punish honey,
It only sweeter grows.

—Emily Dickinson, letter to
Thomas Niles, April 1883, in *Letters of
Emily Dickinson*, 1894, p. 418

J.W. Cross (1885)

George Eliot's husband, John Walter Cross (1840–1924), was a banker who first met the Leweses in Rome in 1869. Cross became a regular visitor to the Priory: he helped the couple purchase their country retreat in Surrey, taught them tennis, and was addressed by both as their "dearest nephew." After Lewes's death in 1878, the thirty-eight-year-old Cross offered the fifty-nine-year-old Eliot his practical and emotional support. George Eliot accepted his offer of marriage in 1880, eight months after his proposal. She died eight months later. Cross, who never remarried, paid homage to her memory with a three-volume biography.

Cross's biography played a crucial part in fashioning the image of the overly serious Eliot which the early twentieth century would uphold. The extract draws attention to Cross's claim that he was letting Eliot speak in her own words, a common Victorian biographical practice that consisted of reproducing large portions of diary entries or letters with little connecting narrative. Yet Cross is open about the fact that he has not left Eliot's words intact. In effect, Cross's method involved removing much of the humor and controversy in Eliot's life and writings. Readers and critics were disappointed with the result: most famously, the prime minister William Gladstone quipped that "it is not a Life at all. It is a Reticence, in three Volumes."

Another notable element of this extract is the way in which it echoes numerous nineteenth-century biographies of female writers in insisting that Eliot's greatest pleasure lay in her domestic life rather than her work. Elizabeth Gaskell's groundbreaking 1857 biography of Charlotte Brontë had set the model for lives of female authors in which "woman" and "artist" were considered almost separately. Eliot undoubtedly took great pleasure in "the joys of the hearthside" that she shared with Lewes. However, she had learned to depend somewhat less on what Cross alludes to as the "love of her friends," many of whom had turned their backs on her after she began co-habitating with Lewes. It is also clear that, though the writing of Eliot's novels often prompted bouts of depression and self-doubt in the author, she took both great joy and pride in her work.

With the materials in my hands I have endeavoured to form an *autobiography* (if the term may be permitted) of George Eliot. The life has been allowed to write itself in extracts from her letters and journals. Free from the obtrusion of any mind but her own, this method serves, I think, better than any other open to me, to show the development of her intellect and character.

In dealing with the correspondence, I have been influenced by the desire to make known the woman, as well as the author, through the presentation of her daily life.

On the intellectual side there remains little to be learnt by those who already know George Eliot's books. In the twenty volumes which she wrote and published in her lifetime, will be found her best and ripest thoughts. The letters now published throw light on another side of her nature—not less important, but hitherto unknown to the public—the side of the affections.

The intimate life was the core of the root from which sprung the fairest flowers of her inspiration. Fame came to her late in life, and, when it presented itself, was so weighted with the sense of responsibility, that it was in truth a rose with many thorns, for George Eliot had the temperament that shrinks from the position of a public character. The belief in the wide, and I may add in the beneficent, effect of her writing, was no doubt the highest happiness, the reward of the artist which she greatly cherished: but the joys of the hearthside, the delight in the love of her friends, were the supreme pleasures in her life.

By arranging all the letters and journals so as to form one connected whole, keeping the order of their dates, and with the least possible interruption of comment, I have endeavoured to combine a narrative of day-to-day life with the play of light and shade, which only letters, written in various moods, can give, and without with no portrait can be a good likeness. I do not know that the particular method in which I have treated the letters has ever been adopted before. Each letter has been pruned of everything that seemed to me irrelevant to my purpose—of everything that I thought my wife would have wished to be omitted.

—J.W. Cross, *George Eliot's Life as Related in Her Letters and Journals*, vol. 1, 1885, pp. v–vii

Henry James "George Eliot's Life" (1885)

The New York–born writer Henry James (1843–1916) first met the Leweses on May 9, 1869, when he visited the Priory with some friends. Though James encountered Eliot in chaotic circumstances (Lewes's twenty-five-year-old son, Thornie, was dying of tuberculosis), he commented to his father on how pleasant and "magnificently ugly" Eliot had appeared.

In this extract, taken from a review of Cross's 1885 biography of Eliot, James writes shrewdly about the strict views of the young George Eliot and the pleasure she took in self-renunciation, much like Maggie Tulliver in *The Mill on the Floss*. The extract picks up on the contrast between Eliot's younger and later selves, while suggesting that Eliot never fully cast off her youthful evangelical seriousness but continued to waver, like many of her characters, between conventionality and independence, conservatism and radicalism.

It was not till Marian Evans was past thirty, indeed, that she became an author by profession, and it may accordingly be supposed that her early letters are those which take us most into her confidence. This is true of those written when she was on the threshold of womanhood, which form a very full expression of her feelings at the time. The drawback here is that the feelings themselves are rather wanting in interest—one may almost say in amiability. At the age of twenty Marian Evans was a deeply religious young woman, whose faith took the form of a narrow evangelism. Religious, in a manner, she remained to the end of her life, in spite of her adoption of a scientific explanation of things; but in the year 1839 she thought it ungodly to go to concerts and read novels. . . . These first fragments of her correspondence, first glimpses of her mind, are very curious; they have nothing in common with the later ones but the deep seriousness of the tone. Serious, of course, George Eliot continued to be to the end; the sense of moral responsibility, of the sadness and difficulty of life, was the most inveterate part of her nature. But the provincial strain in the letters from which I have quoted is very marked: they reflect a meagerness and grayness of outward circumstance; have a tinge as of Dissent in a small English town, where there are brick chapels in back streets. This was only a moment in her development; but there is something touching in the contrast between such a state of mind and that of the woman before whom, at middle age, all the culture of the world unrolled itself, and towards whom fame and fortune and an activity which at the earlier period she would have thought very profane pressed with rapidity.

—Henry James, "George Eliot's Life,"
The Atlantic Monthly, vol. 55,
May 1885, pp. 669–670

Margaret Oliphant "The Life and Letters of George Eliot" (1885)

The life of the Scottish novelist Margaret Oliphant (1828–97) was marked by tragedy as she witnessed the successive deaths of her seven children and her husband. Oliphant's prodigious literary output—she published more than a hundred books—was in large part due to the necessity of providing for her family. Though she was said to have been Queen Victoria's favorite novelist, Oliphant, who was known for her strong Anglican faith, frequently expressed dis-ease about women entering the male-dominated public sphere, which has led to her being commonly labeled an antifeminist writer.

Oliphant's novels were sometimes compared with those of George Eliot. *Salem Chapel* was mistakenly attributed to Eliot when it was published in 1862, an attribution that Eliot vigorously rejected. However, in her *Autobiography*, published posthumously in 1990, Oliphant noted that "no one will even mention me in the same breath with George Eliot. And that is just.... I would not buy their fame with their disadvantages, but I do feel very small, very obscure, beside them, rather a failure all round."

The following extract sheds further light on how Eliot's relationship with Lewes was perceived. Curiously, Oliphant vastly underplays the public response to the scandal. The discovery of the relationship led many of Eliot's friends and family members, including her brother, to reject her; those men who continued to visit the couple were rarely bold enough to bring their wives. Public opinion began to thaw somewhat only after the publication of *The Mill on the Floss* (1860), when Eliot's literary importance was becoming clear. Though some continued to condemn Eliot, people gradually became more willing to concede that the couple's enduring relationship was as close as possible to a legal marriage. The reclusive state kept by Eliot and remarked on by Oliphant was to a great degree determined by Eliot's sensitivity to gossip and condemnation rather than by explicit choice. Similarly, Eliot's early reviews were by no means as timid as Oliphant argues. The passage, with its implications that the public was too kind about both Eliot's life and works, suggests Oliphant's jealousy of her artistic superior. Oliphant anticipates many twentieth-century descriptions of Eliot with her rather sour description of the awe surrounding the novelist.

It was not long before it became known that this purest preacher of domestic love, of fidelity, and self-sacrifice, had, in her own person, defied the laws and modest traditions that guard domestic life, and had taken a step which in all other cases deprives a woman of the fellowship and sympathy of other women, and of the respect of men. But the rule which holds universally from the duchess to the dressmaker, and which even the least straitlaced of moralists would think it dangerous to loosen, was abrogated for her, and the world agreed to consider that permissible or even justifiable in her special case which neither in that of the dressmaker nor the duchess there would be any question of tolerating. To attain this position is a triumph such as scarcely any woman before her has known. Men have got themselves pardoned for all breaches of the law, but women much more rarely. To attain it required more than great literary gifts, more even than genius: a great personal influence, an individual charm or power quite beyond the sway of ordinary laws, seems necessary to account for it. Yet personally the mistress of this great influence was something like a recluse, appearing never in public, and in private only under such restrictions as made the approach to her court a privilege. Perhaps this retirement had something to do with the effect produced. A kind of awe was thus made to mingle with the general admiration. When the first burst of applause was over, and it began to be possible to hint a criticism, even the most daring skirmishers of literature, those bold sappers to whom nothing is sacred, held their breath as they threw a furtive arrow into that sacred enclosure. They fired and ran away, terrified to be identified, knowing the penalty of discovery. A hedge of spears, but more effectual still an atmosphere in which opposition could not breathe, surrounded the oracle. That wide and voiceless public which speaks by purchase, and records its opinion on the publishers' account-books (dear public, precious, irresponsible, whose utterance is as the verdict of the gods!) silently recorded, in its own effectual inarticulate way, its approval even of the less worthy productions of the idol; and society held her peculiar views as to its most fundamental institution and its most sacred beliefs to be palliated—in her case and for her alone.

—MARGARET OLIPHANT, "The Life and Letters of George Eliot," *Edinburgh Review*, vol. 161, April 1885, p. 515

THOMAS ADOLPHUS TROLLOPE (1887)

Thomas Adolphus Trollope (1810–92) was the son of the popular novelist and travel writer Frances Trollope (1779–1863) and brother of the novelist Anthony Trollope (1815–82). Trollope became his mother's agent and editor, while working on his own historical studies and novels. Their home in

Italy, Villino Trollope, became a gathering place for intellectuals and artists such as the Brownings, Harriet Beecher Stowe, and George Eliot. In the following extract, Trollope offers one of the many descriptions of Eliot's physical appearance that appeared during and after her lifetime. It was common to compare her to Savonarola, Dante, Wordsworth, or Cardinal Newman, and acquaintances frequently alluded to her "equine" features. George Eliot was keenly aware of her lack of conventional beauty. Though she was able to joke about it, it was a painful subject for her, and she remained wary throughout her life of sitting for portraits.

She was not, as the world in general is aware, a handsome, or even a personable woman. Her face was long; the eyes not large nor beautiful in colour—they were, I think, of grayish blue—the hair, which she wore in old-fashioned braids coming low down on either side of her face, of a rather light brown. It was streaked with grey when I last saw her. Her figure was of middle height, large-boned and powerful. Lewes often said that she inherited from her peasant ancestors a frame and constitution originally very robust. Her head was finely formed, with a noble and well-balanced arch from brow to crown. The lips and mouth possessed a power of infinitely varied expression. George Lewes once said to me when I made some observation to the effect that she had a sweet face (I meant that the face expressed great sweetness), "You might say what a sweet hundred faces! I look at her sometimes in amazement. Her countenance is constantly changing." The said lips and mouth were distinctly sensuous in form and fullness.

She has been compared to the portraits of Savonarola (who was frightful) and of Dante (who though stern and bitter-looking, was handsome). *Something* there was of both faces in George Eliot's physiognomy. Lewes told us in her presence, of the exclamation uttered suddenly by some one to whom she was pointed out at a place of public entertainment—I believe it was at a Monday Popular Concert in St. James's Hall. "That," said a bystander, "is George Eliot." The gentleman to whom she was thus indicated gave one swift, searching look and exclaimed *sotto voce*, "Dante's aunt!" Lewes thought this happy, and he recognised the kind of likeness that was meant to the great singer of the *Divine Comedy*. She herself playfully disclaimed any resemblance to Savonarola. But, although such resemblance was very distant—Savonarola's peculiarly unbalanced countenance being a strong caricature of hers—some likeness there was.

Her speaking voice was, I think, one of the most beautiful I ever heard, and she used it *conscientiously*, if I may say so. I mean that she availed herself of its modulations to give thrilling emphasis to what was profound in her utterances, and sweetness to what was gentle or playful. She bestowed great care too on her enunciation, disliking the slipshod mode of pronouncing which is so common.

—Thomas Adolphus Trollope,
What I Remember, vol. 2, 1887, p. 295–297

Grant Allen (1895)

The Canadian-born writer Grant Allen (1848–99) initially worked as a professor of philosophy. In this role, he developed theories of evolution based on the works of Herbert Spencer, to whom he dedicated his first book, *Physiological Aesthetics* (1877). Allen remains best known, however, for his novel *The Woman Who Did* (1895). The work, a founding text of the "new woman" fictional genre, narrates the story of a strong-minded woman, Herminia Barton, who decides to live, unmarried, with the man she loves. The work caused immense controversy and was rapidly countered by two promarriage novels entitled *The Woman Who Didn't*.

The following extract—taken from a scene in which Herminia explains her views to her lover, Alan Merrick—reveals how, a decade after Eliot's death, her relationship with Lewes was still the object of debate. Herminia's complaint that Eliot adopted her unconventional lifestyle by necessity rather than as part of a feminist argument—in effect, that she was not sufficiently unconventional—is highly atypical for its period and anticipates later twentieth-century views.

When George Eliot chose to pass her life with Lewes on terms of equal freedom, she defied the man-made law; but still, there was his wife to prevent the possibility of a legalized union. As soon as Lewes was dead, George Eliot showed she had no principle involved, by marrying another man. Now, *I* have the rare chance of acting otherwise; I can show the world from the very first that I act from principle, and from principle only.

—Grant Allen, *The Woman Who Did*, 1895, p. 47

May Clarissa Gillington Byron (1912)

The English author May Clarissa Gillington Byron (1861–1936) was the author of numerous popular biographies narrating fictionalized "days spent with" romantic and Victorian authors, including Lord Byron, John

Keats, Ralph Waldo Emerson, and Walt Whitman. Byron, who sometimes published under the pseudonym Maurice Clare, was also the author of cookbooks, children's books, and poetry.

Byron used preexisting articles and biographies to depict her fictional "day spent with" George Eliot. The account is interesting for the way it rehearses many of the stereotypes of early-twentieth-century depictions of the novelist: her ugliness, her withering intellect, her seemingly self-inflicted illnesses and indulgent complaints, and, above all, her entire lack of humor. The passage anticipates the vicious attacks on eminent Victorians led by Lytton Strachey, though it lacks Strachey's wit.

The big, bony, heavy-featured woman, who appears in her own eyes as only capable of "kindling unpleasant sensations, with a palpitating heart and awkward manners," and who is the object of unfaltering, enthusiastic worship on the part of so many friends, comes slowly out of her bedroom into her large study on the first floor, and casts a somewhat deprecating glance upon her writing-table, strewn with papers. In front of this table stands a cast of the Melian Æsculapius: it looks at her with a dumbly self-reproachful air, as of one whose skill availed nought to counteract her almost incessant ill-health. The books lying here and there are almost suggestive of their owner's most constant *malaises*,—headache and cold feet: their very titles are oppressive to the average mind. For George Eliot, or Mrs. Lewes, as she is more usually known, is reading aloud to Mr. Lewes, o' nights, such imposing and monumental works as Plato's *Republic*, Nisard's *History of French Literature*, Lecky's *History of Morals*, and Herbert Spencer's *Psychology*; not to mention the consumption of such *hors d'œuvres* and "kickshaws" as the works of Lucretius, Theocritus, Sainte Beuve, Becker's *Charicles*, and a vast variety of minor volumes in five or six different languages. It would be difficult, indeed, to gather, from the ponderous character of her miscellaneous reading that this woman is the creator of such immortal types, "brimming with quaint provincial humour" as Mrs. Poyser (*Adam Bede*) or Aunt Glegg (*Mill on the Floss*). Still more difficult, when you realize, from personal acquaintance with her, the extraordinary seriousness of George Eliot,—the gravity with which, in her eyes, the smallest detail of life is weighted. "The sense of the importance of every action and every word, indeed of every influence which she might exercise over her fellow-creatures . . . the momentous issues of the thoughts and emotions which slowly build up the moral character,"—these have deprived her of that sense of laughter, in ordinary affairs, which is such a help and solace to its possessor. She never says a smile-provoking thing:

never writes one in her letters: her vivid and admirable perception of all that makes for gaiety is exclusively confined to her novels.

—Maurice Clare [May Clarissa Gillington Byron], *A Day with George Eliot*, 1912, pp. 2–4

WILLIAM HALE WHITE
"GEORGE ELIOT AS I KNEW HER" (1915)

William Hale White (1831–1913) was an English writer and civil servant. Having turned his back on a career in the ministry, White was offered work by John Chapman at the *Westminster Review* and lived for a time at 142 Strand alongside George Eliot. During this time, he fell in love with Eliot, though he never declared his feelings. White's most famous publication, *The Autobiography of Mark Rutherford* (1881), shows the eponymous hero experiencing a number of spiritual crises, resigning from his ministry, and falling in love with Theresa, a character inspired by Eliot.

The following passage reflects the ardent admiration that White continued to feel for Eliot long after his depature from 142 Strand. Eliot's relationship with Chapman was more complex than White could have guessed: there is evidence to suggest that Eliot and Chapman were lovers for a short while. Chapman remained friends with the Leweses after Eliot had stopped editing the *Westminster Review*, though the relationship soured when Chapman was instrumental in revealing the true identity of "George Eliot."

White's testimony forms a rare tribute to Eliot's personal and artistic courage at a time when it was fashionable to dismiss her. It is curious that (as Herminia declares in Allen's novel *The Woman Who Did*) Eliot, who during her lifetime was accused of flouting social conventions, was reproached after her death for having been too conventional. Interestingly, White defends Eliot by playing with the word *respectable,* which provoked so much scorn among the modernists, and by casting her as intellectually curious and forward thinking.

I fancy that one of the reasons why she and Chapman did not agree was that she did not like his somewhat disorderly ways. She has been accused of 'respectability.' Even Sir Leslie Stephen in his scholarly essay describes her as 'eminently respectable.' It is not very easy to understand what is meant by this word. If there is any meaning in it worth preservation, it is conformity to usage merely for the sake of conformity, and perhaps, more precisely, it is mental compromise. I deny that in either of these senses George Eliot was 'respectable.' She never terminated inquiry till she had gone as far as her powerful intellect permitted her to go, and she never refused to act upon her investigation. If she did not outrage the world by indecency, it was not because she was 'respectable,' but because she had not deduced indecency as the final outcome of thinking or the highest achievement of art.

—MARK RUTHERFORD [WILLIAM HALE WHITE],
"George Eliot as I Knew Her," in *Last Pages from a Journal*, 1915, p. 133

GENERAL

George Eliot's reputation experienced a striking rise and fall. At its peak, she was considered the greatest living English writer; at its lowest point, she was deemed "negligible." Several of the following extracts illustrate this shift in popularity. The publication of *Adam Bede* marked the beginning of her literary fame. For all the controversies surrounding Eliot's personal life, she rapidly gained respectability as a writer; shortly after the publication of *The Mill on the Floss*, she was informed that Queen Victoria counted herself among the author's admirers. The publication of a new novel by Eliot was always something of an event, and the extract from Oscar Browning's biography offers insight into why each novel struck a chord with its readers.

Though critics recognized Eliot's importance, many writers, both during and after Eliot's lifetime, echoed the popular notion that her novels can be divided into two groups. Readers felt greater affection for Eliot's early novels, and in particular *Adam Bede* and *Silas Marner*. For many, it was in these earlier works that Eliot seemed to draw most extensively on her youth in the Midlands and depicted rural England with charm and comparative gentleness. In comparison, the later novels seemed difficult and demanding: *Romola* was burdened with the fruit of Eliot's extensive research, *Middlemarch* was deemed by some to lack the warmth of the earlier works, and *Daniel Deronda* put off many readers with its sustained investigation into Jewish identity. During Eliot's lifetime, critics such as Leslie Stephen and Anthony Trollope openly discussed this apparent shift in her style and concerns, even as they reaffirmed their admiration for Eliot's intellectual achievements and artistic supremacy.

This supremacy became increasingly questioned as the century drew to a close and new fictional modes, together with the somewhat otherworldly portrait of Eliot produced by her biographies, seemed to distance her from the reading public. Like many Victorian novelists, she became the target of modernist writers eager to sweep away the style and concerns of their predecessors in order to make way for new literary experiments. Few Victorian novelists, however, were treated as harshly as Eliot: her apparent seriousness and the moralizing interventions of her narrators marked her for attacks of unusual strength. The extracts in this section narrate this gradual decline, interrupted here and there by lone voices that continued to insist on the enduring worth of Eliot's novels. William Ernest Henley's short chapter on Eliot opens the attacks with its satirical account of Eliot's concerns and style. George Saintsbury is a less aggressive writer and offers a more nuanced account of why Eliot appeared to have lost touch with readers. With W.C. Brownell and Ford Madox Ford, the accusations regain vigor: the two passages provide vivid illustrations of the most extreme end of the modernist position against Victorian writers. Richard Burton, writing between the two, makes a somewhat solitary case for Eliot's modernity. However, the most important modernist critical response to George Eliot is undoubtedly Virginia Woolf's 1919 essay, which offered a first step toward the critical rehabilitation of George Eliot, a process that would only gain force with the publication of F.R. Leavis's *The Great Tradition* in 1948.

The following passages also include extracts by writers who, rather than assessing the entirety of Eliot's literary career, seek to evaluate Eliot's contributions in two different areas of her art: her philosophical outlook and her style. Edward Dowden and Vida D. Scudder both provide interesting reflections on how Eliot's interest in science—and evolution in particular—feeds into her moral and social philosophy. George Willis Cooke is similarly interested in her philosophy and, though he is skeptical of the positivist ideas that Eliot explored, his essay is a balanced assessment of her views. Reflections on Eliot's style are peppered throughout the extracts. Noteworthy extracts include Mary Elizabeth Braddon's commentary on Eliot's narrative voice, Edmund Clarence Stedman's fair assessment of her talents as a poet, and Stephen on her humor. Henley, who dwells on what he calls her "Death's-Head Style," and W.C. Brownell, who goes further with the startling statement that she "has no style" at all, register a judgment that happily has since been overturned.

Mary Elizabeth Braddon (1863)

The English novelist Mary Elizabeth Braddon (1835–1915) achieved fame through her popular and often controversial novels, of which the most widely read today are *Lady Audley's Secret* (1861) and *Aurora Floyd* (1862). Like Eliot, she attracted negative attention by living, unmarried, with her publisher John Maxwell, whose wife was confined to a mental institution. Braddon, together with writers such as Wilkie Collins, was labeled a "sensation novelist" for her reliance on crimes, including bigamy and murder, to build her exciting, breathless narratives. Critics often accused the sensation novelists of having a corrupting influence on female readers.

The following passage from *Aurora Floyd* provides a striking illustration of the way in which Eliot's writing filtered down into popular culture. The allusion to Eliot shows how the novelist was often enjoyed for the epigrammatic quality of her writing, most powerfully displayed in *Adam Bede*'s Mrs. Poyser. More intriguing is the way in which, by invoking Eliot to describe her character, the leading sensation novelist claims a common ground with the leading realist novelist. The relationship between the two genres is a curious one, as sensation novelists would often insist that their improbable plots were based on facts and everyday life, while Eliot's plots were not entirely devoid of sensational plot devices, from Hetty's last-minute rescue in *Adam Bede* to the use of mistaken identities and blackmail in *Felix Holt*.

Mr. James Conyers is, perhaps, no worse than other men of his station, but he is decidedly no better. He is only very much handsomer; and you have no right to be angry with him because his opinions and sentiments are exactly what they would have been if he had had red hair and a pug nose. With what wonderful wisdom has George Eliot told us that people are not any better because they have long eyelashes! Yet it must be that there is something anomalous in this outward beauty and inward ugliness; for, in spite of all experience, we revolt against it, and are incredulous to the last, believing that the palace which is outwardly so splendid can scarcely be ill furnished within.

—Mary Elizabeth Braddon,
Aurora Floyd, vol. 2, 1863, pp. 57–58

Edward Dowden "George Eliot" (1872)

Edward Dowden (1843–1913) was an Irish scholar and poet. He became known for his works on Shakespeare and Shelley, of whom he published a two-volume biography in 1866. Here, Dowden helpfully pinpoints one of the themes running through all of Eliot's works: the conflict between private desires and communal duties. Eliot was not the only Victorian novelist to take up the theme ("Condition of England" novels, for example, frequently explored the same question). However, she makes the theme her own by, as Dowden stresses, approaching her characters almost scientifically and reiterating the importance of self-renunciation. Dowden brings to the fore a central tension in Eliot's works and beliefs: her radicalism counterbalanced by her respect for "the formal contract." This can help to explain why the fluctuation in Eliot's reputation has depended in part on whether critics stressed the more radical or the more conservative aspects of her work.

The tragic aspect of life, as viewed by this great writer, is derived from the Titanic strife of egoistic desires with duties which conscience confesses, and those emotions which transcend the interests of the individual. It seems to her no small or easy thing to cast away the noblest characters she has conceived, certainly all those characters in presenting which a personal accent seems least doubtfully recognizable—the heroical feminine characters or those that might have been heroical, characters of great sensibility, great imaginative power, great fervour of feeling—Maggie, Romola, Fedalma, Armgart—cling with passionate attachment to the joy which must needs be renounced. The dying to self is the dying of young creatures full of the strength and the gladness of living. The world is indeed cruel; to be happy is so sweet. If the joy were ignoble it could be abandoned with less anguish and remorse, but it is pure and high. . . .

The same doctrine of the necessity of self-renunciation, of the obligation laid upon men to accept some other rule of conduct than the desire of pleasure, is enforced in the way of warning with terrible emphasis. Tito Melema, Arthur Donnithorne, Godfrey Cass, Maggie Tulliver, are in turn assailed by one and the same temptation—to deny or put out of sight certain duties to others, to gratify some demand for egoistic pleasure or happiness, or to avoid some wholesome necessary pain. Arthur, vain affectionate, susceptible, owed no one a grudge, and would have liked to see everyone about him happy, and ready to acknowledge that a great part of their happiness was due to the handsome young landlord. Tito was clever and beautiful, kind and gentle in his manners, without a thought of anything cruel or base. And Godfrey was full of easy good nature; and Maggie of a wealth of eager love. But in the linked necessity of evil, each of these, beginning with a soft yielding to egoistic desires, becomes capable of deeds or of wishes that are base and cruel. . . .

The scientific observation of man, and in particular the study of the mutual relations of the individual and society, come to reinforce the self-renouncing dictates of the heart. To understand any individual apart from the whole life of the race is impossible. We are the heirs intellectual and moral of the past; there is no such thing as naked manhood; the heart of each of us wears livery which it cannot throw off. Our very bodies differ from those of primeval savages—differ it may be, from those of extinct apes only by the gradual gains of successive generations of ancestors. Our instincts, physical and mental, our habits of thought and feeling, the main tendency of our activity, these are assigned to us by the common life which has preceded and which surrounds our own. 'There is no private life,' writes George Eliot in *Felix Holt*, 'which has not been determined by a wider public life, from the time when the primeval milkmaid had to wander with the wanderings of her clan, because the cow she milked was one of a herd which had made the pastures bare.' . . .

It will be readily seen how this way of thinking abolishes rights, and substitutes duties in their place. Of rights of man, or rights of woman, we never hear speech from George Eliot. But we hear much of the duties of each. The claim asserted by the individual on behalf of this or that disappears, because the individual surrenders his independence to collective humanity, of which he is a part. And it is another consequence of this way of thinking that the leadings of duty are most often looked for, not within, in the promptings of the heart, but without, in the relations of external life, which connects us with our fellow-men. Our great English novelist does not preach as her favourite doctrine the indefeasible right of love to gratify itself at the expense of law; with the correlative right, equally indefeasible, to cast away the marriage bond as soon as it has became a painful incumbrance. She regards the formal contract, even when its spirit has long since died, as sacred and of binding force. Why? Because it is a formal contract. 'The light abandonment of ties, whether inherited or voluntary, because they had ceased to be pleasant, would be the uprooting of social and personal virtue.' Law is sacred. Rebellion, it is true, may be sacred also. There are moments of life 'when the soul must dare to act upon its warrant, not only without external law to appeal to, but in the face of a law which is not unarmed with Divine lightnings—lightnings that may yet fall if the warrant has been false.' These moments, however, are of rare occurrence, and arise only in extreme necessity. . . . Maggie returns to St Oggs: Fedalma and Don Silva part: Romola goes back to her husband's house.

—Edward Dowden, "George Eliot,"
Contemporary Review, vol. 20,
August 1872, pp. 415–420

Edmund Clarence Stedman (1875)

The American writer Edmund Clarence Stedman (1833–1908) pursued simultaneous careers as a man of letters and a stockbroker. Significant works include *Victorian Poets* (1875) and *Poets of America* (1885), in which he champions the works of Edgar Allan Poe and Walt Whitman. Stedman later undertook the monumental *Library of American Literature* (1888–90).

Stedman offers a fair estimate of Eliot's qualities as a poet, which rarely reflected her genius. Her verse drama *The Spanish Gypsy* (1868) suffered, as *Romola* did, from excessive research. Both her publisher Blackwood and her readers expressed little enthusiasm for the work. Stedman's praise for "O may I join the choir invisible!" (1867), which he included in his *Victorian Anthology* (1895), is, however, largely warranted. The poem anticipates the ideas most fully expressed in *Middlemarch* that obscure lives contribute to the human progress through the "sweet presence of a good diffused." The poem has survived the longest: it was recited at her funeral, and was quoted by the archbishop of Canterbury at the Queen Mother's funeral service in 2002.

George Eliot's metrical work has special interest, coming from a woman acknowledged to be, in her realistic yet imaginative prose, at the head of living female writers. She has brought all her energies to bear, first upon the construction of a drama, which was only a *succès d'estime,* and recently upon a new volume containing "The Legend of Jubal" and other poems. The result shows plainly that Mrs. Lewes, though possessed of great intellect and sensibility, is not, in respect to metrical expression, a poet. Nor has she a full conception of the simple strength and melody of English verse, her polysyllabic language, noticeable in the moralizing passages of *Middlemarch,* being very ineffective in her poems. That wealth of thought which atones for all her deficiencies in prose does not seem to be at her command in poetry. *The Spanish Gypsy* reads like a second-rate production of the Byronic school. "The Legend of Jubal" and "How Lisa Loved the King" suffer by comparison with the narrative poems, in rhymed pentameter, of Morris, Longfellow, or Stoddard. A little poem in blank-verse, entitled "O may I join the choir invisible!" and setting forth her conception of the "religion of humanity," is worth all the rest of her poetry, for it is the outburst of an exalted soul, foregoing personal immortality and compensated by a vision of the growth and happiness of the human race.

—Edmund Clarence Stedman,
Victorian Poets, 1875, p. 254

LESLIE STEPHEN "GEORGE ELIOT" (1881)

Leslie Stephen (1832–1904) was an English writer and editor. Stephen initially seemed destined for a career in the Church, but the influence of works by Comte, Darwin, and Spencer and his own inclinations led him to acknowledge his agnosticism and resign as a tutor at Cambridge. Stephen threw himself into literature instead and published reviews, essays, and biographies. In 1871, the publisher George Smith appointed him editor of *The Cornhill Magazine*, a periodical whose authors included Edmund Gosse, Henry James, and Thomas Hardy. He is best known now as the editor (and, from 1890, co-editor with Sidney Lee) of the monumental *Dictionary of National Biography*. Stephen published a number of important works on George Eliot, including the following article published shortly after her death, her entry in the *DNB,* and a biography published in 1902. In 1919, Stephen's daughter, Virginia Woolf, published her own important essay on George Eliot.

The following article was Stephen's first sustained attempt to evaluate Eliot's career. His cautious comments about the vagaries of fortune are apt in light of Eliot's dip in popularity toward the end of the nineteenth century, but Stephen is nevertheless keen to establish her importance. The essay sheds light on three key issues that affected Eliot's reputation: the popular belief that she failed to live up to the genius of her early novels, the humor of those early works, and her gender.

Though Stephen accords Eliot high praise, he remains aware of the criticisms of her work that had accumulated toward the end of her life. The general consensus was that Eliot's later, more intellectual, novels had a lesser appeal than her earlier works. Stephen defends Eliot's right to mold the novel as she desired but joined his fellow critics in objecting when such intellectualism threatened, in his view, to overmaster her novels. They largely agreed that Eliot's particular contribution to English literature was the study of "English country life" and felt uneasy when she departed from that sphere or complicated it with philosophical reflections.

The essay provides a good survey of Eliot's reception, as Stephen picks out for special attention those moments and characters in her novels that were repeatedly held up for praise, such as Mrs. Poyser in *Adam Bede* and the "Rainbow Inn" scenes in *Silas Marner*. Contemporary readers such as Stephen relished these portraits and scenes for their gentle humor, which they found diminished in the later works. Eliot's reputation as a humorist diminished sharply at the turn of the century—indeed, in his 1902 biography of her, Stephen wrote that women are generally "wanting in humour" altogether.

Though a sympathetic and lucid reviewer of Eliot's works, Stephen could not resist considering her as a "woman," and often called upon gender stereotypes to discuss her. Though most readers initially believed George Eliot to be a man, Stephen makes confident assertions about her "thoroughly feminine nature." The capacity to see the "poetry and pathos" in the commonplace is given as evidence for this, even though such a statement closely echoes Wordsworth's words in the preface to the *Lyrical Ballads*. That Eliot's male heroes are often unconvincingly masculine was a more frequent complaint. Throughout this review, Stephen wavers between judging Eliot as a preeminent Victorian novelist and evaluating her as a woman, limited by her feminine concerns.

Had we been asked, a few weeks ago, to name the greatest living writer of English fiction, the answer would have been unanimous. No one—whatever might be his special personal predilections—would have refused that title to George Eliot. To ask the same question now would be to suggest some measure of our loss. In losing George Eliot we have probably lost the greatest woman who ever won literary fame, and one of the very few writers of our day to whom the name "great" could be conceded with any plausibility. We are not at a sufficient distance from the object of our admiration to measure its true elevation. We are liable to a double illusion on the morrow of such events. In political life we fancy that all heroism is extinct with the dead leader, whilst there are within the realm five hundred good as he. Yet the most daring optimist can hardly suppose that consolatory creed to be generally true in literature. If contemporaries sometimes exaggerate, they not unfrequently underestimate their loss. When Shakespeare died, nobody imagined—we may suspect—that the English drama had touched its highest point. When men are crossing the lines which divide one of the fruitful from one of the barren epochs in literature, they are often but faintly conscious of the change. It would require no paradoxical ingenuity to maintain that we are even now going through such a transition. The works of George Eliot may hereafter appear as marking the termination of the great period of English fiction which began with Scott. She may hereafter be regarded as the last great sovereign of a literary dynasty, who had to bequeath her sceptre to a comparatively petty line of successors: though for anything that we can say to the contrary—it may also be true that the successor may appear to-morrow, or may even be now amongst us in the shape of some writer who is struggling against a general want of recognition.

Ephemeral critics must not pretend to pronounce too confidently upon such questions. They can only try to say, in Mr. Browning's phrase, how it strikes a contemporary. And a contemporary is prompted by the natural regret to stray into irrelevant reflections, and dwell needlessly in the region of might-have-beens. Had George Eliot lived a little longer, or begun to write a little earlier, or been endowed with some additional quality which she did not in fact possess, she might have done greater things still. It is very true, and true of others besides George Eliot. It often seems as if even the greatest works of the greatest writers were but fragmentary waifs and strays—mere indications of more splendid achievements which would have been within their grasp, had they not been forced, like weaker people, to feel out the way to success through comparative failure, or to bend their genius to unworthy tasks. So, of the great writers in her own special department, Fielding wasted his powers in writing third-rate plays till he was five-and-thirty, and died a broken-down man at forty-seven. Scott did not appear in the field of his greatest victories till he was forty-three, and all his really first-rate work was done within the next ten years. George Eliot's period of full activity, the time during which she was conscientiously doing her best under the stimulus of high reputation, lasted some twenty years; and so long a space is fully up to the average of the time allowed to most great writers. If not a voluminous writer, according to the standard of recent novelists, she has left enough work, representative of her powers at their best, to give a full impress of her mind.

So far, I think, we have little reason for regret. When once a writer has managed to express the best that was in him to say, the question of absolute mass is trifling. Though some very great have also been very voluminous writers, the immortal part of their achievement bears a slight proportion to the whole. Goethe lived to a good old age, and never lapsed into indolence: yet all of Goethe that is really of the highest excellence will go into some half-dozen volumes. Putting aside Scott, hardly any great English writer has left a greater quantity of work representing the highest level of the author's capacity than is equivalent to the *Scenes of Clerical Life*, *Adam Bede*, the *Mill on the Floss*, *Silas Marner*, *Romola*, and *Middlemarch*. Certainly, she might have done more. She did not begin to write novels till a period at which many popular authors are already showing symptoms of exhaustion, and indulging in the perilous practice of self-imitation. Why, it may be said, did not George Eliot write immortal works in her youth, instead of translating German authors of a heterodox tendency? If we could arrange all such things to our taste, and could foresee a writer's powers from the beginning, we might have ordered matters differently. Yet one may observe that there is another side to the question. Imaginative minds often ripen quickly; and much of the finest poetry in the language derives its charm from the freshness of youth. But writers of the contemplative order—those whose best works represent the general experience of a rich and thoughtful nature—may be expected to come later to their maturity. The phenomenon of early exhaustion is too common in these days to allow us to regret an occasional exception. If during her youth George Eliot was storing the thoughts and emotions which afterwards shaped themselves into the *Scenes of Clerical Life*, we need not suppose that the time was wasted. Certainly, I do not think that any one who has had a little experience in such matters would regard it as otherwise than dangerous for a powerful mind to be precipitated into public utterance. The Pythagorean probation of silence may be protracted too long; but it may afford a most useful discipline: and I think that there is nothing preposterous in the supposition that George Eliot's work was all the more powerful because it came from a novelist who had lain fallow through a longer period than ordinary.

If it is rather idle to pursue such speculations, it is still more idle to indulge in that kind of criticism which virtually comes to saying that George Eliot ought to have been Walter Scott or Charlotte Brontë. You may think her inferior to those writers; you may dislike her philosophy or her character; and you are fully justified in expressing your dislike. But it is only fair to ask whether the qualities which you disapprove were mere external and adventitious familiarities or the inseparable adjunct of those which you admire. It is important to remember this in considering some of the common criticisms. The poor woman was not content simply to write amusing stories. She is convicted upon conclusive evidence of having induged in ideas; she ventured to speculate upon human life and its meaning, and still worse, she endeavoured to embody her convictions in imaginative shapes, and probably wished to infect her readers with them. This was, according to some people, highly unbecoming in a woman and very inartistic in a novelist. I confess that, for my part, I am rather glad to find ideas anywhere. They are not very common; and there are a vast number of excellent fictions which these sensitive critics may study without the least danger of a shock to their artistic sensibilities by anything of the kind. But if you will permit a poor novelist to indulge in such awkward possessions, I cannot see why he or she should not be allowed occasionally to interweave them in her narrative, taking care of course to keep them in their proper place. Some of that mannerism which offends many critics represents in fact simply George Eliot's way of using this privilege. We are indeed told dogmatically that a novelist should never indulge in little asides to the reader. Why not? One main advantage of a novel, as it seems to me, is precisely that it leaves room for a freedom in such matters which is incompatible with the requirements, for example, of dramatic writing. I can enjoy Scott's downright story-telling, which never reminds you obtrusively of the presence of the author; but with all respect for Scott, I do not see why his manner should be the sole type and model for all his successors. I like to read about Tom Jones or Colonel Newcome; but I am also very glad when Fielding or Thackeray puts his puppets aside for the moment and talks to me in his own person. A child, it is true, dislikes to have the illusion broken, and is angry if you try to persuade him that Giant Despair was not a real personage like his favourite Blunderbore. But the attempt to produce such illusions is really unworthy of work intended for full-grown readers. The humorist in particular knows that you will not mistake his puppet-show for reality, nor does he wish you to do so. He is rather of opinion that the world itself is a greater puppet-show, not to be taken in too desperate earnest. It is congenial to his whole mode of thought to act occasionally as chorus, and dwell upon some incidental suggestion. The solemn critic may step forward, like the physician who attended Sancho Panza's meal, and waive aside the condiment which gives a peculiar relish to the feast. It is not prepared according to his recipe. But till he gives me some better reason for obedience than his *ipse dixit*, I shall refuse to respect what would destroy many charming passages and obliterate touches which clearly contribute to the general effect of George Eliot's work.

Were it not indeed that some critics in authority have dwelt upon this supposed defect, I should be disposed simply to plead "not guilty," for I think that any one who reads the earlier books with the criticism in his mind, and notes the passages which are really obnoxious upon this ground, will be surprised at the rarity of the passages to which it applies. One cannot help suspecting that what is really offensive is not so much the method itself as the substance of the reflections introduced, and occasionally the cumbrous style in which they are expressed. And upon these points there is more to be said. But it is more desirable, if one can do it, to say what George Eliot was than what she was not; and to try to catch the secret of her unique power rather than to dwell upon shortcomings, some of which, to say the truth, are so obvious that it requires little critical acumen to discover them, and a decided tinge of antipathy to dwell upon them at length.

What is it, in fact, which makes us conscious that George Eliot had a position apart; that, in a field where she had so many competitors of no mean capacity, she stands out as superior to all her rivals; or that, whilst we can easily imagine that many other reputations will fade with a change of fashion, there is something in George Eliot which we are confident will give delight to our grandchildren as it has to ourselves? To such questions there is one obvious answer at hand. There is one part of her writings upon which every competent reader has dwelt with delight, and which seems fresher and more charming whenever we come back to it. There is no danger of arousing any controversy in saying that the works of her first period, the *Scenes of Clerical Life*, *Adam Bede*, *Silas Marner*, and the *Mill on the Floss*, have the unmistakable mark of high genius. They are something for which it is simply out of the question to find any substitute. Strike them out of English literature, and we feel that there would be a gap not to be filled up; a distinct vein of thought and feeling unrepresented; a characteristic and delightful type of social development left without any adequate interpreter. A second-rate writer can be more or less replaced. When you have read Shakespeare, you can do very well without Beaumont and Fletcher, and a study of the satires of Pope makes it unnecessary to plod through the many volumes filled by his imitators. But we feel that, however much we may admire the other great English novelists, there is none who would make the study of George Eliot superfluous. The sphere which she has made specially her own is that quiet English country life which she knew in early youth. It has been described with more or less vivacity and sympathy by many observers. Nobody has approached George Eliot in the power of seizing its essential characteristics and exhibiting its real charm. She has done for it what Scott did for the Scotch peasantry, or Fielding for the eighteenth century Englishman, or Thackeray for the higher social stratum of his time. Its last traces are vanishing so rapidly amidst the changes of modern revolution, that its picture could hardly be drawn again, even if there were an artist of equal skill and penetration. And thus, when the name of George Eliot is mentioned, it calls up, to me at least, and, I suspect, to most readers, not so much her later and more ambitious works, as the exquisite series of scenes so lovingly and vividly presented in the earlier stage: snuffy old Mr. Gilfil, drinking his gin-and-water in his lonely parlour, with his faithful Ponto snoring on the rug and dreaming of the early romance of his life; and the inimitable Mrs. Poyser in her exquisite dairy, delivering her soul in a series of pithy aphorisms, bright as the little flames in Mr. Biglow's pastoral, that "danced about the chancy on the dresser;" and the party in the parlour of the "Rainbow" discussing the evidences for "ghoses;" or the family conclaves in which the affairs of the Tulliver family were discussed from so many and such admirably contrasted points of view. Where shall we find a more delightful circle, or quainter manifestations of human character, in beings grotesque, misshapen, and swathed in old prejudices, like the mossy trees in an old-fashioned orchard, which, for all their vagaries of growth, are yet full of sap and capable of bearing mellow and toothsome fruit? "It was pleasant to Mr. Tryan," as we are told in Janet's Repentance, "to listen to the simple chat of the old man to walk in the shade of the incomparable orchard and hear the story of the crops yielded by the red-streaked apple-tree, and the quite embarrassing plentifulness of the summer pears to drink in the sweet evening breath of the garden as they sat in the alcove—and so, for a short interval, to feel the strain of his pastoral task relaxed." Our enjoyment is analogous to Mr. Tryan's. We are soothed by the atmosphere of the old-world country life, where people, no doubt, had as many troubles as ours, but troubles which, because they were different, seem more bearable to our imagination. We half wish that we could go back to the old days of stage-coaches and wagons and shambling old curates in "Brutus wigs," preaching to slumberous congregations enshrouded in high-backed pews, contemplating as little the advent of railways as of a race of clergymen capable of going to prison upon a question of ritual.

So far, indeed, it can hardly be said that George Eliot is unique. She has been approached, if she has not been surpassed, by other writers in her idyllic effects. But there is something less easily paralleled in the peculiar vein of humour which is the essential complement of the more tender passages. Mrs. Poyser is necessary to balance the solemnity of Dinah Morris. Silas Marner would lose half his impressiveness if he were not in contrast with the inimitable party in the "Rainbow" parlour. Omit the few pages in which their admirable conversation is reported, and the whole harmony of the book would be altered. The change would be as fatal as to strike out a figure in some perfect composition, where the most trifling accessory may really be an essential part of the whole design. It might throw some light upon George Eliot's peculiar power if we could fairly analyse the charm of that little masterpiece. Psychologists are very fond of attempting to define the nature of wit and humour. Hitherto they have not been very successful, though, of course, their failure cannot be due to any want of personal appreciation of those qualities. But I should certainly despair of giving any account of the pleasure which one receives from that famous conflict of rustic wits. Why are we charmed by Ben Winthorp's retort to the parish clerk: "It's your inside as isn't right made for music; it's no better nor a hollow stalk;" and the statement that this "unflinching frankness was regarded by the company as the most piquant form of joke;" or by the landlord's ingenious remarks upon the analogy between a power of smelling cheeses and perceiving the supernatural; or by that quaint stumble into something surprising to the speaker himself by its apparent resemblance to witty repartee, when the same person says to the farrier: "You're a doctor, I reckon, though you're only a cow-doctor; for a fly's a fly, though it may be a horse-fly"? One can understand at a proper distance how a clever man comes to say a brilliant thing, and it is still more easy to understand how he can say a thoroughly silly thing, and, therefore, how he can simulate stupidity. But there is something mysterious in the power possessed by a few great humorists of converting themselves for the nonce into that peculiar condition of muddle-headedness dashed with grotesque flashes of common-sense which is natural to a half-educated mind. It is less difficult to draw either a perfect circle or a purely arbitrary line than to see what will be the proportion of the regular figure on some queer, lopsided, and imperfectly-reflecting surface. And these quaint freaks of rustic intelligence seem to be rags and tatters of what would make wit and reason in a cultivated mind, but when put together in this grotesque kaleidoscopic confusion suggests, not simple nonsense, but a ludicrous parody of sense. To reproduce the effect, you have not simply to lower the activity of the reasoning machine, but to put it together on some essential plan, so as to bring out a new set of combinations distantly recalling the correct order. We require not a new defect of logic, but a new logical structure.

There is no answer to this as to any other such problems. It is enough to take note of the fact that George Eliot possessed a vein of humour, of which it is little to say that it is incomparably superior, in depth if not in delicacy, to that of any feminine writer. It is the humour of a calm contemplative mind, familiar with wide fields of knowledge, and capable of observing the little dramas of rustic life from a higher standing-point. It is not—in these earlier books at any rate—that she obtrudes her acquirements upon us; for if here and there we find some of those scientific illusions which afterwards became a kind of mannerism, they are introduced without any appearance of forcing. It is simply that she is awake to those quaint aspects of the little world before her which only show their quaintess to the cultivated intellect. We feel that there must be a silent guest in the chimney-corner of the "Rainbow," so thoroughly at home with the natives as to put no stress upon their behaviour, and yet one who has travelled out of sight of the village spire, and known the thoughts and feelings which are stirring in the great world outside. The guest can at once sympathise and silently criticize; or rather, in the process of observation, carries on the two processes simultaneously by recognising at once the little oddities of the microcosm, and yet seeing them as merely one embodiment of the same thoughts and passions which present themselves on a larger scale elsewhere. It is in this happy combination of two characteristics often disjoined that we have one secret of George Eliot's power. There is the breadth of touch, the large-minded equable spirit of loving contemplative thought, which is fully conscious of the narrow limitations of the actor's thoughts and habits, but does not cease on that account to sympathise with his joys and sorrows. We are on a petty stage, but not in a stifling atmosphere, and we are not called upon to accept the prejudices of the actors or to be angry with them, but simply to understand and be tolerant. We have neither the country idyl of the sentimentalist which charms us in some of George Sand's stories of French life, but in which our enjoyment is checked by the inevitable sense of unreality, nor the caricature of the satirist who is anxious to proclaim the truth that base passions and grovelling instincts are as common in country towns as in court and city. Everything is quietly set before us with a fine sense of its wider relations, and yet with a loving touch, significant of a pathetic yearning for the past, which makes the whole picture artistically charming. We are reminded in Mr. Gilfil's love-story how, whilst poor little Tina was fretting over her wrongs, the "stream of human thought and deed was hurrying and broadening around." "What were our little Tina and her trouble in this mighty torrent, rushing from one awful unknown to another? Lighter than the smallest centre of quivering life in the water-drop hidden and uncared for as the pulse of anguish in the breast of the tiniest bird that has fluttered down to its nest with the long-sought food, and has found the nest torn and empty." It is this constant reference, tacit or express, suggested by pathetic touches, and by humorous exhibition of the incongruities and contrasts of the little drama of village life to the outer world beyond, and to the wider universe in which it too is an atom, that distinctly raises George Eliot above the level of many merely picturesque descriptions of similar scenes. We feel that the artist is at an intellectual elevation high enough to be beyond the illusions of the city fashion; but the singular charm springs out of the tender affection which reproduces the little world left so far behind and hallowed by the romance of early association.

George Eliot's own view of the matter is given in more than one of these objectionable "asides" of which we have had to speak. She entreats us to try to see the poetry and the pathos, the tragedy and the comedy, to be found in the experience of poor dingy Amos Barton. She rarely looks, she says, at "a bent old man or a wizened old woman" without seeing "the past of which they are the shrunken remnant; and the unfinished romance of rosy cheeks and bright eyes seems sometimes of feeble interest and significance compared with that drama of hope and love which has long ago reached its catastrophe, and left the poor soul, like a dim and dusty stage, with all its sweet garden scenes and fair perspectives overturned and thrust out of sight." To reflect that we ought to see wizened old men and women with such eyes is of course easy enough; to have such eyes really to see what we know that we ought to see is to possess true genius. George Eliot is not laying down a philosophical maxim to be proved and illustrated, but is attempting to express the animating principle of a labour of love. Mr. Gilfil, the person who suggests this remark, is the embodiment of the abstract principle, and makes us feel that it is no empty profession. Everybody has noticed how admirably George Eliot has portrayed certain phases of religious feeling with which, in one sense, she had long ceased to sympathise. Amongst the subsidiary actors in her stories, none are more tenderly and lovingly touched than the old-fashioned parsons and dissenting preachers Barton and Gilfil and Tryan, and Irwin and Dinah Morris in *Adam Bede*, and Mr. Lyon in *Felix Holt*. I do not know that they or their successors would have much call to be grateful. For, in truth, it is plain enough that the interest is in the kindly old-fashioned parson, considered as a valuable factor in the social system, and that his creed is not taken to be the source of his strength; whilst the few Methodists and the brethren in Lantern Yard are regarded as attaining a very imperfect and stammering version of truths capable of being very completely dissevered from their dogmatic teaching. In any case, her breach with the creed of her youth involved no breach of the ties formed by early reverence for its representatives. The change involved none of the bitterness which is sometimes generated by a spiritual revolt. Dickens—who is sometimes supposed to represent the version of modern Christianity—could apparently see nothing in a dissenting preacher but an unctuous and sensual hypocrite—a vulgarised Tartuffe such as Stiggins and Chadband. If George Eliot had been the mere didactic preacher of mere critics, she might have set before us mere portraits of spiritual pride or clerical charlatanism. But, whatever her creed, she was too deep a humorist, too thoughtful and too tender, to fall into such an error. She never sinned against the "natural piety" which should bind our days together. The tender regard which she had retained for all the surroundings of her youth did not fail towards those whose teaching had once roused her reverence, and which could never become the objects of indiscriminate antipathy.

In this one may perhaps say George Eliot was a true woman. Women, indeed, can be fully as bitter in their resentment as the harsher sex; but their bitterness seems to be generated in the attempt to outdo their masculine rivals, and to imply perverted rather than deficient sensibility. They seldom exhibit pachydermatous indifference to their neighbour's emotions. The so-called masculine quality in George Eliot—her wide and calm intelligence—was certainly combined with a thoroughly feminine nature; and the more one reads her books and notes her real triumphs, the more strongly this comes out. The poetry and pathos which she seeks to reveal under commonplace surroundings is found chiefly in feminine hearts. Each of the early books is the record of an ordeal endured by some suffering woman. In the *Scenes of Clerical Life* the interest really centres in the women whose fate is bound up with the acts of the clerical heroes; it is Janet and Molly Barton in whom we are really interested; and if poor little Tina is too weak to be a heroine, her vigorous struggle against the destinies is the pivot of the story. That George

Eliot succeeded remarkably in some male portraits, and notably in Tom Tulliver, is undeniable. Yet the men were often simply women in disguise. The piquancy, for example, of the famous character of Tito is greatly due to the fact that he is the voluptuous, selfish, but sensitive character, not unfamiliar in the fiction which deals with social intrigues, but generally presented to us in feminine costume. We are told of Daniel Deronda, upon whose character an extraordinary amount of analysis is expended, that he combined a feminine affectionateness with masculine inflexibility. To our perceptions, the feminine vein becomes decidedly the most prominent; and this is equally true of such characters as Philip Wakem and Mr. Lyon. Adam Bede, indeed, to mention no one else, is a thorough man. He represents, it would seem, that ideal of masculine strength which Miss Brontë used with curious want of success to depict in Louis Moore the firm arm, the offer of which (as we are told *à propos* of Maggie Tulliver and the offensive Stephen Guest) has in it "something strangely winning to most women." Yet if Adam Bede had shown less Christian forbearance to young Squire Donnithorne, we should have been more convinced that he was of masculine fibre throughout.

Here we approach more disputable matters. George Eliot's early books owe their charm to the exquisite painting of the old country-life—an achievement made possible by a tender imagination brooding over a vanishing past—but, if we may make the distinction, they owe their greatness to the insight into passions not confined to one race or period. Janet Dempster would lose much of her charm if she were transplanted from Milby to London; but she would still be profoundly interesting representing a marked type of feminine character. Balzac—or somebody else—said, or is said to have said that there were only possible plots in fiction. Without pledging oneself to the particular number, one may admit that the number of radically different motives is remarkably small. It may be added that even great writers rarely show their highest capacity in more than one of these typical situations. It is not hard to say which is George Eliot's favourite theme. We may call it—speaking with proper reserve—the woman in need of a confessor. We may have the comparatively shallow nature, the poor wilful little Tina, or Hetty or Tessa—the mere plaything of fate, whom we pity because in her childish ignorance she is apt, like little Red Ridinghood, to mistake the wolf for a friend, though not exactly to take him for a grandmother. Or we have the woman with noble aspirations—Janet, or Dinah, or Maggie, or Romola, or Dorothea, or, may we add, Daniel Deronda—who recognises more clearly her own need of guidance, and even in failure has the lofty air of martyrdom. It is in the setting such characters before us that George Eliot has achieved her highest triumphs, and made some of her most unmistakable failures. It is here that we meet the complaint that she is too analytic; that she takes the point of view of the confessor rather than the artist; and is more anxious to probe the condition of her heroines' souls, to give us an accurate diagnosis of their spiritual complaints, and an account of their moral evolution, than to show us the character in action. If I must give my own view, I must venture a distinction. To say that George Eliot's stories are interesting as studies of human- nature, is really to say little more than that they deserve serious attention. There are stories—and very excellent and amusing stories—which have comparatively little to do with character; histories of wondrous and moving events, where you are fascinated by the vivacity of the narrator without caring much for the passions of the actors—such stories, in fact, as compose the Arabian Nights, or the voluminous works of the admirable Alexandre Dumas. We do not care to understand Aladdin's sentiments, or to say how far he differed from Sinbad and Camaralzaman. The famous musketeers have different parts to play, and so far different characters; but one does not care very much for their psychology. Still, every serious writer must derive his power from his insight into men and women. A Cervantes or Shakespeare, a Scott, a Fielding, a Richardson or Thackeray, command our attention by forcible presentation of certain types of character; and, so far, George Eliot's does not differ from her predecessors'. Nor, again, would any truly imaginative writer give us mere abstract analyses of character, instead of showing us the concrete person in action. If George Eliot has a tendency to this error it does not appear in her early period. We can see any of her best characters as distinctly, we know them by direct vision as intimately, as we know any personage in real or fictitious history. We are not put off with the formulae of their conduct, but persons are themselves revealed to us. Yet it is, I think, true that her stories are pre-eminently studies of character in this sense, that her main and conscious purpose is to set before us the living beings in what may be called, with, due apology, their statical relations—to show them, that is, in their quiet and normal state, not under the stress of exceptional events. When we once know Adam Bede or Dinah Morris, we care comparatively little for the development of the plot. Compare, for example, *Adam Bede* with the *Heart of Midlothian*, the first half of which seems to me to be one of the very noblest of all fictions, though the latter part suffers from the conventional madwoman and the bit of commonplace intrigue which Scott fancied himself bound to introduce. Jeanie Deans is, to my mind, a more powerfully drawn and altogether a more substantial and satisfactory young woman than Dinah Morris, who, with all her merits, seems to me, I will confess, to be a bit of a prig. The contrast, however, to which I refer is in the method rather than in the characters or the situation. Scott wishes to interest us in the magnificent trial scene, for which all the preceding narrative is a preparation; he is content to set the Deans family before us with a few amazingly vigorous touches, so that we may thoroughly enter into the spirit of the tremendous ordeal through which poor Jeanie Deans is to pass in the conflict between affection and duty. We first learn to know her thoroughly by her behaviour under that overpowering strain. But in *Adam Bede* we learn first to know the main actors by their conduct in a number of little scenes, most admirably devised and drawn, and serving to bring out, if not a more powerful, a more elaborate and minute manifestation of their inmost feelings. When we come to the critical parts in the story, and the final catastrophe, they are less interesting and vivid than the preliminary detail of apparently insignificant events. The trial and the arrival of the reprieve are probably the weakest and most commonplace passages; and what we really remember and enjoy are the little scenes on the village green, in Mrs. Poyser's dairy, and Adam Bede's workshop. We have there learnt to know the people themselves, and we scarcely care for what happens to them. The method is natural to a feminine observer who has learnt to interpret character by watching its manifestations in little everyday incidents, and feels comparatively at a loss when having to deal with the more exciting struggles and calamities which make a noise in the world. And therefore, as I think, George Eliot is always more admirable in careful exposition—in setting her personages before us—than in dealing with her catastrophes, where, to say the truth, she sometimes seems to become weak just when we expect her full powers to be exerted.

This is true, for example, of *Silas Marner*, where the inimitable opening is very superior to the sequel. It is still more conspicuously true of the *Mill on the Floss*. The first part of that novel appears to me to mark the culmination of her genius. So far, it is one of the rare books which it is difficult to praise in adequate language. We may naturally suspect that part of the singular vividness is due to some admixture of an autobiographical element. The sonnets called *Brother and Sister*—perhaps her most successful poetical effort—suggest that the adventures of Tom and Maggie had some counterpart in personal experience. In any case, the whole account of Maggie's childhood, the admirable pathos of the childish yearnings, and the quaint chorus of uncles and aunts, the adventure with the gipsies, the wanderings by the Floss, the visit to Tom in his school, have a freshness and brilliance of colouring showing that the workmanship is as perfect as the sentiment is tender. But when Maggie ceases to be the most fascinating child in fiction, and becomes the heroine of a novel, the falling off is grievous. The unlucky affair with Stephen Guest is simply indefensible. It may, indeed, be urged—and urged with plausibility—that it is true to nature; it is true, that is, that women of genius—and, indeed, other women—do not always show that taste in the selection of lovers which commends itself to the masculine mind. There is nothing contrary to experience in the supposition that the imagination of an impulsive girl may transfigure a very second-rate young tradesman into a lover worthy of her; but this does not excuse the author for sharing the illusion. It is painfully true that some women, otherwise excellent, may be tempted, like Janet Dempster, to take to stimulants. But we should not have been satisfied if her weakness had been represented as a creditable or venial peculiarity, or without a sense of the degradation. So it would, in any case, be hardly pleasant to make our charming Maggie the means of illustrating the doctrine that a woman of high qualities may throw herself away upon a low creature; but when she is made to act in this way, and the weakness is not duly emphasised, we are forced to suppose that George Eliot did not see what a poor creature she has really drawn. Perhaps this is characteristic of a certain feminine incapacity for drawing really masculine heroes, which is exemplified, not quite so disagreeably, in the case of Dorothea and Ladislaw. But it is a misfortune, and all the more so because the error seems to be gratuitous. If it was necessary to introduce a new lover, he should have been endowed with some qualities likely to attract Maggie's higher nature, instead of betraying his second-rate dandyism in every feature. But the engagement to Philip Wakem, who is at least a lovable character, might surely have supplied enough tragical motive for a catastrophe which would not degrade poor Maggie to common clay. As it is, what promises to be the most perfect story of its kind ends most pathetically indeed, but yet with a strain which jars most painfully upon the general harmony.

The line so sharply drawn in the *Mill on the Floss* is also the boundary between two provinces of the whole region. With Maggie's visit to St. Ogg's, we take leave of that part of George Eliot's work which can be praised without important qualification—of work so admirable in its kind that we have a sense of complete achievement. In the later stories we come upon debatable ground: we have to recognise distinct failure in hitting the mark, and to strike a balance between the good and bad qualities, instead of simply recognising the thorough harmony of a finished whole. What is the nature of the change? The shortcomings are, as I have said, obvious enough. We have, for example, the growing tendency to substitute elaborate analysis for direct presentation; there are such passages, as one to which I have referred, where we are told that it is necessary to understand Deronda's character at five-and-twenty in order to appreciate the effect of after-events; and where we have an elaborate discussion which would be perfectly admissible in the discussion of some historical character, but which, in a writer who has the privilege of creating history, strikes us as an evasion of a difficulty. When we are limited to certain facts, we are forced to theorise as to the qualities which they indicate. Real people do not always get into situations which speak for themselves. But when we can make such facts as will reveal character, we have no right to give the abstract theory for the concrete embodiment. We perceive when this is done that the reflective faculties have been growing at the expense of the imagination, and that, instead of simply enriching and extending the field of interest, they are coming into the foreground and usurping functions for which they are unfitted. The fault is palpable in *Romola*. The remarkable power not only of many passages but of the general conception of the book is unable to blind us to the fact that, after all, it is a magnificent piece of cram. The masses of information have not been fused by a glowing imagination. The fuel has put out the fire. If we fail to perceive this in the more serious passages, it is painfully evident in those which are meant to be humorous or playful. People often impose upon themselves when they are listening to solemn rhetoric, perhaps because, when we have got into a reverential frame of mind, our critical instincts are in abeyance. But it is not so easy to simulate amusement. And if anybody, with the mimicry of Mrs. Poyser or Bob Jakin in his mind, can get through the chapter called "A Florentine Joke" without coming to the conclusion that the jokes of that period were oppressive and wearisome ghosts of the facetious, he must be one of those people who take in jokes by the same faculty as scientific theorems. If we are indulgent, it must be on the ground that the historical novel proper is after all an elaborate blunder. It is really analogous to, and shows the weakness of, the various attempts at the revival of extinct phases of art with which we have been overpowered in these days. It almost inevitably falls into Scylla or Charybdis; it is either a heavy mass of information striving to be lively, or it is really lively at the price of being thoroughly shallow, and giving us the merely pretty and picturesque in place of the really impressive. If any one has succeeded in avoiding the horns of this dilemma, it is certainly not George Eliot. She had certainly very imposing authorities on her side; but I imagine that *Romola* gives unqualified satisfaction only to people who hold that academical correctness of design can supply the place of vivid directness of intuitive vision.

Yet the situation was not so much the cause as the symptom of a change. When George Eliot returned to her proper ground, she did not regain the old magic. *Middlemarch* is undoubtedly a powerful book, but to many readers it is a rather painful book, and it can hardly be called a charming book to any one. The light of common day has most unmistakably superseded the indescribable glow which illuminated the earlier writings.

The change, so far as we need consider it, is sufficiently indicated by one circumstance. The "prelude" invites us to remember Saint Theresa. Her passionate nature, we are told, demanded a consecration of life to some object of unselfish devotion. She found it in the reform of a religious order. But there are many modern Theresas who, with equally noble aspirations, can find no worthy object for their energies. They have found "no coherent social faith and order," no sufficient guidance for their ardent souls. And thus we have now and then a Saint Theresa, "foundress of nothing, whose loving heart-beats and sobs after an unattained goodness tremble off and are dispersed among hindrances instead of centering in some long recognisable deed." This, then, is the keynote of *Middlemarch*. We are to have one more variation on the theme already treated in various form; and Dorothea Brooke is to be the Saint Theresa with lofty aspirations to pass through a searching ordeal, and, if she fails in outward results, yet to win additional nobility from failure. And yet, if this be the design, it almost seems as if the book were intended for elaborate irony. Dorothea starts with some admirable, though not very novel, aspirations of the social kind, with a desire to improve drainage and provide better cottages for the poor. She meets a consummate pedant, who is pitilessly ridiculed for his petty and hidebound intellect, and immediately takes him to be her hero and guide to lofty endeavour. She fancies, as we are told, that her spiritual difficulties will be solved by the help of a little Latin and Greek. "Perhaps even Hebrew might be necessary—at least the alphabet and a few roots—in order to arrive at the core of things and judge soundly on the social duties of the Christian." She marries Mr. Casaubon, and of course is speedily undeceived. But, curiously enough, the process of enlightenment seems to be very partial. Her faith in her husband receives its death-blow as soon as she finds out—not that he is a wretched pedant, but that he is a pedant of the wrong kind. Will Ladislaw points out to her that Mr. Casaubon is throwing away his labour because he does not know German, and is therefore only abreast of poor old Jacob Bryant in the last century, instead of being a worthy contemporary of Prof. Max Müller. Surely Dorothea's error is almost as deep as ever. Casaubon is a wretched being because he has neither heart nor brains—not because his reading has been confined to the wrong set of books. Surely a man may be a prig and a pedant, though he is familiar with the very last researches of German professors. The latest theories about comparative mythology may be familiar to a man with a soul comparable only to a dry pea in a bladder. If Casaubon had been all that Dorothea fancied, if his knowledge had been thoroughly up to the mark, we should still have pitied her for her not knowing the difference between a man and a stick. Unluckily, she never seems to find out that in this stupendous blunder, and not in the pardonable ignorance as to the true value of his literary labours, is the real source of her misfortune. In fact, she hardly seems to grow wiser even at the end; for when poor Casaubon is as dead as his writings, she takes up with a young gentleman, who appears to have some good feeling, but is conspicuously unworthy of the affections of a Saint Theresa. Had *Middlemarch* been intended for a cutting satire upon the aspirations of young ladies, who wish to learn Latin and Greek, when they ought to be nursing babies and supporting hospitals, these developments of affairs would have been in perfect congruity with the design. As it is, we are left with the feeling that aspirations of this kind scarcely deserve a better fate than they meet, and that Dorothea was all the better for getting the romantic aspirations out of her head. Have not the commonplace people the best of the argument?

It would be very untrue to say that the later books show any defect of general power. I do not think, for example, that there are many passages in modern fiction so vigorous as the description of poor Lydgate, whose higher aspirations are dashed with a comparatively vulgar desire for worldly success, gradually engulfed by the selfish persistence of his wife, like a swimmer sucked down by an octopus. On the contrary, the picture is so forcible and so lifelike that one reads it with a sense of actual bitterness. And as in *Daniel Deronda*, though I am ready to confess that Mordecai and Daniel are to my mind intolerable bores, I hold the story of Grandecourt and Gwendolen to be, though not a pleasant, a singularly powerful study of the somewhat repulsive kind. And it may certainly be said both of *Romola* and of *Middlemarch*, that they have some merits of so high an order that the defects upon which I have dwelt are felt as blemishes, not as fatal errors. If there is some misunderstanding of the limits of her own powers, or some misconception of true artistic conditions, nobody can read them without the sense of having been in contact with a comprehensive and vigorous intellect, with high feeling and keen powers of observation. Only one cannot help regretting the loss of that early charm. In reading *Adam Bede*, we feel first the magic, and afterwards we recognise the power which it implies. But in *Middlemarch* we feel the power, but we ask in vain for the charm. Some such change passes over any great mind which goes through a genuine process of development. It is not surprising that the reflective powers should become more predominant in later years; that reasoning should to some extent take the place of intuitive perception; and that experience of life should give a sterner and sadder tone to the implied criticism of human nature. We are prepared to find less spontaneity, less freshness of interest in the little incidents of life, and we are not surprised that a mind so reflective and richly stored should try to get beyond the charmed circle of its early successes, and to give us a picture of wider and less picturesque aspects of human life. But this does not seem to account sufficiently for the presence of something jarring and depressing in the later work.

Without going into the question fully, one thing may be said: the modern Theresa, whether she is called Dorothea, or Maggie, or Dinah, or Janet, is the central figure in the world of George Eliot's imagination. We are to be brought to sympathise with the noble aspirations of a loving and unselfish spirit, conscious that it cannot receive any full satisfaction within the commonplace conditions of this prosaic world. How women are to find a worthier sphere of action than the mere suckling of babes and chronicling of small beer is a question for the Social Science Associations. Some people answer it by proposing to give women votes or degrees, and others would tell us that such problems can only be answered by reverting to Saint Theresa's method. The solution in terms of actual conduct lies beyond the proper province of the novelist. She has done all that she can do if she has revealed the intrinsic beauty of such a character, and its proper function in life. She should make us fall in love with Romola and Maggie, and convert us to the belief that they are the true salt of the earth.

Up to a certain point her success is complete, and it is won by high moral feeling and quick sympathy with true nobility of character. We pay willing homage to these pure and lofty feminine types, and we may get some measure of the success by comparing them with other dissatisfied heroines whose aspirations are by no means so lofty or so compatible with delicate moral sentiment. But the triumph has its limits. In the sweet old-world country life a Janet or a Dinah can find some sort of satisfaction from an evangelical preacher, or within the limits of the Methodist church. If the thoughts and ways of her circle are narrow, it is in harmony with itself, and we may feel its beauty without asking awkward questions. But as soon as Maggie has left her quiet fields and reached even such a centre of civilisation as St. Ogg's, there is a jar and a discord. *Romola* is in presence of a great spiritual disturbance where the highest aspirations are doomed to the saddest failure; and when we get to *Middlemarch* we feel that the charm has somehow vanished. Even in the early period, Mrs. Poyser's bright common-sense has some advantages over Dinah Morris's high-wrought sentiment. And in *Middlemarch* we feel more decidedly that high aspirations are doubtful qualifications; that the ambitious young devotee of science has to compound with the quarrelling world, and the brilliant young Dorothea to submit to a decided clipping of her wings. Is it worth while to have a lofty nature in such surroundings? The very bitterness with which the triumph of the lower characters is set forth seems to betray a kind of misgiving. And it is the presence of this feeling, as well as the absence of the old picturesque scenery, that gives a tone of melancholy to the later books. Some readers are disposed to sneer, and to look upon the heroes and heroines as male and female prigs, who are ridiculous if they persist and contemptible when they fail. Others are disposed to infer that the philosophy which they represent is radically unsatisfactory. And some may say that, after all, the picture is true, however sad, and that, in all ages, people who try to lift their heads above the crowd must lay their account with martyrdom and be content to be uncomfortable. The moral, accepted by George Eliot herself, is indicated at the end of *Middlemarch*. A new Theresa, she tells us, will not have the old opportunity any more than a new Antigone would "spend heroic piety in daring all for the sake of a brother's funeral; the medium in which these ardent deeds took shape is for ever gone." There will be many Dorotheas, and some of them doomed to worse sacrifices than the Dorothea of *Middlemarch*, and we must be content to think that her influence spent itself through many invisible channels, but was not the less potent because unseen.

Perhaps that is not a very satisfactory conclusion. I cannot here ask why it should not have been more satisfactory. We must admit that there is something rather depressing in the thought of these anonymous Dorotheas feeling about vaguely for some worthy outlet of their energies, taking up with a man of science and discovering him to be an effete pedant, wishing ardently to reform the world, but quite unable to specify the steps to be taken, and condescending to put up with a very commonplace life in a vague hope that somehow or other they will do some good. Undoubtedly we must admit that, wherever the fault lies, our Theresas have some difficulty in fully manifesting their excellence. But with all their faults, we feel that they embody the imperfect influence of a nature so lofty in its sentiment, so wide in its sympathies, and so keen in its perceptions, that we may wait long before it will be adequately replaced. The imperfections belong in great measure to a time of vast revolutions in thought which produce artistic discords as well as philosophic anarchy. Lower minds escape the difficulty because they are lower; and even to be fully sensitive to the deepest searchings of heart of the time is to possess a high claim on our respect. At lowest, however we may differ from George Eliot's teaching on many points, we feel her to be one who, in the midst of great perplexities, has brought great intellectual powers to setting before us a lofty moral ideal, and, in spite of manifest shortcomings, has shown certain aspects of a vanishing social phase with a power and delicacy unsurpassed in her own sphere.

—Leslie Stephen, "George Eliot,"
The Cornhill Magazine, vol. 43,
1881, pp. 152–168

ANTHONY TROLLOPE (1883)

Anthony Trollope (1815–82), one of the leading English novelists of his time, was the celebrated author of the Barsetshire series and Palliser series. Trollope first met G.H. Lewes at a dinner given by the publisher George Smith; Trollope later convinced Lewes to act as the first editor of the *Fortnightly Review*, which Trollope had co-founded. Despite his frequent visits to the Leweses' home, Trollope succumbed to the popular prejudice against Eliot insofar as he did not introduce his wife to the novelist. Nevertheless, Eliot and Trollope held great respect for each other's works.

The following passage asserts Eliot's preeminence in Victorian fiction. It also represents the common opinion that Eliot, by having drifted away from the simpler works with which she had launched her caeer, had lost the ear of the public. Indeed, Trollope had warned Eliot after reading the first part of *Romola*: "do not fire too much over the heads of your readers" (*Letters of Anthony Trollope*: 115–116). There is truth in the idea that Eliot's mind was of a strongly intellectual bent and that this sometimes got the better of her writing, as in *Romola*. Many readers formed similar objections to *Middlemarch* and *Daniel Deronda*, though the suggestion that in those novels the "philosopher" overshadows the "portrait-painter" seems singularly unfair.

At the present moment George Eliot is the first of English novelists, and I am disposed to place her second of those of my time. She is best known to the literary world as a writer of prose fiction, and not improbably whatever of permanent fame she may acquire will come from her novels. But the nature of her intellect is very far removed indeed from that which is common to the tellers of stories. Her imagination is no doubt strong, but it acts in analysing rather than in creating. Everything that comes before her is pulled to pieces so that the inside of it shall be seen, and be seen if possible by her readers as clearly as by herself. This searching analysis is carried so far that, in studying her latter writings, one feels oneself to be in company with some philosopher rather than with a novelist. I doubt whether any young person can read with pleasure either *Felix Holt, Middlemarch,* or *Daniel Deronda*. I know that they are very difficult to many that are not young.

Her personifications of character have been singularly terse and graphic, and from them has come her great hold on the public,—though by no means the greatest effect which she has produced. The lessons which she teaches remain, though it is not for the sake of the lessons that her pages are read. Seth Bede, Adam Bede, Maggie and Tom Tulliver, old Silas Marner, and, much above all, Tito, in *Romola,* are characters which, when once known, can never be forgotten. I cannot say quite so much for any of those in her later works, because in them the philosopher so greatly overtops the portrait-painter, that, in the dissection of the mind, the outward signs seem to have been forgotten. In her, as yet, there is no symptom whatever of that weariness of mind which, when felt by the reader, induces him to declare that the author has written himself out. It is not from decadence that we do not have another Mrs. Poyser, but because the author soars to things which seem to her to be higher than Mrs. Poyser.

It is, I think, the defect of George Eliot that she struggles too hard to do work that shall be excellent. She lacks ease. Latterly the signs of this have been conspicuous in her style, which has always been and is singularly correct, but which has become occasionally obscure from her too great desire to be pungent. It is impossible not to feel the struggle, and that feeling begets a flavour of affectation. In *Daniel Deronda*, of which at this moment only a portion has been published, there are sentences which I have found myself compelled to read three times before I have been able to take home to myself all that the writer has intended. Perhaps I may be permitted here to say, that this gifted woman was among my dearest and most intimate friends.

—ANTHONY TROLLOPE, *An Autobiography*,
vol. 1, 1883, pp. 66–69

GEORGE WILLIS COOKE "THE LIMITATIONS OF HER THOUGHT" (1884)

George Willis Cooke (1848–1923) was an American writer and Unitarian minister. Ordained in 1872, he coupled his activities as a minister with literary work. Cooke's study of George Eliot was preceded by a similar account of Ralph Waldo Emerson (1881) and followed by a study of Robert Browning (1891). Cooke retired from the ministry in 1899 in order to devote himself to his writing and lecturing, and published extensively on matters ranging from literary criticism to Unitarian history, before returning to the ministry in 1922.

Though Cooke lays too great a stress on Eliot's positivist convictions, he offers a thought-provoking reflection on her philosophy. Eliot was undoubtedly extremely interested in positivism, a philosophy begun by Auguste Comte (1798–1857), which involved the belief that human progress and understanding could be achieved through science. This eventually led to the discipline of sociology. Eliot greatly sympathized with these ideas, yet resisted joining the positivists officially and refused invitations to write works that would explicitly advertise their ideas.

Cooke is wrong to state that any didacticism to be found in her novels concerns positivist ideas, yet he makes a worthwhile attempt to place Eliot in the context of a broader literary and philosophical movement. Cook identifies many of the important themes in the novels such as the importance of the hereditary, tradition versus modernity, the "organic social life," and self-renunciation. It is not surprising that, as a minister, Cooke balks at what he deems to be Eliot's beliefs. Nevertheless, despite Cooke's conclusion about the narrowness of Eliot's outlook, which can be questioned, this exploration of her ideas is balanced and insightful.

It must be remembered that George Eliot does not use the novel merely for the purpose of inculcating certain doctrines, and that her genius for artistic creation is of a very high order. In dealing with her as a thinker and as a moral and religious teacher, she is to be regarded, first of all, as a poet and an artist. Her ethics are subordinate to her art; her religion is subsidiary to her genius. That she always deliberately set about the task of introducing her positivism into the substance of her novels is not to be supposed. This would be to imply a forgetfulness on her part of her own methods, and a prostration of art to purposes she would have scorned to adopt. This is evidently true, however, that certain features of the positive and the evolution philosophy had so thoroughly approved themselves to her mind as to cause them to be accepted as a completely satisfactory explanation of the world, so far as any explanation is possible. So heartily were they received, so fully did they become incorporated with the substance of her thinking, that she viewed all human experiences in their light. They had ceased to be theory and speculation with her. When she thought about the world, when she observed the acts of men, the positivist explanation was at once applied, and instinctively.

That she did teach positivism is unfortunately true, so far as her literary touch and expression is concerned. That philosophy affects all her books with its subtly insinuating flavor, and it gives meaning and bias to most of them. They thus gain in definiteness of purpose, in moral vigor, in minutely faithful study of some phases of human experience, and in a massive impression of thoughtfulness which her work creates. At the same time, they undoubtedly lose in value as studies of life; in free range of expression for her genius, her poetry and her art; and in that spiritual vision which looks forward with keen gazing eyes of hope and confident inquiry.

Her teaching, like most teaching, is a mingled good and evil. In more than one direction her ethical and religious influence was most wholesome and effective. She brought into clear light a few great facts, and made them the more conspicuous by the strong emphasis she gave them. This is, in the main, the method of all teaching and of all progress. Development seldom proceeds in a direct line, but rather, so far as man is concerned, by forcible emphasis laid on some great fact which has been previously neglected. The idealism of a previous age had shown the value of certain facts and tendencies in human nature, but it had exaggerated some faculties and capacities of man, as well as neglected others. In consequence, our own time swings to the other extreme, and cannot have too much of evolution and positivism.

Idealism is in human nature, and will give itself expression. Positivism is also a result of our experience and of our study of the universe, both material and mental; it is a result of the desire for definite knowledge. As a re-action against the excesses of idealism it is a powerful leaven, and it brings into necessary prominence those facts which are neglected by the opposite philosophy. It takes account of facts, and scorns mysticism; and it thus appeals to a deep-seated bias of the time.

George Eliot's books have an interest as an attempt at an interpretation of life from its more practical and realistic side, and not less as a re-action against the influences of very nearly all the great literary minds of the earlier half of the century in England. Under the lead of Coleridge and Wordsworth, and influenced by German thought and literature, a remarkable movement was then developed in English literature. The outcome of that movement has been surpassed only by that of the age of Shakspere. Freshness of thought, love of nature, profound humanitarian convictions, and spontaneity wedded to great largeness of ideas, characterize this period and its noble work. Such an age is almost invariably followed by an age of re-action, criticism, realism and analysis. An instinctive demand for a portrayal of the more positive side of life, and the influence of science, have developed a new literary school. For doctrine it teaches agnosticism, and in method it cares mainly for art and beauty of form. Towards the development of the new school George Eliot has been a leading influence, though her sympathies have not gone with all its tendencies and results.

If Wordsworth exaggerated the importance of the intuitive and personal, George Eliot equally exaggerated the value of the historic and hereditary. It was desirable, however, that the relations of life to the past should be brought out more distinctly by a literary development of their relations to the present, and that the influence of social heredity should be seen as affecting life on all sides. Tradition is a large and persistent element in the better life of the race, while the past certainly has a powerful influence over the present. This fact was neglected by Wordsworth, and especially is it neglected by the intuitive philosophies. They ignore the lessons of the past, and assume that a new and perfect world is to be evoked from the depths of consciousness. That to think a better world is to create a better world, they seem to take for granted, while the fact is that the truer life is the result of a painful and long-continued struggle against adverse conditions. What has been, persists in remaining, and the past, with all its narrowness and prejudices, continues to influence men more powerfully than does clear thought or regard for the truth. Emotion and sentiment cling about what has become sacred with age. Channels for thought and activity having once been made, it is very difficult to abandon them for untried paths approved even by reason.

The historic view is one of much importance, and is likely to be overlooked by the poets and novelists. It is also ignored by the radicals in morals and religion. Much which George Eliot says on this subject is of great value, and may be heeded with the utmost profit. Her words of wisdom, however, lose much of their value because they utterly ignore those spontaneous and supernatural elements of man's higher life which lift it quite out of the region of dependence on history.

There is something to be said in behalf of George Eliot's attitude towards religion, which caused her to hold it in reverence, even when rejecting the objective validity of its dogmas. Yet much more is to be said for that other attitude, which is faithful to the law of reason, and believes that reason is competent to say some truer and larger word on a subject of such vital importance and such constant interest to man. That both reason and tradition are to be listened to reverently is true, but George Eliot so zealously espoused the cause of tradition as to give it an undue prominence. Her lesson was needed, however, and we may be all the better able to profit by it because she was so much an enthusiast in proclaiming its value. The even poise of perfect truth is no more to be had from her pages than from those of others.

The emphasis she laid on feeling and sentiment was a needed one, as a counterpoise to the exaggerations of rationalism. Man does live in his feelings more than in his reason. He is a being of sentiment, a creature of impulse, his social life is one of the affections. In all the ranges of his moral, religious and social life he is guided mainly by his emotions and sentiments. It cannot be said, however, as George Eliot would have us say, that these are human born and have no higher meaning. They are the outgrowth of spiritual reality, as well as of human experience; they repeat the foregleams and foresights of a

> far-off divine event,
> To which the whole creation moves.

Life is enriched and flooded with light by the emotions, and feeling, true and tender and pure, is as much the symbol of humanity as reason itself. It was therefore well that some one should attempt to justify the emotional life against the aspersions of those who have done it grave injustice. It is true that man is not a being who wholly arrives at his method of life through reason, but feeling lends quite as important aid. He does not only think, but he has emotions as well; he not only weighs evidence, but he acts by impulse. He is continually led by the emotions, sentiments and impulses created for him by the life of ages past. Without emotion there could be no art, no poetry and no music. Without emotion there would be no religion and no spiritual life. Sentiment sweetens, beautifies and endears all that is human and natural.

Emotion and the affections, however, seem to be shorn of their highest beauty and glory when they are restricted to a merely earthly origin and compass of power. It is altogether impossible to believe that their own impulse to look beyond the human is a delusion, and that they really have nothing to report that is valid from beyond the little round which man treads. To believe in the human beauty and glory of the feelings, and to rejoice in their power to unite us to our kind, need imply no forgetfulness of their demand for a wider expression and a higher communion.

Her theory of the origin of feeling is not to be accepted. It means something more than an inheritance of ancestral experience. It is the result rather than the cause of reason, for reason has an influence she did not acknowledge, and an original capacity which she never saw. Her view of feeling was mainly theoretical, for she was led in her attitude towards the facts of life, not by sentiment, but by reason. Hers was a thoughtful rather than an impulsive mind, and given to logic more than to emotion.

Her enthusiasm for altruism, her zeal for humanity, lends a delightful feature to her books. It gives a glow and a consecration to her work, and makes her as great a prophet as positivism is capable of creating. And it is no idle power she awakens in her positivist faith in man. She shames those who claim a broader and better faith. Zeal for man is no mean gospel, as she gives life and meaning to it in her books. To live for others, too many are not likely to do. She made altruism beautiful, she made it a consecration and a religion. Those who cannot accept her agnosticism and her positivism may learn much from her faith in man and from her enthusiasm for humanity. No faith is worth much which does not lead to a truer and a more helpful love of man. Any faith is good in so far as it makes us more humane and sympathetic. In this regard, the radicalism of George Eliot was a great advance on much of the freethinking of our century. She desired to build, not to destroy. She was no iconoclast, no hater of what other men love and venerate. Her tendencies were all on the side of progress, good order and social growth.

Her conception of the organic social life of the race is one of great value. It led her to believe in the possibility of a social organization in the future based on science, and better capable of meeting all the wants of mankind than the more personal and competitive methods have done. This belief in the organic unity of the race is not necessarily positivist in its character, for Hegel entertained it as fully as does Herbert Spencer. The larger social life will come, however, as individuals are moved to lead the way, and not alone as the result of a general evolutionary process. On its mental side, her social theory is to be regarded with grave suspicions, for it brings all minds to the same level. No mind of commanding influence is to be found in her books. No powerful intellect gives greatness to any of her plots. Her Felix Holt is not a man of original and positive thought. We accept, but do not enthusiastically admire him. Deronda is a noble character, but he in no sense represents the largest things of which a social leader is capable. He disappoints and is weak, and he has no power to create the highest kind of leadership. In other words, he is not a great man. The world's reformers have been of another temper and mettle. He is no Mazzini, no Luther. George Eliot's social theories left no room for such men. They were superfluous in her social system. The man not to be explained by heredity and tradition had no place in her books; and no genius, no great man, can ever be explained by heredity and tradition alone.

George Eliot evidently desired to destroy individualism as a social force. The individual, according to her teaching, is to renounce himself for the sake of the race. He is to live, not as a personal being, but as a member of the social organization; to develop his altruistic nature, not to perfect his personal character. The finer flavor of personality is brushed mercilessly away by this method.

Reason needs to be justified in opposition to her excessive praise of feeling. Meanwhile, the capacity of man to live a life higher than that of his social state is to be asserted. He is indeed a member of humanity, but humanity does not absorb him to the cost of his personality. Life is strong in those ages in which the individual is able to assert his own personality, in opposition to what is imperfect and untrue in the life of his time. This failure to recognize the worth and capacity of the individual is a most serious defect in George Eliot's work, and mars it in many directions. A very competent critic has shown how serious is the limitation arising in this manner, and permeating her books with a false conception of life.

"So far as George Eliot's life is concerned," says Mr. Stopford Brooke, "she was eager in her self-development, and as eager in her sympathies. But it was a different matter in the main drift of her work. She lowered the power of individualism. Nay, she did not believe in its having any self-caused or God-caused existence. Few have individualized their characters more than she did, and of these characters we have many distinct types. But she individualized them with, I may say, almost the set purpose of showing that their individualism was to be sacrificed to the general welfare of the race. The more her characters cling to their individuality the more they fail in reaching happiness or peace. If they are noble characters, they are finally obliged, through their very nobility, to surrender all their ideals, all their personal hopes, all the individual ends they hoped to develop; and they reach peace finally only through utter surrender of personality in humanity. The characters of her books who do not do this, who cling to their individuality and maintain it, succeed in life, for the most part, if they are strong; are broken to pieces if they are weak; but in all cases, save one, are not the noble but the ignoble characters. The whole of her books is a suppressed attack on individualism, and an exaltation of self-renunciation as the only force of progress, as the only ground of morality. I leave aside here, as apart from the moral side of the subject, the view that individual power or weakness of any kind is the consequence of the past, of race, of physical causes. What a man is found to do is not affected by that, in her view.... No one can deny that the morality is a lofty one, and, as far as it asserts self-renunciation, entirely useful; we have with all our hearts to thank George Eliot for that part of her work. But when sacrifice of self is made, in its last effort, equivalent to the sacrifice of individuality, the doctrine of self-renunciation is driven to a vicious extreme. It is not self-sacrifice which is then demanded, it is suicide. Fully accepted, it would reduce the whole of the human race to hopelessness. That, indeed, is the last result. A sad and fatal hopelessness of life broods over all the nobler characters. All their early ideals are sacrificed, all their early joys depart, all the pictures they formed are blotted out. They gain peace through renunciation, after long failure; some happiness in yielding to the inevitable, and harmonizing life with it; and some blessedness in doing all they can for the progress of those who follow them, for the good of those that are with them. Their self is conquered, not through ennoblement of personality, but through annihilation of personality. And having surrendered their separate personality, they then attain the fitting end, silence forevermore. It is no wonder that no characters are so sad, that none steep the reader in such hopelessness of joy, as the noble characters of the later works of George Eliot. They want the mighty power, the enkindling hopes, the resurrection of life, the joy and rapture which deepens toward death and enables man to take up the ideals of youth again."

If too severe in some directions, this criticism is substantially sound. It does not matter what theory of personality we adopt, in a philosophical sense, if that theory upholds personal confidence and force of will. If it does not do this, the whole result is evil. This lack of faith in personality saddened all the work done by George Eliot. In theory a believer in an everbrightening future, and no pessimist, yet the outcome of her work is dark with despondency and grief.

Life is sad, hard and ascetic in her treatment of it. An ascetic tone runs through all her work, the result of her theories of renunciation. The same sternness and cheerlessness is to be seen in the poetry and painting of the pre-Raphaelites. The joy, freshness and sunniness of Raphael is not to be found in their work. Life is painful, puritanic and depressing to them. Old age seems to be upon them, or the decadence of a people that has once been great. Human nature does not need that this strain be put upon it. Life is stronger when more assertive of itself. It has a right to assert itself in defiance of mere rules, and only when it does so is it true and great. The ascetic tone is one of the worst results of a scientific view of the world as applied to literature; for it is thoroughly false both in fact and in sentiment. The strong, hopeful, youthful look at life is the one which literature demands, and because it is the nearest the heart and spirit of life itself. The dead nation produces a dead literature. The age made doubtful by an excess of science produces a literature burdened with sadness and pain. Great and truthful as it may be, it lacks in power to conquer the world. It shows, not the power of Homer, but the power of Lucretius.

Her altruism has its side of truth, but not all of the truth is in it. Any system of thought which sees nothing beyond man is not likely to find that which is most characteristic in man himself. He is to be fathomed, if fathomed at all, by some other line than that of his own experience. If he explains the universe, the universe is also necessary to explain him. Man apart from the supersensuous is as little to be understood as man apart from humanity. He belongs to a Universal Order quite as much as he belongs to the human order. Man may be explained by evolution, but evolution is not to be explained by anything in the nature of man. It requires some larger field of vision to take note of that elemental law. Not less true is it that mind does not come obediently under this method of explanation, that it demands account of how matter is transformed into thought. The law of thought needs to be solved after mind is evolved.

There is occasion for surprise that a mind so acute and logical as George Eliot's did not perceive that the evolution philosophy has failed to settle any of the greater problems suggested by Kant. The studies of Darwin and Spencer have certainly made it impossible longer to accept Locke's theory of the origin of all knowledge in individual experience, but they have not in any degree explained the process of thought or the origin of ideas. The gulf between the physiological processes in the brain and thought has not been bridged even by a rope walk. The total disparity of mind and matter resists all efforts to reduce them to one. The utmost which the evolution philosophy has so far done, is to attempt to prove that mind is a function of matter or of the physiological process. This conclusion is as far as possible from being that of unity of mind and matter.

That man is very ignorant, and that this world ought to demand the greater share of his attention and energies, are propositions every reasonable person is ready to accept. Granted their truth, all that is necessarily true in agnosticism has been arrived at. It is a persistent refusal to see what lies behind outward facts which gives agnosticism all its practical justification. Art itself is a sufficient refutation of the assertion that we know nothing of what lies behind the apparent. That we know something of causes, every person who uses his own mind may be aware. At the same time, the rejection of the doctrine of rights argues obedience to a theory, rather than humble acceptance of the facts of history. That doctrine of rights, so scorned by George Eliot, has wrought most of the great and wholesome social changes of modern times. Her theory of duties can show no historic results whatever.

To separate George Eliot's theories from her genius it seems impossible to do, but this it is necessary to do in order to give both their proper place. All praise, her work demands on its side where genius is active. It is as a thinker, as a theorizer, she is to be criticised and to be declared wanting. Her work was crippled by her philosophy, or if not crippled, then it was made less strong of limb and vigorous of body by that same philosophy. It is true of her as of Wordsworth, that she grew prosy because she tried to be philosophical. It is true of her as it is not true of him, that her work lacks in the breadth which a large view of the world gives. His was no provincial conception of nature or of man. Hers was so in a most emphatic sense. The philosophy she adopted is not and cannot become the philosophy of more than a small number of persons. In the nature of the case it is doomed to be the faith of a few students and cultured people. It can stir no common life, develop no historic movements, inaugurate no reforms, nor give to life a diviner meaning. Whether it be true or not,—and this need not here be asked,—this social and moral limitation of its power is enough to condemn it for the purposes of literature. In so far as George Eliot's work is artistic, poetic, moral and human, it is very great, and no word too strong can be said in its praise. It is not too excessive enthusiasm to call her, on the whole, the equal of any novelist. Her genius is commanding and elemental. She has originality, strength of purpose, and a profound insight into character. Yet her work is weakened by its attachment to a narrow theory of life. Her philosophy is transitory in its nature. It cannot hold its own, as developed by her, for any great length of time. It has the elements of its own destruction in itself. The curious may read her for her speculations; the many will read her for her realism, her humanity and her genius. In truth, then, it would have been better if her work had been inspired by great spiritual aims and convictions.

—George Willis Cooke,
"The Limitations of Her Thought,"
George Eliot: A Critical Study of Her Life,
Writings and Philosophy, 1884, pp. 413–424

Charlotte Yonge (1888)

The deeply religious English novelist Charlotte Yonge (1823–1901) was strongly influenced by the tractarian John Keble, who supervised her confirmation when she was fifteen. Church themes and religious values play a leading part in her fiction, which she began publishing in 1844. Her family allowed her to pursue her writerly interests on the condition that any profit was donated to charity. Yonge, who published more than two hundred works of fiction and nonfiction, is best known for *The Heir of Redclyffe* (1853), in which a somewhat dissipated youth gradually embraces a more pious life.

Though Yonge's novels are very different from Eliot's, the tractarian writer was still interested in the realist novelist. In 1885, Yonge published an article in the *Monthly Packet* discussing Eliot's life and works through letters written between two characters. "Una" and "Arachne" discuss the novels, reserving the most praise for *Adam Bede*, but struggle to reconcile their admiration for the novels with their condemnation of Eliot's lifestyle. A similar dilemma emerges from the following extract, an excerpt from the novel *Beechcroft at Rockstone*, a little-known family chronicle that explores class distinctions. The confiscation of *Adam Bede* from a child provides an illustration of the way in which Eliot's works could be considered shocking to her contemporaries. *Silas Marner* escaped such censure and was often alluded to as a fairy tale; *Romola* was too respectably serious to be shocking.

She was angered when Aunt Jane put a stop to some sportive passes and chatter on the stairs between Valetta and Alice Mount, and still more so when her aunt took away *Adam Bede* from the former, as not desirable reading at eleven years old.

It was only the remembrance of her mother's positive orders that withheld Gillian from the declaration that mamma always let them read George Eliot; and in a cooler moment of reflection she was glad she had abstained, for she recollected that *always* was limited to mamma's having read most of *Romola* aloud to her and Mysie, and to her having had *Silas Marner* to read when she was unwell in lodgings, and there was a scarcity of books.

—Charlotte Yonge,
Beechcroft at Rockstone,
1880; 1889, pp. 49–50

Oscar Browning (1890)

Oscar Browning (1837–1923) was an English historian and teacher and a fellow of King's College, Cambridge. From 1862, Browning ran a boardinghouse at Eton, where he brought in decorations by William Morris and circulated pre-Raphaelite ideas and art. His attempts at reform were met with vigorous opposition, exacerbated by his homosexuality, and he was dismissed in 1875. Browning developed a close friendship with George Eliot after having invited the Leweses to visit him in 1867. It was Eliot to whom Browning turned after his dismissal, and he considered her the most important woman in his life after his mother. However, Browning would later start a cruel and apparently unfounded rumor that, when Eliot went through Lewes's papers after his death, she found evidence that he had been unfaithful to her and, in disgust, accepted Cross's proposal of marriage.

Here, Browning considers which novels by Eliot made the greatest impact on the reading public. Browning considers the claims of each novel, except *The Mill on the Floss* and *Felix Holt*, to be deemed the best. For *Adam Bede*, it is the insightful portrait of the Midlands and the wit; for *Silas Marner*, a "gem"-like quality and simplicity to which readers responded enthusiastically. Browning departs from popular opinion in writing that "the joints between erudition and imagination cannot be discovered" in *Romola*. He goes on to stress the cultural importance of *Middlemarch* but suggests that, though the novel entered the psyche of the nation, it prompted a less ardent worship from its readers than many of Eliot's other works. Perhaps most compellingly and atypically, Browning chooses *Daniel Deronda* as his personal favorite: he sums up the objections to Eliot's last novel, before recognizing its undoubted artistic ambition. In many ways, this view reflects that of recent criticism, which has sought to rehabilitate *Daniel Deronda* as an important work.

It remains for me to sum up in this last chapter the principal characteristics of George Eliot's art, the lines of development which it followed, and the aims which she set herself in working it out. For this purpose her poetry may be set on one side. It was always subordinate to her prose and, as has been maintained in the foregoing pages, was mainly a concentrated form of expression specially adapted to her more subtle and imaginative thoughts. To deal, then, with her novels: Which of them do we rank the highest? It would probably be difficult to get any large number of people to unite in the same conclusion. The popular vote, as shown by the publishers' account books, is, I believe, in favour of *Adam Bede*. It is not difficult to understand this. The title of the novel—the names of the first created man and of the first English writer—strikes the keynote of its character. The scene is laid in the heart of the Midlands. The story is a simple tale of a thoughtless boy and a ruined girl—simple yet full of tragic pathos. The deeper thought of the book is expressed in the forms of Puritanism, like all deeper thought in the great mass of English people. It is the wittiest of George Eliot's novels. It is written straight out of her own life. Adam Bede was her father, Dinah was her aunt, the name Poyser seems to be compounded of the names of her mother and her stepmother. The story of Hetty was a true one, and may have lain nearer to her heart than is generally supposed. All this goes to justify the popular verdict. Like the ancient wrestler, she drew her strength from mother earth, and in no book did she touch mother earth so closely.

But although this is the popular, it is not the universal opinion. Men of letters, I believe, give the palm to *Silas Marner*. They are attracted by the exquisite workmanship of the story. The plot was constructed by George Eliot out of the merest hint. The story was written in haste, at one gush. It is a perfect gem—a pure work of art, in which the demands of art have alone to be considered. A large class of admirers would give their vote to *Romola*. It is, as I have said before, perhaps, the best historical novel ever written. Replete with learning, weighted with knowledge in every page, the finish is so rare that the joints between erudition and imagination cannot be discovered. Read it when you have never been to Florence, it will make you long to go there; read it when you have learnt to love Florence, it will make you love Florence more; read it when you have studied the Renaissance, which George Eliot had studied so deeply, and you will feel its beauties as those feel the beauties of a symphony of Beethoven who know the score by heart. There is the character of Tito, so special yet so universal, the creature of his own age and yet the creature of any age, the embodiment of weak selfishness which knows not where it goes, now and ever the most fruitful cause of human misery; and Romola herself, a saint living in the world, a prototype of Dorothea. Yet, say others, the book has great inherent faults. All historical novels are inartistic; they are bad, as historical pictures are bad, as programme music is bad. No historical picture represents the scene as it actually occurred; no music ever realized to us the sound of a storm, a nightingale, or a quail. The armour of erudition encumbers the limbs; the wise man, like the brave brothers in *Princess Ida,* throws it off when he goes into action. Again, the novel is not a true picture of Italian life. Men who have lived long in Italy, and have drunk deeply of its spirit, complain that they cannot read the book with pleasure. The life of Tuscany which it describes is to them a nightmare, a Frankenstein, an artificial monster, not living flesh and blood.

I might quote the highest authority for the superiority of *Middlemarch,* in which George Eliot returns to the Midlands. It is a great prose epic, large in size, commanding in structure, affording an ample space for a great artist to work upon. Perhaps even more than *Adam Bede* has it become part of the ordinary furniture of our minds, of the current coin of our thoughts. Casaubon, Will Ladislaw, Mr. Brooke are types which are ever present with us, like Becky Sharpe and Colonel Newcome; and if Dorothea and Lydgate are more remote, it is because they are rarer characters, not because they are less truly drawn. *Middlemarch* gives George Eliot the chiefest claim to stand by the side of Shakespeare. Both drew their inspiration from the same sources, the villages and the country houses which we know so well.

If I am asked the question with which I set out, I always reply—her last novel, *Daniel Deronda.* I know well, only too well, the criticisms which have been levelled at the book from its first appearance to the present day. I have become tired and sick of hearing that the characters are unreal, that there is not a man or woman in the story whom you can take away with you and live with. I know that Daniel is thought to be a prig, and the Jew Mordecai a bore; that Gwendolen is thought impossible, and Grandcourt a stage villain; that the language is held to be strained and uncouth, full of far-fetched tropes and metaphors drawn from unfamiliar science. It is said there is no motive power in the action, no reason for the characters behaving as they behave. What rational person can care for the return of the Jews to Palestine? Is a young man who stakes his life on such an issue worthy of five minutes' consideration? Would a handsome young Englishman, brought up as a Christian at a public school or university, be suddenly overjoyed to find that he was a Jew? No, in *Daniel Deronda* thought and learning have usurped the place of art. It belongs to the worst type of all novels, a novel with a tendency. The influence of George Lewes, which may have strengthened his wife's mind at first, has acquired in this a fatal predominance. Biological studies have ruined her fine sensibility. George Eliot has passed her prime. As in the "Transfiguration" of Raphael, we see in *Deronda* the downward movement of a great mind, a movement which, if followed, would have disastrous effect upon the national literature.

With none of this can I agree. To me *Daniel Deronda* is one step further upwards in the career of a soaring genius who was destined, if life was spared, to achieve greater heights than any to which it had yet risen. It is the result of the normal and regular growth of unrivalled powers which were ever seeking subjects more and more worthy for their exercise. It is as superior to *Adam Bede* as *Hamlet* is superior to *Much Ado about Nothing*. It is an effort to realize the highest purposes of art, to seize the strongest passions, the loftiest heights and the lowest depths of human nature. If it fails in execution it is because the task cannot yet be accomplished. But if the work is ever to be done, the way must be paved by partial failure. It is better to have tried and failed, than never to have tried at all.

—Oscar Browning,
Life of George Eliot, 1890, pp. 140–144

WILLIAM ERNEST HENLEY (1890)

William Ernest Henley (1849–1903) was an English writer. Despite serious health problems, which led to the amputation of his left leg, Henley made his mark as a journalist and editor. As editor of the *Magazine of Art* from 1881 to 1886, he celebrated the works of Rodin and Whistler. He also edited the *National Observer*, which published works by George Bernard Shaw, Thomas Hardy, Rudyard Kipling, and H.G. Wells. Henley is also known as a model for the character of Long John Silver in *Treasure Island* (1881–82), written by his close friend Robert Louis Stevenson.

Henley's caricatural style created a number of sound bites that would help later writers to stereotype George Eliot. Though Henley professes to lay out other people's views, the way in which he does so did far more harm to Eliot's reputation than the original opinions he picks up. Henley's targets are Eliot's didacticism, style, and portrayal of male characters. The "Novel-with-a-Purpose" was an umbrella term used to evoke widely varying didactic works, from those that set out to preach in the most obvious terms to those that seemed to put forward certain moral, political or religious ideas. Eliot's novels undoubtedly display her ideas—to name a few, about duty, the pace of social change, and the narrowness of the female sphere—but they are by no means as didactic as the label "Novel-with-a-Purpose" implies. In her essays in the *Westminster Review*, Eliot made it clear that while she believed that art could and should strive to diffuse moral ideas, the novelist should at all costs avoid preaching. Nevertheless, Eliot was considered for a while, dismissively, as a didactic novelist.

Henley's image of Eliot's "Death's-Head Style" also stuck. Modernist writers were fond of attacking the funereal quality of their ancestors' works and concerns. Many writers had previously expressed their opinion that readers had to work too hard at Eliot's novels, though rarely with Henley's scathing satire.

Again, Henley was not the first to quibble at the portrayal of Eliot's male heroes, a particular bugbear of Leslie Stephen and Henry James. The phrase "governesses in revolt" is yet another of Henley's effective rebukes. The epigrams that follow complete this lighthearted but injurious portrayal of Eliot.

It was thought that with George Eliot the Novel-with-a-Purpose had really come to be an adequate instrument for the regeneration of humanity. It was understood that Passion only survived to point a moral or provide the materials of an awful tale, while Duty, Kinship, Faith, were so far paramount as to govern Destiny and mould the world. A vague, decided flavour of Liberty, Equality, and Fraternity was felt to pervade the moral universe, a chill but seemly halo of Golden Age was seen to play soberly about things in general. And it was with confidence anticipated that those perfect days were on the march when men and women would propose—(from the austerest motives)—by the aid of scientific terminology.

To the Sceptic—(an apostate, and an undoubted male)—another view was preferable. He held that George Eliot had carried what he called the 'Death's-Head Style' of art a trifle too far. He read her books in much the same spirit and to much the same purpose that he went to the gymnasium and diverted himself with parallel bars. He detested her technology; her sensationalism revolted while it amused him; and when she put away her puppets and talked of them learnedly and with understanding—instead of letting them explain themselves, as several great novelists have been content to do—he recalled how Wisdom crieth out in the street and no man regardeth her, and perceived that in this case the fault was Wisdom's own. He accepted with the humility of ignorance, and something of the learner's gratitude, her woman generally, from Romola down to Mrs. Pullet. But his sense of sex was strong enough to make him deny the possibility in any stage of being of nearly all the governesses in revolt it pleased her to put forward as men; for with very few exceptions he knew they were heroes of the divided skirt. To him Deronda was an incarnation of woman's rights; Tito an 'improper female in breeches'; Silas Marner a good, perplexed old maid, of the kind of whom it is said that they have 'had a disappointment.' And Lydgate alone had aught of the true male principle about him.

Epigrams are at best half-truths that look like whole ones. Here is a handful about George Eliot. It has been said of her books—('on several occasions')—that 'it is doubtful whether they are novels disguised as treatises, or treatises disguised as novels'; that, 'while less romantic than Euclid's Elements, they are on the whole a great deal less improving reading'; and that 'they seem to have been dictated to a plain woman of genius by the ghost of David Hume.' Herself, too, has been variously described: as 'An Apotheosis of Pupil-Teachery'; as 'George Sand *plus* Science and *minus* Sex'; as 'Pallas with prejudices and a corset'; as 'the fruit of a caprice of Apollo for the Differential Calculus.' The comparison of her admirable talent to 'not the imperial violin but the grand ducal violoncello' seems suggestive and is not unkind.

—WILLIAM ERNEST HENLEY, *Views and Reviews: Essays in Appreciation*, 1890, pp. 130–132

GEORGE SAINTSBURY
"THREE MID-CENTURY NOVELISTS" (1895)

George Saintsbury (1845–1933) was a leading English literary scholar and critic. Saintsbury gained a reputation as an important critic of contemporary French literature. In the 1880s, he turned his attention to English literature and published numerous articles, anthologies, and editions. He also contributed extensively to the *Saturday Review*, of which he became the assistant editor in 1883. Twelve years later, he took up a professorship at the University of Edinburgh.

The following passage provides a characteristic turn-of-the-century summary of George Eliot's career. Saintsbury begins by stating that Eliot is no longer considered the preeminent novelist she once was, before going on to poke fun at the "worshippers" who gathered around her. Siding with popular opinion, he offers quiet praise for her earlier works and condemnation for the later novels. Saintsbury is perhaps less harsh than many of his contemporaries, and as a critic he is not without insight. (The idea that she took up "will-worship" to "replace the faith that she had cast out, but that was evidently more or less neccessary to her" is, for example, an interesting one.) However, his rather simplistic theories about gender and literary creation, which rehearse a common belief that male artists "create" whereas female artists are essentially autobiographical, seems inappropriate for Eliot. She certainly drew from her own experiences, though she also startled the reading public by successfully portraying individuals from very different walks of life.

Twenty years ago it required, if not a genuine strength of mind, at any rate a certain amount of "cussedness," not to be a George-Eliotite. All, or almost all, persons who had "got culture" admired George Eliot, and not to do so was to be at best a Kenite among the chosen people, at worst an outcast, a son of Edom and Moab and Philistia. Two very different currents met and mingled among the worshippers who flocked in the flesh to St. John's Wood, or read the books in ecstasy elsewhere. There was the rising tide of the aesthetic, revering the creator of Tito. There was the agnostic herd, faithful to the translator of Strauss and the irregular partner of Mr. G. H. Lewes. I have always found myself most unfortunately indisposed to follow any fashion, and I never remember having read a single book of George Eliot's with genuine and whole-hearted admiration. Yet an experience which I once went through enables me, I think, to speak about her at least without ignorance. When *Daniel Deronda* appeared, my friend, the late Dr. Appleton, asked me to review it for the *Academy*. My hands were the reverse of full at the time, and as there were some books of the author's which I had not read, and others which I had not read for some time, I thought it might be worth while to get an entire set and read it through in chronological order, and so "get the atmosphere" before attacking that Ebrew Jew. I have spent many days with less pleasure and less profit than those which I spent on this task. And when I had finished it, I came to an opinion which I have since seen little reason to change.

Something of what has been already said about Charlotte Brontë will apply also to this very different contemporary and craftsfellow of hers. Neither of them seems to have had in any great degree the male faculties of creation and judgment. Both, and Miss Evans especially, had in no ordinary degree the female faculty of receiving, assimilating, and reproducing. During a long and studious youth she received and assimilated impressions of persons, of scenes, of books. At a rather belated crisis of feeling she experienced what I suppose must be called Love, and at the same time was exposed to a fresh current of thought, such as it was. She travelled and enriched her store; she frequented persons of distinction and was influenced by them. And then it came out in novels, at first pretty simple, and really powerful; then less simple, but ingeniously reproductive of certain phases of thought and sentiment which were current; last of all reflective of hardly anything (save in scattered and separate scenes where she always excelled) except strange crotchets of will-worship, which she had taken up to replace the faith that she had cast out, but that was evidently more or less neccessary to her.

She began with those *Scenes of Clerical Life,* which some very fervent worshippers of hers, I believe, put at the head of all her work in merit as in time, but which I should rank decidedly below the best parts of *Adam Bede* and the wonderful opening of *Silas Marner.* Then came the great triumph, *Adam Bede,* itself. Of course it is extremely clever; but no one who calls himself a critic can afford to forget the circumstances in which it appeared. Dickens's best work was done, and his mannerism was already disgusting some readers. Thackeray, though at his very best, had not reached full popularity, and was entirely different in style and subject. Charlotte Brontë was dead or dying,—I forget which; there was nobody else who could even pretend to the first class. How could *Adam Bede* fail?

The Mill on the Floss was not likely, the circumstances being still the same, to diminish the author's vogue, and I suppose it is her best book, though it may not contain her best scenes. The objection which is often made and still oftener felt to the repulsiveness of Maggie's worship of a counter-jumping cad like Stephen, is somewhat uncritical. I suspect that most women resent it, because they feel the imputation to be true: and most men out of a not wholly dissimilar feeling which acts a little differently. *Silas Marner* again has qualities of greatness, though the narrative and characters are slight for a book. But between these earlier novels and the later batch a great gulf is fixed. Hardly after *Silas* do we find anything, except in patches and episodes, that is really "genial" in George Eliot's work. *Felix Holt* and *Middlemarch* are elaborate studies of what seemed to the author to be modern characters and society,—studies of immense effort and erudition not unenlightened by humour, but on the whole dead. *Romola* is an attempt—still more Herculean, and still more against the grain—to resuscitate the past. As for *Daniel Deronda,* it is a kind of nightmare,—a parochial and grotesque idea having thoroughly mastered the writer and only allowed her now and then to get free in the character of Grandcourt and (less often) in that of Gwendolen. I think *Theophrastus Such* has met with rather undeserved contempt, due to the fact that *Deronda* had already begun to sap the foundations of its author's popularity. The poems are laboured and thoroughly unpoetical expositions of crotchet and theory. The essays are neither better nor worse than a vast number of essays by quite second-rate authors.

—George Saintsbury, "Three Mid-Century Novelists," *Corrected Impressions,* 1895, pp. 162–167

Vida D. Scudder "George Eliot and the Social Conscience" (1898)

Julia Vida Dutton Scudder (1861–1954) was an American social reformer and writer, born of missionary parents. A graduate of Smith College (1884), she was one of the first women to study at Oxford University, where she was influenced by John Ruskin. Scudder engaged in feminist and social reform. Back in the United States, she combined literary scholarship at Wellesley College with endeavors to create settlements promoting education in poorer neighborhoods. Scudder became increasingly interested in combining Christian doctrine with socialist ideas, a notion she explores in *Socialism and Character* (1912).

Scudder provides an unusually positive account of Eliot's novels and ideas at a time when the novelist was falling out of favor. The passage offers two elements of interest. First, Scudder pays attention to the importance of evolutionary ideas in Eliot's novels. Second, she overturns the common judgment of Eliot's career: she agrees that the early works are "winning" but finds the later volumes more mature and profound. In both these views, Scudder anticipates more recent criticism.

The interests that controlled English thought between 1830 and 1870 were chiefly religious; and the most obvious fact about George Eliot's novels is their spiritual appeal. To run over the tables of contents in the leading magazines during these years, and compute proportion of subjects, would convince any one that religious speculation dominated all other questions in the mind of the reading public. From the beginning of the period, a yearning for the religious temper met a profound discontent with religious formulae. The most life-communicating men of the day, John Stuart Mill, Cardinal Newman, Spencer, Harrison, Maurice, were all in one way or another of the religious type. The iconoclastic instinct, in matters spiritual, had ceased to give pleasure, and almost every leader of skeptical thought was in his own way making efforts toward construction. A fresh and mighty synthetic principle was introduced into the thought-world as years went on by the scientific theory formulated by the followers of Darwin; and as soon as it appeared and made its significance felt, earnest minds took up the attempt to correlate the religious instinct with evolutionary ethics. Of all the people engaged in this endeavor, George Eliot was the most vividly human. Every one of her books bears witness to the painstaking ardor of her attempts at readjustment, the sincerity of spirit with which she sought to replace the sanctions for high morality once found in dogma by new sanctions, equally stringent, found in natural law.

To transform morals and art by the infusion of evolutionary ideas—to find in the revelation of the forces that had shaped the visible universe a substitute for the old revelation from the Invisible on which humanity had been used to lean—might seem quest absorbing enough for one generation. But progress was breathlessly rapid during that half-century; nor can we fully account for the genesis of George Eliot's books without a new factor. Her work is as important in its social as in its religious aspect. It is profoundly significant as marking the transition between a period preoccupied with relations of life and evolution to that next period, in which we still live, quite as intensely absorbed with the relations of life and democracy. The first order of problems was her chief conscious interest, as it was that of the circle in which she moved; to the second, her books bear witness all the stronger because largely unconscious.

No one, reading her, can fail to see the close connection by which one order of thought led into the other. The tremendous contribution made by evolutionary ethics to the social ideal can hardly be overrated. George Eliot, first of imaginative writers, was alive to the solemn and formative power of heredity and environment, and their shaping force in the determination of duty. From *Romola* to *The Spanish Gypsy* and *Daniel Deronda,* her plots are constructed almost wholly to show how all personal passions and desires, however laudable, should yield if they come in contact with the great principles which carry the race onward toward expanding life. Study of these inexorable principles quickens in thought a new sense of the organic relation of each atom to the social whole. George Eliot's finer characters recognize with wonder or feel with constraining force the relation of the individual experience to that human past from which it sprang, that present which surrounds it, that future which it must help to create. Their intense social consciousness is possible only to an age which had outlived revolution in history, and was facing evolution in thought. Evolutionary ethics directly led the way to an enlarged recognition of social responsibility. This recognition was, as we have seen, entirely lacking in society as pictured by Dickens and Thackeray: George Eliot is the first novelist to show us a society in which it is at work.

Even apart from this great achievement, the social value of her books is high. With her two brilliant predecessors, she completes the social survey of the Victorian novel. She was bred in the country, close in heart and origin to the agricultural life of England; and her early books, *Adam Bede, Silas Marner,* and *The Mill on the Floss,* reflect this life, in all its quaint and leisurely charm. An England uninvaded by competition or spiritual unrest, where telegrams are unknown and the railroad is a distant rumor,—an England unchanged in essentials from the time of Shakespeare,—smiles on us from these fair and serene pages. All this attractive life belongs to the past. To-day, Dolly Winthrop can hardly keep the quaint *naïveté* of her theology, nor can it be easy even in quiet corners to find Mrs. Poyser superintending the butter, or Mrs. Tulliver weeping over the family linen. But George Eliot gave us a real gift in these kindly pictures of the England of her girlhood, showing the honesty and simplicity, the strong uprightness, the tranquil intelligence independent of book-learning, that lingered in the rural population before the word or thing "Proletariat" was thought of.

These early books are the most winning that George Eliot ever wrote. Perhaps this is because the best art has a way of springing from the heart of childish memories; perhaps because her subjects have great intrinsic beauty. To invest the lives of the ignorant and simple with pathos, dignity, and charm was almost a new departure for fiction when she began to create. Nothing more clearly evidences the strength of the impulse which sends our sophisticated world back to nature, than the growth since her day of the attraction which drew her. Under the guidance of Hardy, of Verga, of Tolstoi, we are coming to feel that the noblest art, because the most sincere, is that which reveals the free movement of elemental human passions in the large simplicity of the lives of the poor. George Eliot's early books take their place in a great literary group, strongly expressive of one phase in the most modern social feeling.

But her later books, if they probe less deep into primal instincts, have a more direct bearing on the problems that perplex us, and therefore a keener interest for the artificial creatures that we have become. She turned from those delightful pastorals where the idyllic, the grotesque, and the profoundly human blend in so tranquil a harmony; she described the stirrings of discontent, the seething of new forces, in the England of the central Victorian period. After *Silas Marner,* her books reflect the interests of the eager intellectual circle into which, as a mature woman, she entered in London. Thackeray and Dickens had showed us the life of the average, the majority,—of Poverty and Fashion, equally unintellectual. George Eliot, a few years later, showed the life, the mood, the questions, of the small minority of thinking people.

Never, surely, were books more wistful than those great novels, *Romola, Middlemarch, Daniel Deronda.* Their animus is wholly new: it is neither scorn nor laughter; it is sympathy. This sympathy, more than any other quality, gives to the work of George Eliot a depth of thoughtfulness unsounded by the shallow criticism on life of her predecessors.

—Vida D. Scudder, "George Eliot and the Social Conscience," *Social Ideals in English Letters*, 1898, pp. 180–185

W.C. Brownell "George Eliot" (1900)

William Crary Brownell (1851–1928) was an American literary critic. He contributed articles on Henry James and Matthew Arnold to *The Nation* and later served as editor for Charles Scribner's Sons, in which capacity he provided assistance to Edith Wharton. Brownell's most significant work was his 1909 *American Prose Masters*, which was preceded by *Victorian Prose Masters* (1901).

Brownell's opening sentence provides an apt image for the disfavor into which Eliot had fallen in the early twentieth century. Brownell blames this neglect for the contemporary "surfeit of psychological fiction," which Eliot was primarily responsible for initiating. It is noteworthy that Eliot here is no longer bracketed with Charlotte Brontë or Charles Dickens, as in many earlier critical pieces, but with Thomas Hardy and Henry James. Much of what Eliot's contemporaries considered to be too intellectual in her novels was subsequently being labeled "pedantic."

Brownell is even less generous when it comes to Eliot's style. That Brownell was an admirer of Gallic literature is evidenced by his references to Buffon and La Rochefoucauld. Brownell finds Eliot's style disappointing in that it does not draw attention to itself in the manner of the French writers he enjoys. Much of what Eliot's Victorian readers admired, such as those sentences that "have the force, the ring, of proverbs," is what Brownell objects to as being heavy handed and humorless. Overall, Brownell harshly argues that style is, for Eliot, a kind of necessary evil, a tool to be used to get her message across.

How long is it since George Eliot's name has been the subject of even a literary allusion? What has become of a vogue that only yesterday, it seems, was so great? Of course, every day has its own fiction—even ours, such as it is. But this does not exclude popular interest in august survival—Thackeray, Dickens, Jane Austen, Reade, Trollope, Charlotte Brontë, everyone but Bulwer and George Eliot, I should say. As to Bulwer, perhaps, speculation would be surplusage. The neglect, however, into which so little negligible a writer as George Eliot has indubitably fallen is one of the most curious of current literary phenomena, and an interesting one to consider, since considering it involves also a consideration at the same time of the remarkable genius that is the subject of it. It is probably largely due to the fact that from a purely intellectual point of view people in books or out of them are both less interesting and less idiosyncratic than we were wont to suppose when George Eliot's fame was at its height.

The novelty of psychological fiction was a powerful source of attraction, in the first place. For any such fiction as hers, which keeps one actively thinking not only some but all of the time, the stimulus of novelty is requisite, because only under such stimulus does the mind experience the zest that alone sustains the needed alertness of appreciation. In the second place its *ex vi termini* superiority—surely no stuff of fiction could have the dignity and the significance of the human mind!—gave it an irrefutable claim on our esteem. The novelty has disappeared. We have had a surfeit of psychological fiction since George Eliot's day. Psychology, too, has entered as an element into almost every other variety of fiction. And the glamour of novelty gone, we have been able to discern the defects, once obscured by the qualities, of the purely intellectual element of fiction when it wholly overshadows all others. We now recognize that science had invaded the domain of literature—*dona ferens* and undistrusted. The current reaction, started perhaps, exemplified certainly, by Stevenson—the significance of whose work is purely "literary"—is so great as to have sacrificed seriousness along with science. But it is not necessary to exalt the puerile in order to establish the insufficiency of the pedantic. And to pedantry, however obscurely felt or unconsciously manifested, disproportionate preoccupation with the intellectual element in fiction is apt, popularly, to be ascribed.

George Eliot certainly stands at the head of psychological novelists, and though within far narrower limits she has here and there been equaled—by Mr. Hardy, for example; and in highly differentiated types, in the subtleties and *nuances* of the *genre* by Mr. Henry James—it is probable that the *genre* itself will decay before any of its practitioners will, either in depth or range, surpass its master spirit. As George Eliot herself remarks, "Of all forms of mistake, prophecy is the most gratuitous," but we may conjecture that the psychological novel, in its present explicit sense, will disappear before her own preeminence in the writing of it is successfully challenged. She is, thus, and is likely to remain, a unique figure. More than any other writer's her characters have—and for the serious readers of the future will continue to have—the specifically intellectual interest. This interest, indeed, is so marked in them that one is tempted to call it the only one they possess. What goes on in their minds is almost the sole concern of their creator. Our attention is so concentrated on what they think that we hardly know how they feel, or whether—in many cases, at least, where we nevertheless have a complete inventory of their mental furniture—they feel at all. They are themselves also prodigiously interested in their mental processes. They do a tremendous lot of thinking. In any emergency or crisis their minds fairly buzz, like a wound clock with the pendulum removed. We assist at the spectacle of a cogitation that seems to be pursued by the thinkers themselves with disinterested devotion. At all events the stars of the company not only practise but enjoy mental exercise to an extent not elsewhere to be met with.

I have heard it remarked in qualification of the legitimate interest of Thackeray's characters that they "never seem to have any fun with their minds," and it is certainly true that in the concert of powers of which the nature of Thackeray's personages is composed, the mind does not hold a notable hegemony. The personages themselves are rarely either introspective or mentally energetic for pure love of the exercise. But the drama itself of George Eliot's world is largely an intellectual affair. The soul, the temperament, the heart—in the scriptural sense—the whole nature plays a subordinate part. The plot turns on what the characters think. The characters are individualized by their mental complexions; their evolution is a mental one; they change, develop, deteriorate in consequence of seeing things differently. Their troubles are largely mental perplexities; in her agony of soul, Romola goes to Savonarola and Gwendolen to Deronda for light, not heat. The prescriptions they receive are also terribly explicit—addressed quite exclusively to the reason and wholly unlike that obtained by Nicodemus "by night." The courtship of Esther and Felix Holt is mainly an interchange of "views." There are exceptions—notably Maggie Tulliver and Dorothea, the two characters which have been called, with ample reason, one may guess, autobiographic. But the exceptions accentuate the rule. As a rule the atmosphere of each novel is saturated with thought. Certainly nowhere else in fiction is there any such apotheosis of intellect both express and implied. . . .

One may speak of George Eliot's style as of the snakes in Iceland. She has no style. Her substance will be preserved for "the next ages" by its own pungency or not at all. No one will ever read her for the sensuous pleasure of the process. She is a notable contradiction of the common acceptance of Buffon's *"le style c'est l'homme."* Her very marked individuality expresses itself in a way which may be called a characteristic manner, but which lacks the "order and movement" that Buffon defined style to be when he was defining it instead of merely saying something about it. In itself, moreover, this is not often a felicitous manner. It is inspired by the wish to be pointed, to be complete, to give an impeccable equivalent in expression for the content of thought, to be adequately articulate. In her aim at exactness she neglects even energy. Her statements are scientific, but never even rudimentarily rhetorical, if we except the use of irony, in which she was sometimes very happy. Of modulation she never seems to have thought. Any element of periodic quality, of rhythm, of recurrence, of alternation, succession, inversion, for the sake of effect, decorating instead of merely expressing significance, she would no doubt have eschewed had any ever occurred to her, as plainly it never did. Rhetoric of any degree, in short, probably seemed to her meretricious if—which one doubts—she ever considered it at all. She was the slave of the meaning, hypnotized apparently by the sense, and deaf to the sound, of what she wrote. Her taste was noticeably good in avoiding the pretentious, but her tact was insufficient to save her from the complicated and the awkward. Her puritan predilections should have suggested simplicity to her, but simplicity is the supreme quality which she not only wholly lacks, but never even strives for; the one salient characteristic of her style—of her manner of writing, that is to say—is its complexity.

Thus there are no "passages," either "fine" or in any way sustained, in her works; at least I think of none, and if any exist I suspect they are put into the mouths of some personage with whom they are "in character"—in which case they would be sure to be very well done indeed. Every sentence stands by itself; by its sententious self, therefore. The "wit and wisdom" of the author are crystallized in phrases, not distilled in fluid diction. Their truth strikes us sharply, penetrates us swiftly; the mind tingles agreeably under the slight shock, instead of glowing in expansive accord and dilating with gradual conviction. Often these sentences have the force, the ring, of proverbs—of those of Solomon, too, rather than those of Sancho Panza. Some of them, on the other hand, have the air less of the Sibyl than of "saws," and suggest the wiseacre more than the philosophic moralist. At times they have the trenchant crispness of La Rochefoucauld; at others, even in the novels, the unravelled looseness premonitory of the appalling Theophrastus Such. The manner naturally takes on the character of the substance, and we have thus this formal sententiousness—now epigrammatic, as I say, and now otiose and obscure—because of the writer's exclusive consecration to the content which itself varies, of course, from the pithy to the commonplace. Her defective aesthetic feeling, her lack indeed of the aesthetic sense nowhere comes out more clearly than in this absorption in the significance to the neglect of the aspect of the picture she is presenting. This picture, and even the personages who people it, seem to have for her at least a disproportionate attraction in virtue of their typical to the exclusion of their individual interest—sharply individualized as her characters are in the matter of psychology alone. She seems so impressed with their universal appeal and representative office, with the principle her facts illustrate and enforce, with the ulterior meaning and value of her "criticism of life," as to have at all events distinctly less zest in depicting than in defining her material. For fiction this indubitably means a tame style.

Lacking in aesthetic feeling as she was, she was probably more or less conscious of this. Her attempts to circumvent it are now and then deplorable.

They are invariably verbiage of one kind or another. The refuge of pedantry in its endeavor to escape dulness is apt to be sportiveness, and it is perhaps when she is playful that George Eliot comes nearer pedantry than at any other time. Even in moments when her erudition seems elaborate and essentially inapposite, we are always conscious that it does not seem so to her, and that not only is there no parade about it, but also that neither is it in the least mechanical. It is the native, however awkward, expression of a kind of tempered enthusiasm. At times, certainly, the sense of humor failed her equally with the aesthetic sense, of which in a large—or strict—sense it is, of course, a subdivision; and the artist who could objectively reproduce such humor as that of *Adam Bede,* and *The Mill on the Floss* could also, when it came to self-expression, illustrate the very acme of dulness. Her facetiousness is, at its worst, as bad as Dickens's; and, at her worst, she writes as badly, without the mitigation of his extraordinary high spirits and infectious hilarity. Without, too, his bad taste, though with, as I said, the tactlessness which is the next thing to it. The moral element in taste involves self-respect. And in anything moral George Eliot is never deficient. Her intelligence saves her; it is too serious, it has too much poise, and it sees temptation as a kind of sophistry—temptation, I mean, to put up with the second rate on account of its tinsel, for example. But the tact that shows one when he is hitting and when he is missing the mark, she does not infallibly possess and often when, apparently, she seems to herself to be exhibiting the light touch, she is bravely ponderous. With a little more tact, a little more humor, a little more aesthetic sense, some of her significance might have been even more striking, and certainly some of it would not have seemed so absolutely flat.

But why discuss her style at all, one asks one's self. No one can have any doubt that, though, in general, it serves her well enough, and sometimes expresses adequately the most searching subtleties of observation and reflection, nevertheless its idiosyncrasies are defects. And of style in any large sense surely no great writer ever had so little. Her constant references in her letters to her "art" have an odd sound. Yet even here one's last word must be a recognition of the extraordinary way in which her intellect atones for sensuous deficiencies. Could two better words be found, for a slight example, to characterize the first impression Rome makes on the stranger than "stupendous fragmentariness." One of her characters, "like most tyrannous people, had that dastardly kind of self-restraint which enabled him to control his temper where it suited his convenience to do so." The adverb is felicity itself. And in her letters one can see how safely her intelligence guides her through the museum maze of plastic art for which she had so little native feeling, but in which less than many an aesthetic temperament is she either imposed upon or unappreciative. In art, as in life, she has an acute sense if not a sensitive feeling for what is distinctly worth while.

—W.C. BROWNELL, "George Eliot," *Scribner's Magazine*, December 1900, reprinted in *Victorian Prose Masters*, 1901, pp. 99–124

RICHARD BURTON "GEORGE ELIOT" (1909)

Richard Eugene Burton (1861–1940) was an American poet and critic. After completing his Ph.D. at Johns Hopkins University in 1888, Burton worked in various editorial roles for *The Churchman*, the *Hartford Courant*, and the Lothrop Publishing Company. He was appointed head of the English department at the University of Minnesota in 1906.

Burton provides an unusually positive early-century evaluation of Eliot. In stark contrast to most modern critics, he stresses Eliot's modernity. Burton argues against critics such as Saintsbury who believed that Eliot's talent lay in narrowly reproducing the scenes she had grown up with and instead stresses her imaginative capacity. Eliot's brand of realism is here interpreted as a technique that paved the way for modern fiction. The belief that "modern psychology in the complete sense as method and interest begins in the Novel with Eliot" was echoed by D.H. Lawrence, who declared that "you see, it was really George Eliot who started it all. . . . It was she who started putting all the action inside" (Jessie Chambers Wood, *D. H. Lawrence: a personal record*, 1935).

George Eliot began fiction a decade later than Thackeray, but seems more than a decade nearer to us. With her the full pulse of modern realism is felt a-throbbing. There is no more of the yeas and thous with which, when he would make an exordium, Thackeray addressed the world—a fashion long since laid aside. Eliot drew much nearer to the truth, the quiet, homely verity of her scenes is a closer approximation to life, realizes life more vitally than the most veracious page of *Vanity Fair*. Not that the great woman novelist made the mistake of a slavish imitation of the actual: that capital, lively scene in the early part of *The Mill on the Floss*, where Mrs. Tulliver's connections make known to us their delightsome personalities, is not a mere transcript from life; and all the better for that. Nevertheless, the critic can easily discover a difference between Thackeray and Eliot in this regard, and the ten years between them (as we saw in the case of Dickens and Thackeray) are partly responsible: technique and ideal in literary art were changing fast. George Eliot was a truer realist. She took more seriously her aim of interpreting life, and had a higher conception of her artistic mission. Dickens in his beautiful tribute to Thackeray on the latter's death, speaks of the failure of the author of *Pendennis* to take his mission, his genius, seriously: there was justice in the remark. Yet we heard from the preface to *Pendennis* that Thackeray had the desire to depict a typical man of society with the faithful frankness of a Fielding, and since him, Thackeray states, never again used. But the novelist's hearers were not prepared, the time was not yet ripe, and the novelist himself lacked the courage, though he had the clear vision. With Eliot, we reach the psychologic moment: that deepest truth, the truth of character, exhibited in its mainsprings of impulse and thought, came with her into English fiction as it had never before appeared. It would hardly be overstatement to say that modern psychology in the complete sense as method and interest begins in the Novel with Eliot. For there is a radical difference, not only between the Novel which exploits plot and that which exploits character: but also between that which sees character in terms of life and that which sees it in terms of soul. Eliot's fiction does the latter: life to her means character building, and has its meaning only as an arena for spiritual struggle. Success or failure means but this: have I grown in my higher nature, has my existence shown on the whole an upward tendency? If so, well and good. If not, whatever of place or power may be mine, I am among the world's failures, having missed the goal. This view, steadily to be encountered in all her fiction, gives it the grave quality, the deep undertone and, be it confessed, at times the almost Methodistic manner, which mark this woman's worth in its weakness and its notable strength.

—RICHARD BURTON, "George Eliot,"
Masters of the English Novel: A Study of Principles and Personalities, 1909, pp. 218–220

FORD MADOX FORD
"ENGLISH LITERATURE OF TODAY: I" (1911)

Ford Madox Ford (1873–1939) was an English writer and editor whose maternal grandfather was the painter Ford Madox Brown. Ford played a key part in supporting the modernist movement by founding the *English Review* (1908) and the *Transatlantic Review* (1924), which published works by James Joyce, Gertrude Stein, and Ernest Hemingway. His own novels include *The Good Soldier* (1915) and the trilogy *Parade's End* (1924–28).

It is a powerful illustration of the fluctuation of Eliot's reputation that, in 1911, Ford could confidently state that she is "unreadable." Far from agreeing with Burton about Eliot's modernity, Ford discusses her as a novelist firmly entrenched in the past. Ford, usually a sophisticated writer and critic, misreads Eliot in curious ways. Scorn for what he perceives to be Eliot's "solemnity" leads him to state that Eliot "cared in her heart very little whether or no she would be considered an artist," that her novels are "peopled by supermen" and that hers is an "idealised world." The modernist writer's instinctive dislike of the Victorian temperament means that Trollope is preferred for being so imperfect and for holding such small ambitions. Though Ford never actively championed George Eliot's novels, it is worth noting that his views on the novelist mellowed somewhat in later years.

We have set ourselves the task of determining for the uninstructed reader the difference between the writer of the commercial book and the writer of a book which shall be a work of art. When it comes to results this is a matter of great difficulty, demanding of the analyst a cool faculty of criticism, a broad catholicity and great powers of self-abnegation in the realms of taste. Suppose, for instance, we consider the case of a debatable writer—let us say George Eliot. Here was an authoress almost omnipotent in her power to charm at once the great multitude and the austere critic of her time. She was taken more seriously than any writer of to-day ever has been, or ever will be taken. Yet, to the great bulk of educated criticism of to-day, George Eliot has become a writer unreadable in herself and negligible as a critical illustration. Her character-drawing appears to be singularly wooden: her books without any form, her style entirely pedestrian and her solemnity intolerable. And it is probable that it was this very solemnity that gave to her works all the qualities that make them to men in touch with the life of to-day so entirely unreadable, so exactly like so many heavy cakes. George Eliot was, in fact, a great figure. She was great enough to impose herself upon her day; she probably never sought, though she certainly found, the popularity of sensationalism. Taking herself with an enormous seriousness, she dilated upon sin and its results, and so found the easy success of the popular preacher who deals in horrors. She desired that is to say, to be an influence: she cared in her heart very little whether or no she would be considered an artist.

Let us place her alongside another writer of her day whose ambition did not soar above producing a good "household article." As an artist as a mere writer Anthony Trollope had most of the vices of George Eliot. He is never remarkably engrossing, his writing has no particular justness of phrase, his novels are hardly constructed at all, but meander one into another without any particular bounds, without there being any particular reason why any given book should begin or end here or there. Yet, although Trollope's books do not very much cry aloud to be read, we can take up with interest *Barchester Towers* in a hand from which nervelessly *Adam Bede* drops. The reason is that never taking himself with any attempt at solemnity, Trollope was content to observe and to record, whereas George Eliot, as if she had converted herself into another Frankenstein, went on evolving obedient monsters who had no particular relation to the life of her time monsters who seduced or admitted themselves to be seduced, who murdered their infants or quoted the Scriptures just as it suited the creator of their ordered world. Trollope, on the other hand, observed the world he lived in: his characters walk upon the ground; perhaps they are even a little flat-footed, but his observations have the light of facts, filtered through the screen of a personality. That the personality was not a very rare, was not a very subtle one, is perhaps the reason why we do not read him with very great avidity. But because the personality was so honest so humble and above all, so conscientious, he helps us to live in a real world, he affords us real experiences. And precisely because George Eliot had no conscience, precisely because she gives us a world that never was, peopled by supermen who, we may thank God, never could have been, she is now a moral force practically extinct, is hourly losing impetus. And she has as an artist no existence whatever. Having studied *Das Leben Jesu*, she became inflated by the idea of the writer as prophet, she evolved monstrous works which contained her endless comments upon Victorian philosophy, forgetting that our Lord, Who was the supreme influence, because He was the supreme artist, limited Himself in His recorded fiction to the barest statement of fact, to the merest citation of instance.

Having stated so much we may pause to concede that probably the great majority of humanity would say that the converse of what we have stated is the actual fact. They would say, precisely, that George Eliot was the great artist because she presented them with an unreal, with an idealised world, which is what they demand of art. George Eliot, that is to say, takes them out of themselves. Mr Trollope makes them think. With this, of course, we cannot quarrel, since it is merely a matter of terms. We prefer, that is to say, to consider that the artist is the renderer of human vicissitude, the creator of a world of his own in which conscientiously, as he sees it, effect follows cause.

—Ford Madox Ford,
"English Literature of Today: I,"
The Critical Attitude, 1911, pp. 55–58

Virginia Woolf "George Eliot" (1919)

The English novelist and essayist Virginia Woolf (1882–1941) became one of the most important modernist writers with works such as *Mrs. Dalloway* (1925). Woolf displayed ambivalence toward the Victorians. Like many modernist writers, she sought to distance herself from what she saw as Victorian prudishness, hypocrisy, and hero worship. George Eliot was not immune from her sarcasm—in *To The Lighthouse* (1927) the character Minta Doyle forgets the third volume of *Middlemarch* on the train. Nevertheless, Woolf remained fascinated by the nineteenth century and the lives of its women in particular.

Virginia Woolf's essay on George Eliot, published during the centenary of her birth, was the first important reevaluation of the novelist to appear in the twentieth century. Woolf begins by glancing over some of the more damaging claims made against Eliot by recent critics. It was in a letter to Woolf's father, Leslie Stephen, that George Meredith had mused that, had he been set the task of writing Eliot's biography, he "could not have refrained from touches on the comic scenes of the Priory—with the dais, and the mercurial little showman, and the Bishops about the feet of an errant woman, worshipped as a literary idol and light of philosophy" (*Letters of George Meredith*, II: 439–40). Edmund Gosse had published a similarly dismissive essay on George Eliot. Gosse's disdain for the woman extended also to the novelist—in the same essay he denounced *Middlemarch*, for example, as a "remarkable instance of elaborate mental resources misapplied, and genius revolving, with tremendous machinery, like some great water-wheel, while no water is flowing underneath" (*Aspects and Impressions*: 14). Woolf acknowledges that the iconoclastic modern attitude meant that some writers were being lampooned unfairly.

Woolf does not offer radically new readings of Eliot's novels. Though Woolf famously describes *Middlemarch* as "one of the few English novels written for grown-up people," she sides with the popular opinion that the early novels have the most impact on the reader. However, she insists on their enduring force and distances Eliot from attacks of pomposity. Woolf admires the struggles experienced by Eliot and the courageous choices but finds that these affected her works adversely, much as she states in *A Room of One's Own* that Charlotte Brontë's anger at the limitations of female lives damaged *Jane Eyre*. However, Woolf shared Eliot's interest in hidden lives and provides the foundation for a feminist reading of George Eliot's life and works. The essay, in questioning contemporary depreciations of Eliot and proposing a more careful rereading of her works, marks an important turning point in George Eliot's reputation.

To read George Eliot attentively is to become aware how little one knows about her. It is also to become aware of the credulity, not very creditable to one's insight, with which, half consciously and partly maliciously, one had accepted the late Victorian version of a deluded woman who held phantom sway over subjects even more deluded than herself. At what moment and by what means her spell was broken it is difficult to ascertain. Some people attribute it to the publication of her Life. Perhaps George Meredith, with his phrase about the "mercurial little showman" and the "errant woman" on the daïs, gave point and poison to the arrows of thousands incapable of aiming them so accurately, but delighted to let fly. She became one of the butts for youth to laugh at, the convenient symbol of a group of serious people who were all guilty of the same idolatry and could be dismissed with the same scorn. Lord Acton had said that she was greater than Dante; Herbert Spencer exempted her novels, as if they were not novels, when he banned all fiction from the London Library. She was the pride and paragon of her sex. Moreover, her private record was not more alluring than her public. Asked to describe an afternoon at the Priory, the story-teller always intimated that the memory of those serious Sunday afternoons had come to tickle his sense of humour. He had been so much alarmed by the grave lady in her low chair; he had been so anxious to say the intelligent thing. Certainly, the talk had been very serious, as a note in the fine clear hand of the great novelist bore witness. It was dated on the Monday morning, and she accused herself of having spoken without due forethought of Marivaux when she meant another; but no doubt, she said, her listener had already supplied the correction. Still, the memory of talking about Marivaux to George Eliot on a Sunday afternoon was not a romantic memory. It had faded with the passage of the years. It had not become picturesque.

Indeed, one cannot escape the conviction that the long, heavy face with its expression of serious and sullen and almost equine power has stamped itself depressingly upon the minds of people who remember George Eliot, so that it looks out upon them from her pages. Mr. Gosse has lately described her as he saw her driving through London in a Victoria—

> a large, thick-set sybil, dreamy and immobile, whose massive features, somewhat grim when seen in profile, were incongruously bordered by a hat, always in the height of Paris fashion, which in those days commonly included an immense ostrich feather.

Lady Ritchie, with equal skill, has left a more intimate indoor portrait.

> She sat by the fire in a beautiful black satin gown, with a green shaded lamp on the table beside her, where I saw German books lying and pamphlets and ivory paper-cutters. She was very quiet and noble, with two steady little eyes and a sweet voice. As I looked

> I felt her to be a friend, not exactly a personal friend, but a good and benevolent impulse.

A scrap of her talk is preserved. "We ought to respect our influence," she said. "We know by our own experience how very much others affect our lives, and we must remember that we in turn must have the same effect upon others." Jealously treasured, committed to memory, one can imagine recalling the scene, repeating the words, thirty years later and suddenly, for the first time, bursting into laughter.

In all these records one feels that the recorder, even when he was in the actual presence, kept his distance and kept his head, and never read the novels in later years with the light of a vivid, or puzzling, or beautiful personality dazzling in his eyes. In fiction, where so much of personality is revealed, the absence of charm is a great lack; and her critics, who have been, of course, mostly of the opposite sex, have resented, half consciously perhaps, her deficiency in a quality which is held to be supremely desirable in women. George Eliot was not charming; she was not strongly feminine; she had none of those eccentricities and inequalities of temper which give to so many artists the endearing simplicity of children. One feels that to most people, as to Lady Ritchie, she was "not exactly a personal friend, but a good and benevolent impulse". But if we consider these portraits more closely we shall find that they are all the portraits of an elderly celebrated woman, dressed in black satin, driving in her victoria, a woman who has been through her struggle and issued from it with a profound desire to be of use to others, but with no wish for intimacy, save with the little circle who had known her in the days of her youth. We know very little about the days of her youth; but we do know that the culture, the philosophy, the fame, and the influence were all built upon a very humble foundation—she was the grand-daughter of a carpenter.

The first volume of her life is a singularly depressing record. In it we see her raising herself with groans and struggles from the intolerable boredom of petty provincial society (her father had risen in the world and become more middle class, but less picturesque) to be the assistant editor of a highly intellectual London review, and the esteemed companion of Herbert Spencer. The stages are painful as she reveals them in the sad soliloquy in which Mr. Cross condemned her to tell the story of her life. Marked in early youth as one "sure to get something up very soon in the way of a clothing club", she proceeded to raise funds for restoring a church by making a chart of ecclesiastical history; and that was followed by a loss of faith which so disturbed her father that he refused to live with her. Next came the struggle with the translation of Strauss, which, dismal and "soul-stupefying" in itself, can scarcely have been made less so by the usual feminine tasks of ordering a household and nursing a dying father, and the distressing conviction, to one so dependent upon affection, that by becoming a blue-stocking she was forfeiting her brother's respect. "I used to go about like an owl," she said, "to the great disgust of my brother." "Poor thing," wrote a friend who saw her toiling through Strauss with a statue of the risen Christ in front of her, "I do pity her sometimes, with her pale sickly face and dreadful headaches, and anxiety, too, about her father." Yet, though we cannot read the story without a strong desire that the stages of her pilgrimage might have been made, if not more easy, at least more beautiful, there is a dogged determination in her advance upon the citadel of culture which raises it above our pity. Her development was very slow and very awkward, but it had the irresistible impetus behind it of a deep-seated and noble ambition. Every obstacle at length was thrust from her path. She knew every one. She read everything. Her astonishing intellectual vitality had triumphed. Youth was over, but youth had been full of suffering. Then, at the age of thirty-five, at the height of her powers, and in the fulness of her freedom, she made the decision which was of such profound moment to her and still matters even to us, and went to Weimar, alone with George Henry Lewes.

The books which followed so soon after her union testify in the fullest manner to the great liberation which had come to her with personal happiness. In themselves they provide us with a plentiful feast. Yet at the threshold of her literary career one may find in some of the circumstances of her life influences that turned her mind to the past, to the country village, to the quiet and beauty and simplicity of childish memories and away from herself and the present. We understand how it was that her first book was *Scenes of Clerical Life*, and not *Middlemarch*. Her union with Lewes had surrounded her with affection, but in view of the circumstances and of the conventions it had also isolated her. "I wish it to be understood", she wrote in 1857, "that I should never invite any one to come and see me who did not ask for the invitation." She had been "cut off from what is called the world", she said later, but she did not regret it. By becoming thus marked, first by circumstances and later, inevitably, by her fame, she lost the power to move on equal terms unnoted among her kind; and the loss for a novelist was serious. Still, basking in the light and sunshine of *Scenes of Clerical Life*, feeling the large mature mind spreading itself with a luxurious sense of freedom in the world of her "remotest past", to speak of loss seems inappropriate. Everything to such a mind was gain. All experience filtered down through layer after layer of perception and reflection, enriching and nourishing. The utmost we can say, in qualifying her attitude towards fiction by what little we know of her life, is that she had taken to heart certain lessons not usually learnt early, if learnt at all, among which, perhaps, the most branded upon her was the melancholy virtue of tolerance; her sympathies are with the everyday lot, and play most happily in dwelling upon the homespun of ordinary joys and sorrows. She has none of that romantic intensity which is connected with a sense of one's own individuality, unsated and unsubdued, cutting its shape sharply upon the background of the world. What were the loves and sorrows of a snuffy old clergyman, dreaming over his whisky, to the fiery egotism of Jane Eyre?

The beauty of those first books, *Scenes of Clerical Life*, *Adam Bede*, *The Mill on the Floss*, is very great. It is impossible to estimate the merit of the Poysers, the Dodsons, the Gilfils, the Bartons, and the rest with all their surroundings and dependencies, because they have put on flesh and blood and we move among them, now bored, now sympathetic, but always with that unquestioning acceptance of all that they say and do, which we accord to the great originals only. The flood of memory and humour which she pours so spontaneously into one figure, one scene after another, until the whole fabric of ancient rural England is revived, has so much in common with a natural process that it leaves us with little consciousness that there is anything to criticise. We accept; we feel the delicious warmth and release of spirit which the great creative writers alone procure for us. As one comes back to the books after years of absence they pour out, even against our expectation, the same store of energy and heat, so that we want more than anything to idle in the warmth as in the sun beating down from the red orchard wall. If there is an element of unthinking abandonment in thus submitting to the humours of Midland farmers and their wives, that, too, is right in the circumstances. We scarcely wish to analyse what we feel to be so large and deeply human. And when we consider how distant in time the world of Shepperton and Hayslope is, and how remote the minds of farmer and agricultural labourers from those of most of George Eliot's readers, we can only attribute the ease and pleasure with which we ramble from house to smithy, from cottage parlour to rectory garden, to the fact that George Eliot makes us share their lives, not in a spirit of condescension or of curiosity, but in a spirit of sympathy. She is no satirist. The movement of her mind was too slow and cumbersome to lend itself to comedy. But she gathers in her large grasp a great bunch of the main elements of human nature and groups them loosely together with a tolerant and wholesome understanding which, as one finds upon re-reading, has not only kept her figures fresh and free, but has given them an unexpected hold upon our laughter and tears. There is the famous Mrs. Poyser. It would have been easy to work her idiosyncrasies to death, and, as it is, perhaps, George

Eliot gets her laugh in the same place a little too often. But memory, after the book is shut, brings out, as sometimes in real life, the details and subtleties which some more salient characteristic has prevented us from noticing at the time. We recollect that her health was not good. There were occasions upon which she said nothing at all. She was patience itself with a sick child. She doted upon Totty. Thus one can muse and speculate about the greater number of George Eliot's characters and find, even in the least important, a roominess and margin where those qualities lurk which she has no call to bring from their obscurity.

But in the midst of all this tolerance and sympathy there are, even in the early books, moments of greater stress. Her humour has shown itself broad enough to cover a wide range of fools and failures, mothers and children, dogs and flourishing midland fields, farmers, sagacious or fuddled over their ale, horse-dealers, inn-keepers, curates, and carpenters. Over them all broods a certain romance, the only romance that George Eliot allowed herself—the romance of the past. The books are astonishingly readable and have no trace of pomposity or pretence. But to the reader who holds a large stretch of her early work in view it will become obvious that the mist of recollection gradually withdraws. It is not that her power diminishes, for, to our thinking, it is at its highest in the mature *Middlemarch*, the magnificent book which with all its imperfections is one of the few English novels written for grown-up people. But the world of fields and farms no longer contents her. In real life she had sought her fortunes elsewhere; and though to look back into the past was calming and consoling, there are, even in the early works, traces of that troubled spirit, that exacting and questioning and baffled presence who was George Eliot herself. In *Adam Bede* there is a hint of her in Dinah. She shows herself far more openly and completely in Maggie in *The Mill on the Floss*. She is Janet in *Janet's Repentance,* and Romola, and Dorothea seeking wisdom and finding one scarcely knows what in marriage with Ladislaw. Those who fall foul of George Eliot do so, we incline to think, on account of her heroines; and with good reason; for there is no doubt that they bring out the worst of her, lead her into difficult places, make her self-conscious, didactic, and occasionally vulgar. Yet if you could delete the whole sisterhood you would leave a much smaller and a much inferior world, albeit a world of greater artistic perfection and far superior jollity and comfort. In accounting for her failure, in so far as it was a failure, one recollects that she never wrote a story until she was thirty-seven, and that by the time she was thirty-seven she had come to think of herself with a mixture of pain and something like resentment. For long she preferred not to think of herself at all. Then, when the first flush of creative energy was exhausted and self-confidence had come to her, she wrote more and more from the personal standpoint, but she did so without the unhesitating abandonment of the young. Her self-consciousness is always marked when her heroines say what she herself would have said. She disguised them in every possible way. She granted them beauty and wealth into the bargain; she invented, more improbably, a taste for brandy. But the disconcerting and stimulating fact remained that she was compelled by the very power of her genius to step forth in person upon the quiet bucolic scene.

The noble and beautiful girl who insisted upon being born into the Mill on the Floss is the most obvious example of the ruin which a heroine can strew about her. Humour controls her and keeps her lovable so long as she is small and can be satisfied by eloping with the gipsies or hammering nails into her doll; but she develops; and before George Eliot knows what has happened she has a full-grown woman on her hands demanding what neither gipsies, nor dolls, nor St. Ogg's itself is capable of giving her. First Philip Wakem is produced, and later Stephen Guest. The weakness of the one and the coarseness of the other have often been pointed out; but both, in their weakness and coarseness, illustrate not so much George Eliot's inability to draw the portrait of a man, as the uncertainty, the infirmity, and the fumbling which shook her hand when she had to conceive a fit mate for a heroine. She is in the first place driven beyond the home world she knew and loved, and forced to set foot in middle-class drawing-rooms where young men sing all the summer morning and young women sit embroidering smoking-caps for bazaars. She feels herself out of her element, as her clumsy satire of what she calls "good society" proves.

> Good society has its claret and its velvet carpets, its dinner engagements six weeks deep, its opera, and its faery ball rooms ... gets its science done by Faraday and its religion by the superior clergy who are to be met in the best houses; how should it have need of belief and emphasis?

There is no trace of humour or insight there, but only the vindictiveness of a grudge which we feel to be personal in its origin. But terrible as the complexity of our social system is in its demands upon the sympathy and discernment of a novelist straying across the boundaries, Maggie Tulliver did worse than drag George Eliot from her natural surroundings. She insisted upon the introduction of the great emotional scene. She must love; she must despair; she must be drowned clasping her brother in her arms. The more one examines the great emotional scenes the more nervously one anticipates the brewing and gathering and thickening of the cloud which will burst upon our heads at the moment of crisis in a shower of disillusionment and verbosity. It is partly that her hold upon dialogue, when it is not dialect, is slack; and partly that she seems to shrink with an elderly dread of fatigue from the effort of emotional concentration. She allows her heroines to talk too much. She has little verbal felicity. She lacks the unerring taste which chooses one sentence and compresses the heart of the scene within that. "Whom are you going to dance with?" asked Mr. Knightley, at the Westons' ball. "With you, if you will ask me," said Emma; and she has said enough. Mrs. Casaubon would have talked for an hour and we should have looked out of the window.

Yet, dismiss the heroines without sympathy, confine George Eliot to the agricultural world of her "remotest past", and you not only diminish her greatness but lose her true flavour. That greatness is here we can have no doubt. The width of the prospect, the large strong outlines of the principal features, the ruddy light of the early books, the searching power and reflective richness of the later tempt us to linger and expatiate beyond our limits. But it is upon the heroines that we would cast a final glance. "I have always been finding out my religion since I was a little girl," says Dorothea Casaubon. "I used to pray so much—now I hardly ever pray. I try not to have desires merely for myself...." She is speaking for them all. That is their problem. They cannot live without religion, and they start out on the search for one when they are little girls. Each has the deep feminine passion for goodness, which makes the place where she stands in aspiration and agony the heart of the book—still and cloistered like a place of worship, but that she no longer knows to whom to pray. In learning they seek their goal; in the ordinary tasks of womanhood; in the wider service of their kind. They do not find what they seek, and we cannot wonder. The ancient consciousness of woman, charged with suffering and sensibility, and for so many ages dumb, seems in them to have brimmed and overflowed and uttered a demand for something—they scarcely know what—for something that is perhaps incompatible with the facts of human existence. George Eliot had far too strong an intelligence to tamper with those facts, and too broad a humour to mitigate the truth because it was a stern one. Save for the supreme courage of their endeavour, the struggle ends, for her heroines, in tragedy, or in a compromise that is even more melancholy. But their story is the incomplete version of the story of George Eliot herself. For her, too, the burden and the complexity of womanhood were not enough; she must reach beyond the sanctuary and pluck for herself the strange bright fruits of art and knowledge. Clasping them as few women have ever clasped them, she would not renounce her own inheritance—the difference of view, the difference of standard—nor accept an inappropriate reward. Thus we behold her, a memorable figure, inordinately praised and shrinking from her fame, despondent, reserved, shuddering back into the arms of love as if there alone were satisfaction and, it might be, justification, at the same time reaching out with "a fastidious yet hungry ambition" for all that life could offer the free and inquiring mind and confronting her feminine aspirations with the real world of men. Triumphant was the issue for her, whatever it may have been for her creations, and as we recollect all that she dared and achieved, how with every obstacle against her—sex and health and convention—she sought more knowledge and more freedom till the body, weighted with its double burden, sank worn out, we must lay upon her grave whatever we have it in our power to bestow of laurel and rose.

—Virginia Woolf, "George Eliot,"
Times Literary Supplement,
November 20, 1919, pp. 657–658

WORKS

❖

Although *Scenes of Clerical Life* (1857) was praised by reviewers, it did not make Eliot famous overnight. Responses to the work tended to focus on three elements: the new brand of realism put forward by the work, the open manner in which the novelist tackled religious belief, and the mystery of the author's identity. It was with *Adam Bede* (1859) that the public realized that a significant talent had emerged. Critics again tried to define what seemed to be a new kind of writing by picking up Eliot's own language on Dutch paintings. Faced with a sympathetic portrayal of Methodism, speculations about the author's religious inclinations continued, as the real identity of "George Eliot" remained a secret to all but a small number of people. Had it been known that the creator of Hetty and Arthur Donnithorne was not, as it was assumed, a man, critics may have been harsher: indeed, some were already uncomfortable with the novel's sensational and even, for some, indecent aspects, as the extracts by George Augustus Sala and James Benjamin Kenyon illustrate. Whatever their views of the novel, reviewers tended to agree that Mrs. Poyser was one of its best creations and, indeed, in all of contemporary fiction. Leslie Stephen conveniently summarizes the response to the novel and suggests that, for many readers, *Adam Bede* remained the work by Eliot that they regarded with the most affection long after her later novels had appeared.

By the time *The Mill on the Floss* (1860) was published, readers knew that its author was Marian Evans, who was living unmarried with George Henry Lewes. Though this occasioned numerous snide remarks in personal correspondences, reviewers were still content to praise Eliot's obvious talents. However, many writers began to evaluate Eliot's work in gendered terms—a response she had understandably sought to avoid. Criticism of *The Mill on the Floss* seems to have been strikingly consistent in the decades following its publication. Eliot's depiction of children was praised, Stephen Guest's characterization was deplored, and the final volume was considered artistically and morally weak. Most critics reacted strongly to what they felt was a distinctly darker vision than that presented in her previous works. E.S. Dallas attempted to assess it as an extension of Eliot's realist aesthetic, whereas Algernon Charles Swinburne and John Ruskin offered far less balanced responses. The novel occupied an awkward position in Eliot's canon for a long time: it was often excluded both from the group of her more "charming" depictions of rural life and that of her later, more intellectually ambitious works. Even among Eliot's greatest admirers, it was rarely cited as a favorite work.

Silas Marner (1861) is the novel by Eliot that best weathered the storm surrounding her critical reputation during the early twentieth century for the same reason that critics first praised it after its initial publication. Though some critics found fault with Eliot's use of realism, most writers praised the work's simplicity, which seemed particularly welcome after the torments of *The Mill on the Floss*. Acclaim for its small, talelike scale were usually complemented with a celebration of the "Rainbow Inn" scenes, which a few critics compared to Shakespearean drama.

Romola (1863), on the other hand, has suffered the sharpest depreciation. Richard Holt Hutton and a number of contemporary reviewers praised the work in terms that now seem extravagant. Nevertheless, they also agreed that the laborious advance research carried out by Eliot in preparation for the novel weighed the work down. Critics who later evaluated the entire span of Eliot's career, such as Mathilde Blind and Leslie Stephen, unreservedly adopted this view, and the novel is rarely read today.

When *Felix Holt* (1868) was published, a number of critics, including John Morley, felt that Eliot was returning to the subjects in which she excelled: depictions of the English, predominantly rural, past. John Hutton Balfour Browne and Arthur Sedgwick expressed interest in the fictionalization of Eliot's more radical ideas, which, closely following the Second Reform Act (1867), seemed singularly topical. However, the novel did not have the same impact as *Adam Bede* or *Silas Marner* and, by the early twentieth century, it was, as Browne writes, considered with some justification one of Eliot's minor, more forgettable, works.

The tide turned with *Middlemarch* (1871–72). Whether the reviewers were insistent in their praise, such as Edith Simcox and Sidney Colvin, or more ambivalent, as Henry James and George Parsons Lathrop were, there was a consensus that *Middlemarch* was one of the most important novels published in the nineteenth century. The variety of responses to the novel gives an indication that reviewers recognized that they were dealing with an unusually complex work. Whereas responses to Eliot's earlier novels often voiced similar concerns, here the reviewers considered issues as diverse as Eliot's explorations of the mind (Simcox), the use of scientific concerns and terminology (Colvin), and the complexity of the structure (James). Nevertheless, far fewer readers and critics than today deemed this her greatest novel, and it was certainly not her most popular. The extract by George Parsons Lathrop provides some insight into this: he finds that, as in *Romola*, analysis rather than imagination dominates in *Middlemarch*. Vida D. Scudder's turn-of-the-century response added a new element to discussions of the work by dwelling on the feminist ideas expressed in the work; in doing so, she anticipated one of the ways in which the novel would be celebrated in the later twentieth century.

In many ways, *Daniel Deronda* (1874–76) posed the greatest critical difficulties for contemporary and later reviewers as well. George Saintsbury offers a largely representative picture of the novel's immediate reception. Critics were enthusiastic about the storyline involving Gwendolen and Grandcourt; they were far more skeptical about the success, and even the interest of, the "Jewish episodes," which Joseph Jacobs defended in his 1877 essay. James's lively dialogue demonstrates that the novel provoked more debate than any of Eliot's previous novels. Oliver Elton's frustratingly dismissive response to the novel provides a good indication of early-twentieth-century views of the work, at a time when George Eliot's novels as a whole were out of fashion. Robert Edward Francillon's take on the work atypically acknowledges its importance and perceptively suggests that a time would come when the consensus regarding the work would be overturned, and *Daniel Deronda* would be considered one of Eliot's most interesting and rewarding novels.

SCENES OF CLERICAL LIFE

GEORGE ELIOT (1857)

Eliot's explanation of how she "began to write fiction" revealingly displays both her doubts and her confidence. She is open about the despondency she felt about her creative ability (something that would continue to plague her throughout her lifetime) and "everything else," which included the fear of loneliness. Eliot evokes the key role played by Lewes, who encouraged her while managing her expectations, but also makes it clear that her artistic ambitions existed independently of Lewes. The account anticipates many of the later debates surrounding Eliot's works: critics acknowledged her "wit" and her genius for dialogue, they acknowledged her powers as a "philosopher" (though they often questioned whether the latter were always judiciously employed), they argued about her talents for "dramatic presentation," and debated whether her "pathos" was indeed "better than [her] fun."

September 1856 made a new era in my life, for it was then I began to write fiction. It had always been a vague dream of mine that some time or other I might write a novel; and my shadowy conception of what the novel was to be, varied, of course, from one epoch of my life to another. But I never went further towards the actual writing of the novel than an introductory chapter describing a Staffordshire village and the life of the neighbouring farmhouses; and as the years passed on I lost any hope that I should ever be able to write a novel, just as I desponded about everything else in my future life. I always thought I was deficient in dramatic power, both of construction and dialogue, but I felt I should be at my ease in the descriptive parts of a novel. My "introductory chapter" was pure description, though there were good materials in it for dramatic presentation. It happened to be among the papers I had with me in Germany, and one evening at Berlin something led me to read it to George. He was struck with it as a bit of concrete description, and it suggested to him the possibility of my being able to write a novel, though he distrusted—indeed disbelieved in—my possession of any dramatic power. Still he began to think that I might as well try some time what I could do in fiction; and by and by when we came back to England, and I had greater success than he ever expected in other kinds of writing, his impression that it was worth while to see how far my mental power would go towards the production of a novel, was strengthened. He began to say very positively, "You must try and write a story," and when we were at Teriby he urged me to begin at once. I deferred it, however, after my usual fashion with work that does not present itself as an absolute duty. But one morning, as I was thinking what should be the subject of my first story, my thoughts merged themselves into a dreamy doze, and I imagined myself writing a story, of which the title was, 'The Sad Fortunes of the Reverend Amos Barton.' I was soon wide awake again and told G. He said, "Oh, what a capital title!" and from that time I had settled in my mind that this should be my first story. George used to say, "It may be a failure—it may be that you are unable to write fiction. Or perhaps it may be just good enough to warrant you trying again." Again, "You may write a *chef-d'oeuvre* at once—there's no telling." But his prevalent impression was, that though I could hardly write a *poor* novel, my effort would want the highest quality of fiction, dramatic presentation.

He used to say, "You have wit, description, and philosophy those go a good way towards the production of a novel. It is worth while for you to try the experiment." We determined that if my story turned out good enough, we would send it to Blackwood; but G. thought the more probable result was that I should have to lay it aside and try again. But when we returned to Richmond, I had to write my article on "Silly Novels," and my review of Contemporary Literature for the "Westminster", so that I did not begin my story till September 22. After I had begun it, as we were walking in the park, I mentioned to G. that I had thought of the plan of writing a series of stories, containing sketches drawn from my own observations of the clergy, and calling them 'Scenes from Clerical Life,' opening with "Amos Barton." He at once accepted the notion as a good one—fresh and striking; and about a week afterwards, when I read him the first part of "Amos," he had no longer any doubt about my ability to carry out the plan. The scene at Cross Farm, he said, satisfied him that I had the very element he had been doubtful about—it was clear that I could write good dialogue. There still remained the question whether I could command any pathos; and that was to be decided by the mode in which I treated Milly's death. One night G. went to town on purpose to leave me a quiet evening for writing it. I wrote the chapter from the news brought by the shepherd to Mrs. Hackit, to the moment when Amos is dragged from the bedside, and I read it to G. when he came home. We both cried over it, and then he came up to me and kissed me, saying, "I think your pathos is better than your fun."

—GEORGE ELIOT, cited in John W. Cross, *George Eliot's Life as Related in Her Letters and Journals*, vol. 1, 1885, pp. 414–417

UNSIGNED "SCENES OF CLERICAL LIFE" (1858)

This early review of Eliot's first published work of fiction is representative of the way in which the work was discussed at large: it praises Eliot's faithful depiction of life in a country village, celebrates her "humor and pathos," and notes her "intelligent and comprehensive sympathy." The review is especially prescient for the manner in which it senses a shift in contemporary literary concerns and strives to offer an initial definition of the high realism with which Eliot would come to be associated. The writer is astonished at the extent to which the novelist is "in revolt against the old theory of the necessity of perfection" in fictional characters. The phrase accurately reflects the attacks on artistic idealization that Eliot had expressed in two essays: "The Natural History of German Life" (July 1856) and "Silly Novels by Lady Novelists" (October 1856). In the latter, Eliot had poked fun at a fictional heroine whose "eyes and wit are both dazzling" and who "dances like a sylph, and reads the Bible in the original tongues." The reviewer, struggling to pin down a consistent definition of Eliot's realism, describes it as "copying," a term that was frequently used to discuss her writing and later prompted criticisms that she was insufficiently "creative." The writer also considers the idea of the "romance of reality," a phrase that was again repeatedly used and could be twisted by both novelists and reviewers to include almost anything. (In the preface to *Bleak House*, Dickens similarly stressed that he had "dwelt on the romantic side of familiar things," which under this definition went so far as to include spontaneous combustion!)

Fiction represents the character of the age to which it belongs, not merely by actual delineations of its times, like those of *Tom Jones* and *The Newcomes*, but also in an indirect, though scarcely less positive manner, by its exhibition of the influence of the times upon its own form and general direction, whatever the scene or period it may have chosen for itself. The story of *Hypatia* is laid in Alexandria almost two thousand years ago, but the book reflects the crudities of modern English thought; and even Mr. Thackeray, the greatest living master of costume, succeeds in making his *Esmond* only a joint-production of the Addisonian age and our own. Thus the novels of the last few years exhibit very clearly the spirit that characterizes the period of regard for men and women as men and women, without reference to rank, beauty, fortune, or privilege. Novelists recognize that Nature is a better romance-maker than the fancy, and the public is learning that men and women are better than heroes and heroines, not only to live with, but also to read of. Now and then, therefore, we get a novel, like these *Scenes of Clerical Life*, in which the fictitious element is securely based upon a broad groundwork of actual truth, truth as well in detail as in general.

It is not often, however, even yet, that we find a writer wholly unembarrassed by and in revolt against the old theory of the necessity of perfection in some one at least of the characters of his story. 'Neither Luther nor John Bunyan,' says the author of this book, 'would have satisfied the modern demand for an ideal hero, who believes nothing but what is true, feels nothing but what is excellent, and does nothing but what is graceful.'

Sometimes, indeed, a daring romance-writer ventures, during the earlier chapters of his story, to represent a heroine without beauty and without wealth, or a hero with some mortal blemish. But after a time his resolution fails;—each new chapter gives a new charm to the ordinary face; the eyes grow 'liquid' and 'lustrous,' always having been 'large'; the nose, 'naturally delicate,' exhibits its 'fine-cut lines'; the mouth acquires an indescribable expression of loveliness; and the reader's hoped-for Fright is transformed by Folly or Miss Pickering into a commonplace, tiresome, *novelesque* Beauty. Even Miss Brontë relented toward Jane Eyre; and the weaker novelists are continually repeating, but with the omission of the moral, the story of the *Ugly Duck*. Unquestionably, there is the excuse to be made for this great error, that it betrays the seeking after an Ideal. Dangerous world! The ideal standard of excellence is, to be sure, fortunately changing, and the unreal ideal will soon be confined to the second-rate writers for second-rate readers. But all the great novelists of the two last generations indulged themselves and their readers in these unrealities. It is vastly easier to invent a consistent character than to represent an inconsistent one;—a hero is easier to make (so all historians have found) than a man.

Suppose, however, novelists could be placed in a society made up of their favorite characters,—forced into real, lifelike intercourse with them;—Richardson, for instance, with his Harriet Byron or Clarissa, attended by Sir Charles; Miss Burney with Lord Orville and Evelina; Miss Edgeworth with Caroline Percy, and that marvelous hero, Count Altenburg; Scott with the automatons that he called Waverley and Flora McIvor. Suppose they were brought together to share the comforts (cold comforts they would be) of life, to pass days together, to meet every morning at breakfast; with what a ludicrous sense of relief, at the close of this purgatorial period, would not the unhappy novelists have fled from these deserted heroes and heroines, and the precious proprieties of their romance, to the very driest and mustiest of human bores, gratefully rejoicing that the world was not filled with such creatures as they themselves had set before it as *ideals!*

To copy Nature faithfully and heartily is certainly not less needful when stories are presented in words than when they are told on canvas or in marble. In the *Scenes from Clerical Life* we have a happy example of such copying. The three stories embraced under this title are written vigorously, with a just appreciation of the romance of reality, and with honest adherence to truth of representation in the sombre as well as the brighter portions of life. It demands not only a large intellect, but a large heart, to gain such a candid and inclusive appreciation of life and character as they display. The greater part of each story reads like a reminiscence of real life, and the personages introduced show little signs of being 'rubbed down' or 'touched up and varnished' for effect. The narrative is easy and direct, full of humor and pathos; and the descriptions of simple life in a country village are often charming from their freshness, vivacity, and sweetness. More than this, these stories give proof of that wide range of experience which does not so much depend on an extended or varied acquaintance with the world, as upon an intelligent and comprehensive sympathy, which makes each new person with whom one is connected a new illustration of the unsolved problems of life and a new link in the unending chain of human development.

—UNSIGNED, "Scenes of Clerical Life,"
The Atlantic Monthly, vol. 1,
May 1858, pp. 890–892

RICHARD SIMPSON
"GEORGE ELIOT'S NOVELS" (1863)

Richard Simpson (1820–76) was an English writer and scholar. In 1846, Simpson converted to Roman Catholicism and went on to contribute to and edit *The Rambler*, which became the popular *Home and Foreign Review* in 1862. Simpson often caused controversy for his liberal Catholic views. Passionate about Shakespeare, he also published a number of works on Elizabethan literature. The excerpt included here is useful in reminding us that, though *Scenes* was praised by its reviewers, it was not until *Adam Bede* that Eliot fully caught the attention of the reading public. Eliot's publisher John Blackwood was as ignorant as his readers of the identity of "George Eliot," as it was Lewes who served as liaison between the two. Indeed, Blackwood misunderstood a reference made by Lewes to his "clerical friend" and had to be corrected in his assumption that the novelist was a man of the Church. The conviction that the author was a clergyman, together with Simpson's remark on the liberality of his religious opinions, illustrates the manner in which Eliot refrained from allowing her characters to reflect her own agnosticism. When some readers went on to discover who George Eliot really was, they felt, as Margaret Oliphant wrote, "cheated" that they had been moved by the works of an agnostic.

George Eliot did not burst upon us like a flood, but trickled into fame through the channel of a monthly magazine. Readers who in 1858 took up the *Scenes of Clerical Life*, reprinted from *Blackwood's Magazine*, with the languid expectancy with which the first writings of new novelists are received, were astonished that, instead of an author, they had found a man,—and a man uniting the characteristics of Montesquieu's two classes, those who think for us, and those who amuse us. He was apparently a young clergyman, whose piety was mitigated by irony, who had carefully formed a style on the best models, and who had stored his mind with the results of an intelligent and sympathetic observation of common life. People were struck with his power of putting before them the sorrows of the 'breaking heart that will not break' in Amos Barton, the shut soul's hypocrisy in young Wybrow, and the strength of stormy pity in "Janet's Repentance". The only exception the most orthodox found to make to him was for a liberality, scarcely edifying, in approving indiscriminately every school of religious opinion; but then it was remarked that his object was to bring into vivid light the fundamental agreement underlying all these differences. His liberality was clearly far removed from indifference. Had he not the deepest scorn for sensual hypocrisy, and for the 'dingy ditchwater'? Obviously here was an author on whom the eye of expectation was to be kept open.

—RICHARD SIMPSON, "George Eliot's Novels," *Home and Foreign Review*, vol. 3, October 1863, p. 522

OSCAR BROWNING (1890)

Statements about the autobiographical nature of Eliot's fiction should be approached with caution, as Eliot did not slavishly replicate in her fiction her childhood surroundings and experiences. It is undeniable, however, that she drew heavily on her past, particularly in her early fiction, and Browning's attempts to match the tales with the reality reflect the interest this created among the public. Attentive readers from the Midlands made similar comparisons, and naturally sought out the author who had displayed such an intimate knowledge of their lives. As Browning narrates, Mr. Liggins was put forward as a likely candidate—a rumor that he did nothing to dispel.

The first of the "Scenes of Clerical Life" was drawn, like all other good art, from personal experience. Shepperton Church is Chilvers Colon, a suburb of Nuneaton. In this church Mary Ann Evans was baptized, and she attended it during the whole of her residence at Griff. It stands close to the Vicarage. The "little flight of steps, with their wooden rail running up the outer wall and leading to the children's gallery," still exists, and has not been removed in the restoration of the church. This restoration took place when George Eliot was fifteen and must have made a deep impression upon her mind. The Vicarage is a pleasant-looking, old-fashioned house, with a pretty garden in front, and everything around neat and well ordered. The Rev. Amos Barton was in reality the Rev. John Gwyther, B. A., and Milly Barton was his wife Emma. Mrs. Hackit is supposed to be a sketch of George Eliot's mother. The story told by George Eliot, the struggle of the curate's family to live, the taking of a foreign lady into the family, the death of Mrs. Gwyther, were subjects of common conversation in the neighbourhood during George Eliot's girlhood, and if Mrs. Evans really attended at Milly's death-bed there is a strong reason for her daughter knowing all about it. Indeed, Emma Gwyther did not die till 1836, so that George Eliot probably knew her personally. The story shows the full strength of George Eliot's genius mixed with some weaknesses which disappeared at a later period. The dialogue is admirably dramatic. Her power of objective representation was fully grown from the first. The homely wit so apparent in *Adam Bede* here shows itself as a new force in literature. "You're like the wood-pigeon: it says do do do all day, and never sets about any work itself." "When he tries to preach without book he rambles about and doesn't stick to his text; and every now and then he flounders about like a sheep that has cast itself, and can't get on its legs again." On the other hand, the Greek quotation at the end of chapter iv is not very appropriate, and is probably inserted to keep up the idea that the writer is a man. The opening reflections of chapter v., a defence of uninteresting characters, are too obviously an imitation of Walter Scott, and are rather long in proportion to the story; and the same might be said of other paragraphs. Nanny, however, the servant, is a most life-like creature, and her conversation is as true and racy as any which George Eliot ever penned. It is needless to praise the pathos of Milly's death, not less remarkable for its intense feeling than for its strong self-repression. The criticism of Mr. Blackwood curtailed the conclusion of the story, which related the fate of the children. Most readers would prefer that it had been left in its original state.

"Mr. Gilfil's Love-Story," begun immediately after the conclusion of "Amos Barton," was finished in the Scilly Islands, in May, 1857. It also is laid amongst scenes of her early recollections, although it is not known how far the plot is based on fact. The introduction of the Italian element, which the writer could only have learnt superficially from travel, points to the coming *Romola*. It is also remarkable that these first two stories depend for their interest on the incongruity between English and foreign views of life and conduct. Cheverell Manor is Arbury Hall, in the grounds of which George Eliot was born. Sir Christopher Cheverell is Sir Roger Newdigate, a family already commemorated by the Oldinports of "Amos Barton." He rebuilt and redecorated his ancient family seat precisely in the manner described in the novel. Maynard Gilfil was the ward of Sir Christopher, who—when at Milan had adopted a little Italian orphan girl, and had brought her up at Cheverell.

It is said that Sir Roger Newdigate had adopted a village girl with a beautiful voice. Tina, the Italian girl, is destined to be Maynard's wife, whereas she is heart and soul in love with Captain Wybrow, Sir Christopher's heir, whom he wishes to marry to a rich heiress, Miss Archer. Wybrow has no intention of marrying the penniless Italian, but he makes love to her, and excuses himself to his betrothed by alleging Tina's importunity. Tina, furious with passion and jealousy secretes a dagger, she scarcely knows with what object, and going to meet Wybrow in the woods, finds him stretched on the ground dead of heart disease. She runs away, but is recovered and marries Gilfil. She dies within the year and "Maynard Gilfil's love went with her into deep silence for evermore." He sits down in his bare dining-room, whilst in another part of the house, cleaned by his servants once a quarter, is a chamber with an oriel window, with a dainty looking-glass over a dressing-table, "a faded satin pin-cushion with the pins rusted in it, a scent-bottle and a large green fan lay on the table, and on a dressing-box by the side of the glass was a work-basket and an unfinished baby-cap, yellow with age, lying in it." "Such was the locked-up chamber in Mr. Gilfil's house, a sort of visible symbol of the secret chamber in his heart, where he had long turned the key on early hopes and early sorrows, shutting up for ever all the passion and the poetry of his life."

The Knebley Church of the story is Astley Church, about a mile from Arbury, topping a hill with a fine view. The ruins of Astley Castle are close by. Here Mr. Gilfil officiated in the afternoon, "in a wonderful little church with a checkered pavement, which had once rung to the iron-tread of military monks, with coats of arms in clusters on the lofty roof, marble warriors and their heads without noses occupying a large proportion of the area, and the twelve apostles, with their heads very much on one side, holding didactic ribbons, painted in fresco on the walls." There is a similar church on a hill at Norbury in Derbyshire, amidst the scenery of *Adam Bede*.

The epilogue to "Mr. Gilfil's Love-Story," written on Fortification Hill, Scilly Islands, one sunshiny morning, contains a lovely passage of universal application, which throws a strong light upon George Eliot's philosophy:

> It is with men as with trees: if you lop off their finest branches, into which they are pouring their young life-juice, the wounds will be healed over with some rough boss, some odd excrescence, and what might have been a grand tree expanding into liberal shade is but a whimsical misshapen trunk. Many an irritating fault, many an unlovely oddity, has come of a hard sorrow, which has crushed and maimed the nature just when it was expanding into plenteous beauty; and the trivial erring life, which we visit with our harsh

blame, may be but as the unsteady motion of a man whose best limb is withered.

"Janet's Repentance," the last of the "Scenes," had been begun in the Scilly Islands, on April 18, 1857, but the greater part of it was written in Jersey, where the Leweses had delightful lodgings, at Gorey in the Bay of Granville, within sight of the castle of Montorgueil. "It was a sweet beautiful life we led there. Good creatures the Amys, our host and hostess, with their nice boy and girl, and the little white kid the family pet. No disagreeable sounds to be heard in the house, no unpleasant qualities to hinder one from feeling perfect love to these simple people." They spent their time in long rambles and long readings; George Eliot reading aloud *Drape's Physiology* in the "grave evening hours." They dined at five. George Eliot's strength increased in this delicious quiet, and she had fewer interruptions to meet, from headache, than she had experienced since Christmas. She writes to Blackwood on June 2nd: "Lewes seems to have higher expectations from the third story than from either of the preceding; but I can form no judgment myself, until I have quite finished a thing, and see it aloof from my actual self. I can only go on writing what I feel, and waiting for the proof that I have been able to make others feel." Strangely enough, Blackwood did not like the story. He thought that it dealt too much with clerical matters, and George Eliot proposed that the series should close with No. 2, and that "Janet's Repentance" should be included if the tales were republished in a volume. The Leweses returned to Park Shot at the end of July, probably for the sake of their children's holidays; and there "Janet's Repentance" was finished on October 9th. *Adam Bede*, the thought of which had already begun to burgeon in the author's mind, was begun on October 22nd. She writes in her diary at the former date: "I had meant to carry on the series, and especially I longed to tell the story of the "Clerical Tutor," but my annoyance at Blackwood's want of sympathy in the first part (although he came round to admiration at the third part) determined me to close the series and republish them in two volumes." She received £180 for the first edition of the "Scenes of Clerical Life."

"Janet's Repentance" is, again, full of early recollections. Milby is Nuneaton, so-called from a convent of nuns founded in the reign of King Stephen in later days a flourishing factory town. The main details of the story are said to be based on actual occurrences. Dempster is the representation of a well-known lawyer. The virtues of his wife Janet still live in the recollections of her fellow-townspeople. Mr. Tryan was curate at the Stockingford chapel-of-ease. Mr. Pilgrim was a well-known doctor. Although George Eliot declared that Mr. Tryan was not a portrait of any clergyman living or dead, and was an ideal character, yet it is probable that she frequently introduced into her writings more exact representations of living people than she was herself aware. The name Milby Mill belongs to a corn-mill in the town standing on the River Anker. The "Red Lion" still flourishes as the "Bull." Mr. Pilgrim, the doctor, has all the trace of a real character.

> I have known Mr. Pilgrim discover the most unexpected virtues in a patient seized with a promising illness. A good inflammation fired his enthusiasm, and a lingering dropsy dissolved him into charity. Gradually, however, as his patients became convalescent, his view of their character became more dispassionate. When they could relish mutton-chops he began to admit that they had foibles, and by the time they had swallowed their last dose of tonic he was alive to their most inexcusable faults.

"Dempster's" House in Church Street, "an old-fashioned house with an overhanging upper storey," still exists. "Outside it had a face of rough stucco, and casement windows with green panes and shutters; inside it was full of long passages and rooms with low ceilings." Stockingford, which lies about two miles from Nuneaton, between that town and Arbury, is called Paddiford Common in the story. It was up Church Street that Mr. Tryan passed "through a pelting shower of nicknames and bad puns, with an ad libitum accompaniment of groans, howls, hisses, and hee-haws."

It is scarcely to be wondered at that, when the incognito of George Eliot was so carefully preserved and yet the tales were so full of local incident and colour an attempt should have been made to claim the authorship for another. This was the origin of the myth of Joseph Liggins, who was for some time supposed to be George Eliot. A table-rapper had spelt out the name of the great unknown as Liggers. Mr. Liggins of Nuneaton, a broken-down gentleman of very poor literary pretensions, did not reject the honour which was thrust upon him. He called himself George Eliot, and was more proud than ever after the appearance of *Adam Bede*. A deputation of Dissenting parsons went out to see him, and found him washing his slop-basin at a pump. At a later period a subscription was got up for him, and George Eliot and Mr. Blackwood found it necessary to interfere. The myth was at last killed, though not without some difficulty, and there is little doubt that this absurd mistake delayed for some time the discovery of the true George Eliot.

—Oscar Browning,
Life of George Eliot, 1890, pp. 47–54

May Tomlinson "The Beginning of George Eliot's Art: A Study of Scenes of Clerical Life" (1919)

May Copeland Tomlinson Hamilton (1870–1924) wrote a number of articles on George Eliot, including a piece on humor in her works. Tomlinson also translated some of Balzac's novels into English. Her essay on *Scenes of Clerical Life* was published at a time when Eliot's novels were highly unpopular, yet Tomlinson makes no reference to the ongoing critical debate. Instead, she feeds into the idea that Eliot's early works are the most successful. By defining Eliot's appeal as a nostalgic one, however, Tomlinson does little to reinstate Eliot as an important novelist.

The exquisiteness of George Eliot's *Scenes of Clerical Life* grows on one—as one advances in years, I was going to say, and there is no need to withdraw the modifying clause. Youth, I think, is less susceptible to the quality of exquisiteness, less consciously appreciative of what is delicately fine. As the years go on, one seeks quiet enjoyment; the merely specious and the merely exciting no longer satisfy; the ear listens more willingly to the tender plaintive minor tones; the eye turns more readily to the quietly tinted scenes, sights more in harmony with those upon which the inward eye dwells.

If it be true that a full relish of these *Clerical Scenes* implies a wealth which age alone confers, it is no less true that their exquisiteness could only have sprung from a mind enriched with a bountiful store of memories. Their tone is tenderly pensive; their mood is retrospective. This retrospective note is struck at once. "Shepperton church was a very different looking building five-and-twenty years ago." So runs the opening sentence of "Amos Barton." The second *Scene* begins thus: "When Mr. Gilfil died, thirty years ago, there was general sorrow in Shepperton." "Janet's Repentance" opens with a conversation, but, in the first paragraph of the second chapter, we are told that "more than a quarter of a century has slipped by since then." . . .

A few words must be said concerning the style and diction of these clerical tales. The deathbed scene in "Amos Barton," which no lover of George Eliot can possibly read, even for the twentieth time, without deep and tearful emotion, will ever remain a consummate example of simple pathos secured through the use of plain, homely words and straightforward, unembellished statement. All the fairies that attend artistic creation must have guided the pen that produced that impeccable eighth chapter. Nothing short of instinct could have prompted the manner of it. And indeed throughout the *Scenes* one finds a greater simplicity of style, less circumlocution, and less inclination to philosophic dissertation, than characterizes George Eliot's later fiction. If it were less difficult to make a selection, I should like to choose a few excerpts from the *Clerical Scenes*, illustrative not only of their general style but of that pervading spirit—that indescribable sweetness, that ineffable tenderness—which is their life and immortality. My choice might be the closing paragraph of "Janet's Repentance" or it might be that picture of the fire-lighted room, with Janet, an image of life and strength, in loving tendance on the man, now feeble and suffering, who had guided her feet into ways of purity and holiness; or that unexpected meeting with Mr. Tryan, when Janet tries her persuasive powers and they go back together along the lane; or that lovely description of Tina's reawakening; or the story of Tina's end and of how "Maynard Gilfil's love went with her into deep silence for-evermore."

—May Tomlinson, "The Beginning of George Eliot's Art: A Study of Scenes of Clerical Life," *Sewanee Review*, vol. 27, 1919, p. 320–329

ADAM BEDE

Jane Welsh Carlyle (1859)

Jane Welsh Carlyle (1801–66), the wife of the "sage" Thomas Carlyle (1795–1881), received some of the leading artistic and political figures of the time at her home. Jane Carlyle gained a reputation during her lifetime as a brilliant and witty letter writer. Her lively letter to Eliot captures some of the excitement with which *Adam Bede* was greeted within literary circles. Jane also echoes Eliot's own ambitions for the story: Eliot had written to her publishers in October 1857 that she wished the novel to be "full of the breath of cows and the scent of hay" (*GE Letters*, II: 387–88). Though Jane thanked Eliot for sending a copy of *Adam Bede*, the Carlyles did not entirely refrain from gossiping about the Leweses and did not invite them to their home.

The Book was actually *Adam Bede*, and *Adam Bede* "justified my enthusiasm"; to say the least!

Oh yes! It was as good as *going into the country for one's health*, the reading of that Book was!—Like a visit to Scotland *minus* the fatigues of the long journey, and the grief of seeing friends grown old, and Places that knew me knowing me no more! I could fancy in reading it, to be seeing and hearing once again a crystal-clear, musical, Scotch stream, such as I long to lie down beside and—*cry* at (!) for gladness and sadness; after long stifling sojourn in the South; where there is no *water* but what is stagnant or muddy!

In truth, it is a beautiful most *human* Book! Every *Dog* in it, not to say every man woman and child in it, is brought home to one's 'business and bosom,' an individual fellow-creature! I found myself in charity with the whole human race when I laid it down—the *canine* race I had *always* appreciated—"not wisely but too well!"—the *human,* however,—

Ach!—*that* has troubled me—as badly at times as "twenty gallons of milk on one's mind"! For the rest; why you are so good to *me* is still a *mystery,* with every appearance of remaining so!

—Jane Welsh Carlyle, letter to
Thomas Carlyle, February 20, 1859,
cited in *The George Eliot Letters*, ed.
Gordon S. Haight, vol. 3, 1954–55, pp. 17–18

Charles Dickens (1859)

Charles Dickens (1812–70), one of the most popular English novelists of the Victorian period, first encountered Eliot in May 1852 at a meeting organized by John Chapman to discuss the publishing industry. Seven years later, Dickens expressed his admiration for *Scenes of Clerical Life*, ignorant of the fact that he had previously encountered its author. In the following extract, he records his even greater delight with *Adam Bede*. As a result, Dickens attempted to convince Eliot to publish her new novel, *The Mill on the Floss*, in his recently founded periodical *All the Year Round*. (She declined, partly out of a reluctance to publish in rapid installments.) The letter displays the tribute paid from the leading novelist of the day to one who would soon be considered to have equal claims to that title. Dickens was also sufficiently perspicuous to have guessed Eliot's gender. (In a review for *Bentley's Quarterly Review* published in July 1859, the essayist and editor Anne Mozley publicly expressed a similar opinion.)

Adam Bede has taken its place among the actual experiences and endurances of my life. Every high quality that was in the former book [*Scenes of Clerical Life*], is in that, with a World of Power added thereunto. The conception of Hetty's character is so extraordinarily subtle and true, that I laid the book down fifty times, to shut my eyes and think about it. I know nothing so skilful, determined, and uncompromising. The whole country life that the story is set in, is so real, and so droll and genuine, and yet so selected and polished by art, that I cannot praise it enough to you. And that part of the book which follows Hetty's trial (and which I have observed to be not as widely understood as the rest), affected me far more than any other, and exalted my sympathy with the writer to its utmost height. You must not suppose that I am writing this to *you*. I have been saying it over and over again, here and elsewhere, until I feel in a ludicrously apologetic state for repeating myself on this paper.

I cannot close this note without touching on two heads. Firstly (Blackwood not now being the medium of communication), if you should ever have the freedom and inclination to be a fellow labourer with me, it would yield me a pleasure that I have never known yet and can never know otherwise; and no channel that even you could command, should be so profitable as to yourself. Secondly, I hope you will let me come to see you when we are all in or near London again, and tell you—as a curiosity—my reasons for the faith that was in me that you were a woman, and for the absolute and never-doubting confidence with which I have waved all men away from *Adam Bede*, and nailed my colors to the Mast with 'Eve' upon them.

—CHARLES DICKENS, letter to George Eliot,
July 10, 1859, cited in *The George Eliot Letters*, ed.
Gordon S. Haight, vol. 3, 1954–55, pp. 114–115

E.S. DALLAS "ADAM BEDE" (1859)

The English writer Eneas Sweetland Dallas (1828–79) contributed numerous anonymous articles to leading newspapers and periodicals and became a member of the staff on *The Times* in 1855. Dallas's strong opening provides a sense of the groundbreaking nature of the novel: it confirmed that Eliot was an author to be taken seriously. Like Lewes, Dallas praises Eliot for having mastered both comedy and pathos. He also underlines the importance of sympathy, which would become an ongoing theme in both Eliot's novels and discussions of them.

Dallas also pays tribute to the element of the novel that received the highest praise: Mrs. Poyser, who delighted readers with her pithy sayings. (Eliot had to refute suggestions that she had borrowed traditional expressions and proverbs.) The success of Mrs. Poyser had its drawbacks, though: her speeches were often enjoyed separately from the novel in which they appeared. More importantly, as Dallas anticipates, readers returned continuously to Eliot's novels hoping to find similar instances of wit and quaintness and were more than not displeased when they found these lacking.

There can be no mistake about *Adam Bede*. It is a first-rate novel, and its author takes rank at once among the masters of the art. Hitherto known but as the writer of certain tales to which he gave the modest title of *Scenes*, and which displayed only the buds of what we have here in full blossom, he has produced a work which, after making every allowance for certain crudities of execution, impresses us with a sense of the novelist's maturity of thought and feeling. Very seldom are so much freshness of style and warmth of emotion seen combined with so much solid sense and ripened observation. We have a pleasant feeling of security in either laughing or crying with such a companion. We need not fear to yield ourselves entirely to all the enchantments of the wizard whose first article of belief is the truism which very few of us comprehend until it has been knocked into us by years of experience—that we are all alike—that the human heart is one. All the novelists and all the dramatists that have ever lived have set themselves to exhibit the differences between man and man. Here, they seem to say, are circumstances precisely similar, and yet mark how various are the characters which grow out of these circumstances. The Pharisee in the Temple felt that he was different from other men, thanking his God for it; and which of us, in the immaturity of experience, is not forced chiefly to consider the differences between ourselves and other men, often utterly forgetting the grand fact of an underlying unity? Here we see monsters, and there we see angels, alien faces and inaccessible natures. It is only after much beating about, long intercourse with society, and many strange discoveries and detections, that the truism which we never doubted becomes a great reality to us, and we feel that man is like to man even as face answers to face in a glass. . . .

There is not much of a story it will be seen. The great charm of the novel is rather in the characters introduced than in the action which they carry on. All the characters are so true, and so natural, and so racy that we love to hear them talk for the sake of talking. They are so full of strange humours and funny pretty sayings that we entirely overlook the want of movement in the story. Besides which, when the dialogue ceases, the author's reflections are so pointed, and his descriptions are so vivid, that we naturally think more of what we have than of what we have not. There is not a character in the novel which is not well drawn, and even if the portrait is but a sketch still it is a true one. We have not mentioned the name of Mr. Irwine, the parson, who is very carefully drawn, nor of his mother, who is touched off in a more rapid manner; and yet the former is a very important personage in the dialogue, and is a fine moral influence throughout the tale. He is a very favourable specimen of the moral preachers of the close of the last century, and the author has placed him in contrast to the more Scriptural style of which Dinah Morris, the youth Methodist, is the representative. He sympathises strongly with both, but leans most to the side of those moral teachers who have been somewhat harshly judged he thinks. Comparing Mr. Irwine with the curate of an "evangelical" turn who succeeded him, he makes Mr. Poyser pronounce this judgement:—"Mr. Irwine was like a good meal o' victual; *you are the better for him without thinking on it*; but Mr. Ryde is like a dose o'physic; he gripes you and worrets you, and after all he leaves you much the same." Irwine is a noble man, with a fine presence and a kindly, catholic nature. He was a silent influence, who did not trouble his parish much with theological "notions," but gave them the example of a kind heart, and demanded from them the reward of honest lives. "It's summat like to see such a man as that i' the desk of a Sunday," says that rattling Mrs. Poyser. "As I say to Poyser, it's like looking at a full crop o' wheat, or a pasture with a fine dairy o'cows in it; it makes you think the world's comfortable-like." The tolerance with which an author who is comfortable to conceive the character of Dinah Morris, and to sympathize with her religious views, is thus pleased to regard a very opposite type of the religious character—a type which many worthy people, no doubt, would be disposed to brand as utterly irreligious, is one of the finest things in the novel, and affords a very good illustration of the tendency of the author to beat down all external differences, and bring into the light the grand points of a genuine resemblance. You fancy that there can be nothing in nature more diverse than the spiritually-minded, praying, and preaching Dinah Morris, and the carnally-minded, easy, gentlemanly Mr. Irwine. I tell you, again and again, says Mr. Elliot, that there is no difference between them. . . .

The gem of the novel is Mrs. Poyser, who, for that combination of shrew remark and homely wit with genuine kindliness and racy style which is so taking in Mr. Samuel Weller, is likely to outvie all the characters of recent fiction, with the single exception of the hero we have named. Mrs. Poyser, in her way, is as amusing as either Mrs. Gamp or Mrs. Nickleby, and much more sensible. Wife of a rough and ready farmer, she is a great woman. She is the firstling of the author's mind, which he is not likely to surpass, even as that glorious Sam Weller, the firstling of Mr. Dickens's pen, has not been outshone by any successor. Mrs. Poyser pervades the novel.

—E.S. Dallas, "Adam Bede," *The Times*, April 12, 1859, p. 5

George Augustus Sala
"The Cant of Modern Criticism" (1867)

George Augustus Sala (1828–95) was an English journalist. His article "The Key of the Street," published in Dickens's periodical *Household Words* in 1851, brought him to public attention. From 1857 until his death, he devoted much of his efforts to the *Daily Telegraph*. He also published five novels and took on editorial duties for a number of publications including *Temple Bar* (1860–63), *Banter* (1867–68), and *Sala's Magazine* (1892–93).

Sala's article was written as an attempt to defend the novels of his friend Mary Elizabeth Braddon and the genre of the sensation novel that was then coming under attack. Sala's method of defence is to point to more "respectable" works that were praised even though they contained similarly improbable or violent incidents. The piece provides a curious instance in which the realist novelist George Eliot is bracketed with authors working in a very different strain. Nevertheless, the piece usefully reminds us how Eliot stretched, at times, the tenets of realism to include the sensational.

Do I intend to maintain that the modern, the contemporary novel of life and character and adventure—the outspoken, realistic, moving, breathing fiction, which mirrors the passions of the age for which it is written, is preferable to the silly sentimentalities of Lady Blessington and Mrs. Gore, to the aristocratic highwaymen and intellectual assassins of *Paul Clifford* and *Eugene Aram*,—or to the dead thieves, bullies, doxies, and turnkeys who were galvanized by Mr. Harrison Ainsworth? Unhesitatingly I say I do. *Jane Eyre* was to all intents and purposes a "sensational" novel, and some fastidious parents might forbid their daughters to read a book in which there is a deliberate attempt at bigamy; in which there is a mad wife who tries to burn her husband's house down; in which the flogging of a girl at school is minutely described; and in which an impulsive little governess sits on a blind gentleman's knee, and pulls his beautiful dark hair about—likening it to the hair of Samson. *Adam Bede* too is clearly "sensational." There is murder, and there is frailty in it.

—George Augustus Sala,
"The Cant of Modern Criticism,"
Belgravia, vol. 4, November 1867, p. 52.

James Benjamin Kenyon "George Eliot" (1901)

James Benjamin Kenyon (1858–1924) was an American poet and minister for the Methodist Episcopal Church. His volumes of poetry include *From out of the Shadows* (1886) and *In Realms of Gold* (1887). Kenyon's *Loiterings* in *Old Fields* contains chapters on Tennyson, William Morris, John Keats, Dante Gabriel Rossetti, James Russell Lowell, and Robert Louis Stevenson.

The following extract considers some of the negative attention that *Adam Bede* received. The first charge—that Eliot misrepresented the Methodists—seems easily dismissed. Though Eliot herself was not a Methodist, the portrait of Dinah was in part inspired by a story told by Eliot's Methodist aunt and drew on her own childhood experiences. More interesting is the accusation of indelicacy. Though *Adam Bede* was widely admired, a number of readers were taken aback by the depiction of Hetty's pregnancy: the *Examiner* published a review in March 1859 criticizing the novel's "almost obstetric accuracy of detail." As Kenyon notes, that *Adam Bede* could be perceived as scandalous seems odd, though it is important to recall that such a reaction also formed part of the novel's reception. Though Kenyon is correct in assuming that few turn-of-the-century readers or critics responded with similar opprobrium, he is a little too optimistic regarding the return to popularity of mid-Victorian novelists.

Adam Bede has been criticised on at least two grounds: first, it is alleged that the story presents a false and distorted portrayal of "the people called Methodists;" and, second, that in certain portions of the book subjects tabooed in polite circles are treated with indelicacy. As to the first objection, anyone familiar with the history of early Methodism in England will exonerate the author of Adam Bede from the charge of inaccuracy or a willful perversion of facts. It cannot be denied that, amid the varying phases, the stirring scenes, and the intense agitation of rude but earnest human nature, early Methodism produced strange and diverse developments both of piety and conduct. The second charge would scarcely be insisted on in these days by any person at all familiar with the products of some recent writers of fiction though the signs of a healthful reaction against the pruriency of much recent so-called literature, and the demand for Stevenson's, Weyman's, Doyle's, Hope's, and Crockett's romances of derring-do and chivalrous adventure, indicate a return to good old Sir Walter's knightly tales, and the generous and sweetly human pages of Thackeray, Dickens, Hawthorne, Reade, Trollope, and Kingsley.

—James Benjamin Kenyon, "George Eliot,"
Loitering in Old Fields, 1901, pp. 124–125

Leslie Stephen (1902)

Stephen gives a thorough account of the genesis and reception of *Adam Bede* and places the novel in its contemporary context. The list of novels that appeared shortly before and after *Adam Bede* confirms Stephen's declaration that it was a "flowering time of genius" and illustrates the particular niche occupied by Eliot. However, by stressing that such novels appeal to his "old-fashioned tastes" and going on to compare her to Sir Walter Scott, Stephen does little to recommend Eliot to an early-twentieth-century audience. Stephen's personal fondness for the work is prompted in part by the underlying mellowness he detects in the novel ("Even the seducer," he notes, "is a thoroughly amiable, if rather weak, young man"), which he and many others found absent from the later works. For Stephen, Eliot's leniency toward her characters goes hand in hand with her sympathetic vision of the past. Like many of Eliot's most perceptive critics, he finds that "conservatism really underlay her acceptance, in the purely intellectual sphere, of radical opinions," which is confirmed by Eliot's description of herself as "conservative rather than destructive" (*GE Letters*, IV: 472).

She finished *Janet's Repentance* on 9th October 1857, and began *Adam Bede* on 22nd October. She completed the first volume by the following March; wrote the second during a following tour in Germany; and after returning to England at the beginning of September, completed the third volume on 16th November. It was published in the beginning of 1858. When recording these dates in her journal she gives also an interesting account of the genesis of the book. It was suggested by an anecdote which she had heard from an aunt, the Methodist preacher, Mrs. Samuel Evans. Mrs. Evans, she says, was a "very small, black-eyed woman, who in the days of her strength could not rest without exhorting and remonstrating in season and out of season." She had become much gentler when, at the age of about sixty, she visited Griff and made the acquaintance of her niece. She was very "loving and kind"; and the niece, then under twenty, given to strict reticence about her "inward life," was encouraged to confide in her aunt. This, as already quoted, shows the affectionate relationship which sprang up. They only met twice afterwards, and Mrs. Evans died in 1849. The anecdote which Mrs. Evans had told was of a girl who was hanged for child-murder. Mrs. Evans had passed a night in prayer with her and induced her to make a confession. She afterwards accompanied the criminal in the cart to the place of execution. George Eliot had been deeply affected by this account, and while writing her first story spoke of it to Lewes. He observed, with his keen eye to business, that the prison scene would make an effective incident in a story. The novel was accordingly worked out with a view to this climax. Mrs. Evans was transformed into Dinah Morris, though materially altered in the process. The child-murder implies the seducer, Arthur Donnithorne, and the true lover, Adam Bede. For

Adam Bede, she took her father as in some degree the model, though again carefully avoiding direct portraiture. These points established, the general situation is defined, and the development follows simply and naturally. Lewes was responsible for two important points. He was convinced by the first three chapters that Dinah Morris would be the centre of interest for readers. She had there been introduced as preaching and receiving an offer of marriage from Seth Bede. He inferred that she should be the "principal figure at the last"; and the remainder of the story was written with this end "constantly in view." Lewes's other remark was that Adam Bede was becoming too passive. He ought to be brought into more direct collision with Arthur Donnithorne. George Eliot was impressed by this suggestion; and one night, while listening to "William Tell" at the Munich Opera, the fight between the two lovers came upon her as a "necessity." An account of the way in which a work of genius has been created is always interesting; and in this case, I think that it helps to explain some important characteristics of the story.

Adam Bede, whatever else may be said of it, placed the author in the first rank of the "Victorian" novelists. Some of us can still look back with fondness to the middle of the last century, and recall the period which seems—to our old-fashioned tastes at least—to have been a flowering time of genius. Within a few years on either side of 1850 many great lights of literature arose or culminated. By *David Copperfield*, which appeared in 1850, Dickens' popular empire, one may say, was finally established; and if his best work was done, his admirers steadily increased in number. Thackeray's *Vanity Fair*, *Pendennis*, *Esmond*, and *The Newcomes* came out between 1847 and 1855. Miss Brontë's short and most brilliant apparition lasted from 1847 to 1853. The versatile Bulwer was opening a new and popular vein by *The Caxtons* and *My Novel* in 1850 and 1853, preaching sound domestic morality and omitting the True and the Beautiful. All Charles Kingsley's really powerful works of fiction—*Alton Locke*, *Yeast*, *Hypatia*, and *Westward Ho!*—appeared between 1850 and 1855. Mrs. Gaskell had first made a mark by *Mary Barton* in 1848, which was followed by *Cranford* and *North and South*, the last in 1855. Trollope, after some failures, was beginning to set forth the humours of Barsetshire by the *Warden* in 1855; and Charles Reade became a popular novelist by *Christie Johnstone* in 1853, and *Never too late to Mend* in 1856. In 1855, I may add, Mr. George Meredith's *Shaving of Shagpat* was praised and reviewed by George Eliot; but the author had long to wait for a general recognition of his genius. Anyhow, an ample and attractive feast was provided for those who had the good fortune to be at the novel-reading age in the fifties. The future historian of literature may settle to his own satisfaction what was the permanent value of the different stars in this constellation, and what was the relation which

George Eliot was to bear to her competitors. He will no doubt analyse the spirit of the age and explain how the novelists, more or less unconsciously, reflected the dominant ideas which were agitating the social organism. I am content to say that a retrospect, coloured perhaps by some personal illusion, seems to suggest a very comfortable state of things. People, we are told, were absurdly optimistic in those days; they had not learned that the universe was out of joint, and were too respectable to look into the dark and nasty sides of human life. The generation which had been in its ardent youth during the Reform of 1832 believed in progress and expected the millennium rather too confidently. It liked plain common-sense. Scott's romanticism and Byron's sentimentalism represented obsolete phases of feeling, and suggested only burlesque or ridicule. The novelists were occupied in constructing a most elaborate panorama of the manners and customs of their own times with a minuteness and psychological analysis not known to their predecessors. Their work is, of course, an implicit "criticism of life." Thackeray's special bugbear, snobbism, represents the effete aristocratic prejudices out of which the world was slowly struggling. Dickens applied fiction to assail the abuses, which were a legacy from the old order—debtors' prisons, and workhouses, and Yorkshire schools, and the "circumlocution office." The "social question" was being treated by Kingsley and Mrs. Gaskell. But little was said which had any direct bearing upon those religious or philosophical problems in which George Eliot was especially interested. The novelists when they approach such topics speak with sincere respect of religious belief, though they obviously hold also that true Christianity is something very different from the creeds which are nominally accepted by the churches. They regard such matters as generally outside of their sphere, and simply accept the view of the sensible layman with a prejudice against bigotry and priestcraft. Here was one special province for the new writer. George Eliot alone came to fiction from philosophy. She was, as we have sufficiently seen, familiar with the speculations of her day, and had accepted the most advanced rationalist opinions. But, on the other hand, she had a strong religious sentiment which asserted itself the more as she abandoned the dogmatic system. She puts this emphatically in her letters at the time. She had, as she tells M. D'Albert in 1859, abandoned the old spirit of "antagonism" which had possessed her ten years before. She now sympathises with "any faith in which human sorrow and human longing for purity have expressed themselves." She thinks, too, that Christianity is the highest expression of the religious sentiment that has yet found its place in the history of mankind, and has the "profoundest interest in the inward life of sincere Christians in all ages." She has ceased, she says a little later, to have any sympathy with freethinkers as a class, and holds that a "spiritual blight comes with no faith." It is characteristic that Buckle, who was startling the world at this time, inspires her with "personal dislike," as "an irreligious conceited man." It is therefore intelligible that she should take a Methodist preacher for her centre of interest. Methodism, she says, in the opening of *Adam Bede*, was a "rudimentary culture" for the simple peasantry; it "linked their thoughts with the past," and "suffused their souls with the sense of a pitying, loving, infinite presence, sweet as summer to the homeless needy." Methodism, to some of her readers, may mean "low-pitched gables up dingy streets, sleek grocers, sponging preachers, and hypocritical jargon—elements which are regarded as an exhaustive analysis of Methodism in many fashionable quarters." Certainly that would be true of readers of Dickens. Stiggins and Chadband and their like were wonderful caricatures, but imply a very summary "analysis." The difference is significant. George Eliot had gone much further than Dickens in explicit rejection of the popular religion, considered as a system of doctrine; but she found her ideal heroine in one of its typical representatives. . . .

The memory of Mrs. Samuel Evans brought up a vivid picture of the little world in which she moved; though her world, as represented by Adam Bede and Mrs. Poyser themselves, looked upon Methodism as rather an intruding and questionable force than as the spiritual leaven which was to redeem it. George Eliot, meaning to set forth the beauty of Dinah Morris's character, incidentally comes to draw a more attractive picture of the sinners whom she ought to have awakened. Dinah gives up preaching when the Society decides against the practice, whereas her prototype, it is said, joined another sect rather than be silenced. Dinah settles down by her domestic hearth, and Adam remains a sound Churchman. He admits in his old age, we are told, that the excellent vicar, Mr. Irwine, "didn't go into deep speritial experience," and only preached short moral sermons. Apparently Adam thought none the worse of him. He quotes Mrs. Poyser's dictum that Mr. "Irwine was like a good meal o' victual; you were the better for him without thinking on it; and Mr. Ryde [his successor] was like a dose of physic; he gripped you and worreted you, and after all he left you much the same." We get the impression that Mrs. Poyser and Adam took the most judicious view; and that the rustic congregation, with its "ruddy faces and bright waistcoats," which reposed in the great square pews and listened to Mr. Irwine's moral without attaching any particular meaning to theological formula, did very well without stronger spiritual stimulants. "The world," in Sir W. Besant's formula, "went very well then." *Adam Bede*, like *Waverley*, might have had for a second title *'Tis Sixty Years Since*; and the verdict seems to be that the simple society of that period was sound at the core; wholesome and kindly, if not very exciting. The pathos to be found in commonplace lives was the main topic of the *Scenes of Clerical Life*; and now, looking back with fondness to her early days, and through them to the early days of her parents, George Eliot finds a beauty not in the individuals alone, but in the whole quiet humdrum order of existence of the rustic population. Everybody is treated with a kindly touch. Even the seducer, Arthur Donnithorne, instead of being the wicked baronet who generally appears on such occasions, is a thoroughly amiable, if rather weak, young man, who is not aware of the sufferings of his victim till too late, and then does all he can to obviate unpleasant consequences. "At present," she says, writing a little later, my "mind works with most freedom and the keenest sense of poetry in my remotest past, and there are many strata to be worked through before I can begin to use, *artistically*, any material I may gather in the present." The world of Adam Bede clearly is the world of her first years, harmonized by loving memories and informed, no doubt, with more beauty than it actually possessed. Her philosophy, indeed, reminds her that the range of ideas of her characters was singularly narrow and hopelessly obsolete. She has no sympathy with the romanticism which leads to reactionary fancies. She is perfectly well aware of the darker sides of the past, though she does not insist upon them. She has herself breathed a larger atmosphere. Only her affectionate recognition of the merits of the old world makes one feel how much conservatism really underlay her acceptance, in the purely intellectual sphere, of radical opinions.

The *Scenes of Clerical Life* had made a more decided success with critics than with the public. *Adam Bede* had an equal and triumphant success with both classes. The original agreement with Blackwood had been for £800 for four years' copyright. Seven editions and 16,000 copies were printed during the first year (1859). Blackwood acknowledged the success generously by another check for £800, and gave back the copyright. He offered at the same time £2000 for 4000 copies of her next novel, and proposed to pay at the same rate for subsequent editions. The pecuniary success put her at once and permanently beyond the reach of any pecuniary pressure. Meanwhile she had received hearty greetings on all sides. In April she notes that she has left off recording the "pleasant letters and words" that had come to her: "the success has been so triumphantly beyond anything I had dreamed of, that it would be tiresome to put down particulars." "Shall I ever," she asks herself, "write another book as true as *Adam Bede*?" The "weight of the future presses on me and makes itself felt even more than the deep satisfaction of the past and present." Old friends had been delighted. One of them, Mme. Bodichon, had discovered the authorship, though she had only inferred it from extracts in the reviews. Her friends the Brays were not so perspicacious, and were "overwhelmed with surprise" when in June she revealed the secret to them. She reopened her acquaintance with M. D'Albert by announcing to him that she had "turned out" to be, like him, "an artist," though in words, not with the pencil. Mr. Herbert Spencer wrote an "enthusiastic" letter, and declared that he felt the better for reading the book. Mrs. Carlyle felt herself in "charity with the whole human race" after the same experience, though her husband apparently could not be persuaded to try whether his views of the race could be softened by the same application. Letters from Froude and John Brown of *Rab and his Friends* called forth grateful acknowledgments. Fellow-novelists were equally warm. Dickens made her personal acquaintance, and begged for a novel in *Household Words*. Charles Reade declared that "Adam Bede was the finest thing since Shakespeare." Mrs. Gaskell said how "earnestly, fully, and *humbly*" she admired both *Adam Bede* and its precursors. "I never read anything so complete and beautiful in fiction in my life before." Bulwer, with less expansiveness, pronounced the book to be "worthy of great admiration," and congratulated Blackwood upon his discovery. He thought, it seems, from a later note, that the defects of the book were the use of dialect and the marriage of Adam Bede. "I would have my teeth drawn," says George Eliot, "rather than give up either."

—Leslie Stephen, *George Eliot*, 1902, pp. 64–84

THE MILL ON THE FLOSS

Unsigned "The Mill on the Floss" (1860)

Although, as this anonymous reviewer notes, *The Mill on the Floss* was less popular than its predecessor, readers once more paid tribute to Eliot's masterful use of dialogue, her humorous touches, and her ability to depict a world that rarely appeared in print. The passage shows how critics now talked in familiar terms about Eliot's Dutch realism and frequently borrowed artistic terms to describe her writing: she "paints" and "draws."

With the secret of George Eliot's identity revealed, critics began to feel more comfortable about assessing her place in contemporary literary culture. The fact that the author had turned out to be a woman prompted comparisons with other female novelists and Charlotte Brontë in particular. This reviewer, keen that the author should not be able to pass as male for long, complains that Eliot deals with matters that "are better omitted from the scope of female meditation." It was the final volume of the novel that occasioned the greatest objections from readers. The passionate relationship between Maggie and Stephen, critics complained, was improbable, immoral, and unbalanced the novel. There is much to be said for the structural weakness of the final volume (which Eliot herself admitted to); however, this reviewer's objections hinge on anxieties about "feminine delicacy" and the boldness of the "modern female novelist."

A year ago, most readers who had just finished *Adam Bede* would have been greatly surprised to hear two things which we now know to be true. It would have been very strange news that *Adam Bede* was written by a woman, and it would have been equally surprising to learn that within a twelvemonth the authoress would produce another tale quite worthy to rank beside its predecessor. Now that we are wise after the event, we can detect many subtle signs of female authorship in *Adam Bede*; but at the time it was generally accepted as the work of a man. To speak the simple truth, without affectation of politeness, it was thought to be too good for a woman's story. It turns out that a woman was not only able to write it, but that she did not write it by any lucky accident. The *Mill on the Floss* may not, perhaps, be so popular as *Adam Bede*, but it shows no falling off nor any exhaustion of power. We may think ourselves very fortunate to have a third female novelist not inferior to Miss Austen and Miss Brontë; and it so happens that there is much in the works of this new writer that reminds us of these two well-known novelists without anything like copying. George Eliot has a minuteness of painting and a certain archness of style that are quite after the manner of Miss Austen, while the wide scope of her remarks, and her delight in depicting strong and wayward feelings, show that she belongs to the generation of Currer Bell, and not to that of the quiet authoress of *Emma*. Where all excel, it is of no use to draw up a sort of literary class-list, and pronounce an opinion as to the comparative merits of these three writers; but no one can now doubt that the lady who, with the usual pretty affectation of her sex, likes to look on paper as much like a man as possible, and so calls herself George Eliot, has established her place in the first rank of our female novelists.

She has done us all one great kindness, for she has opened up a field that is perfectly new. She has, for the first time in fiction, invented or disclosed the family life of the English farmer, and the class to which he belongs. She paints farmers and their wives and children, and their equals in the little villages and towns around them, and brings before us their settled opinions, convictions, and humours. Both in her present novel and in *Adam Bede* she throws the date of her story back a few years, and paints the farmers of a past generation. Perhaps the type is altering now, and is too much mixed up with other forms of English social life to present salient peculiarities to the eye of the novelist. But George Eliot not only draws the farmer of other days and his wife, but she multiplies the shapes which she makes these people assume. In the *Mill on the Floss* there is a whole volume devoted to depicting the ways and doings of persons in the rank of Mr. and Mrs. Poyser. It is scarcely possible that new friends of this sort in novels should please us quite so much as the old ones, for we have no longer the sensation of pleased surprise that any one can describe such people. But if Mrs. Poyser remains unequalled, the great variety of characters, all distinct and yet all hitherto unanticipated, who figure in the first volume of the *Mill on the Floss*, show that the range of the writer's observation goes far beyond one or two specimens. The most conspicuous of these characters are three sisters who belong to the family of Dodson, and are possessed with an immovable belief in the innate superiority of everything Dodson. These sisters have married three men dissimilar enough in taste and temper to have each an individual and distinct existence, and yet with a general resemblance in the cast and level of their minds which stamps them as belonging to the same class and the same generation. There is nothing in which George Eliot succeeds more conspicuously than in this very nice art of making her characters like real people, and yet shading them off into the large group which she is describing. Some notion of what it requires to make a good novelist may be obtained by reflecting on all that is implied in the delineation of three farmer's daughters and their husbands, with separate and probable characters, and in allotting them suitable conversation, and following the turns and shifts of their minds within the narrow limits of the matters that may be supposed to interest them. It is this profusion of delineative power that marks the *Mill on the Floss*, and the delineations are given both by minute touches of description and by dialogues. To write dialogue is much harder than merely to describe, and George Eliot trusts greatly to the talk of her farmers' wives in order to make her conception of these sisters come vividly before us. . . .

Passion, and especially the passion of love, is so avowedly the chief subject of the modern novel that we can scarcely quarrel with a novelist because the passion she chooses to describe is of a very intense kind. We all know that love is neither a smooth-going nor a strictly decorous and prudential affair, and there are many emotions in female breasts, even when the sufferer is judged by her acquaintance to be an ordinary sort of person, which would shock friends and critics if put down in black and white. But there is a kind of love-making which seems to possess a strange fascination for the modern female novelist. Currer Bell and George Eliot, and we may add George Sand, all like to dwell on love as a strange overmastering force which, through the senses, captivates and enthralls the soul. They linger on the description of the physical sensations that accompany the meeting of hearts in love. Curiously, too, they all like to describe these sensations as they conceive them to exist in men. We are bound to say that their conceptions are true and adequate. But we are not sure that it is quite consistent with feminine delicacy to lay so much stress on the bodily feelings of the other sex. No one could be less open to the charge of thinking lightly of purity than George Eliot. She proclaims in every page the infinite gain of virtue. In her new novel she has set herself to describe the dreadful results of giving feeling the victory. But she lets her fancy run on things which are not wrong, but are better omitted from the scope of female meditation. The heroine, for example, is in love with a man who passionately loves her, but as each is pre-engaged, they are separated by duty and honour. All goes on very well until one day the lover, when alone with the heroine, takes to watching her arm. Its beauties are minutely described, as well as the effect gradually produced on him. At last, in a transport of passion, he rushes forward, seizes on the lovely arm, and covers it with kisses. There is nothing wrong in writing about such an act, and it is the sort of thing that does sometimes happen in real life; but we cannot think that the conflict of sensation and principle raised in a man's mind by gazing at a woman's arm is a theme that a female novelist can touch on without leaving behind a feeling of hesitation, if not repulsion, in the reader. In points like these, it may be hesitated, if not repulsion, in the reader. In points like these, it may be observed that men are more delicate than women. There are very few men who would not shrink from putting into words what they might imagine to be the physical effects of love in a woman. Perhaps we may go further, and say that the whole delineation of passionate love, as painted by modern female novelists, is open to very serious criticism. There are emotions over which we ought to throw a veil; and no one can say that, in order to portray an ardent and tender love, it is necessary to describe the conquest of a beautiful arm over honour and principle. As it seems to us, the defect of the *Mill on the Floss* is that there is too much that is painful in it. And the authoress is so far led away by her reflections on moral problems and her interest in the phases of triumphant passion, that she sacrifices her story. We have such entire changes of circumstances, and the characters are exhibited under such totally different conditions of age and mental development, that we get to care nothing for them. The third volume seems to belong to quite a new story. The Dodsons have faded away, and the young woman with the overmastering passion is very slightly connected with the little Maggie of the Mill who makes her appearance at the beginning of the novel. As in *Adam Bede*, the interest fades off towards the end; and we are not sorry when the tremendous machinery of a flood is called in to drown off two of the principal characters. We hope that some time George Eliot will give us a tale less painful and less discursive.

There is something in the world and in the quiet walks of English lower life besides fierce mental struggles and wild love. We do not see why we should not be treated to a story that would do justice to George Eliot's powers, and yet form a pleasing and consistent whole.

—Unsigned, "The Mill on the Floss,"
Saturday Review, vol. 9, April 14,
1860, p. 470–471

E.S. Dallas "The Mill on the Floss" (1860)

Dallas, one of Eliot's most sophisticated critics, offers an intelligent reading of the novel: he picks up on the echoes of Greek tragedy running throughout the work and notes that there is a religious quality to the novel even though religion is "conspicuous by its absence"—a paradox that runs throughout Eliot's novels.

Having been introduced to the rural world in *Adam Bede*, readers found the farmers and their families in *The Mill on the Floss* to be of a very different kind. Critics were united in their praise of Eliot's depiction of childhood. However, they found the Dodsons and Tullivers to be far more sordid than Eliot had either desired or anticipated. Unlike her two previous novels, Eliot seemed to give little "poetry to peasant life" here. Dallas notes the narrator's interruption in the middle of the novel (much as in *Adam Bede*) in which this stark realism is justified. For Dallas, as for other critics, the novel's bleakness combined with the narrator's explanation that such realism is justified in artistic and moral terms led to the idea of Eliot as a "preacher" intent on making readers both "think and feel." This labeling of Eliot as a preacher became a recurring theme in criticism: it was one of the main reasons early-twentieth-century readers were so eager to dismiss her and why F.R. Leavis, in *The Great Tradition* (1948), sought to reestablish her as one of the most important of English novelists.

This emmetlike life of the Tullivers and Dodsons is essentially, as "George Eliot" preaches, a sordid life—irradiated by no sublime principles, no romantic visions, no active, self-renouncing faith, moved by none of those wild, uncontrollable passions which create the dark shadows of crime and misery—without that primitive rough simplicity of wants, that hard, submissive, ill-paid toil, that childlike spelling out of what nature has written, which gives its poetry to peasant life—a life so sordid that even sorrow hardly suffices to lift it above the level of the tragic-comic. We commend these half-dozen pages, in which the author, midway in her work, has stopped to criticize it and to explain her intention to the notice of all who wish to understand, as well as to enjoy what a writer of undoubted genius has invited us to read. Without attending to the clue thus furnished by the author, her object wil be overlooked and full justice will not be done to her work. We must point out, however, that the object which the author has set herself of painting in all its nakedness, hideousness, and littleness the life of respectable brutishness which so many persons lead, illumined by not one ray of spiritual influence, by no suspicion of a higher life, of another world, of a surrounding divinity,—lifts the present work out of the category of ordinary novels. The author is attempting not merely to amuse us as a novelist, but, as a preacher, to make us think and feel. The riddle of life as it is here expounded is more like a Greek tragedy than a modern novel. In form we have the modern novel, with its every-day incidents and its humorous descriptions, but in spirit we have the Greek play, with its mysterious allusions and its serious import. In the highest sense we might call this a religious novel, only that description is liable to be misunderstood, and especially as religion is chiefly "conspicuous by its absence." We read on, wondering why these mean, prosaic people, the Dodsons ever live; wondering why a brilliant novelist asks us to make their acquaintance and to become interested in their paltry existence, when suddenly the author breaks in upon us with the criticism to which we have already referred, and which we have partly quoted. She says in effect:—"You, reader, are oppressed by all this meanness—disgusted at all this hardness—perplexed that I should think it worthy of your notice. I perfectly agree with you; but such is life, and it is in the midst of such a life, the most marked quality of which is the utter absence of poetry or religion, that many of us grow up—it was in the midst of such a desert that my little heroine, Maggie, bloomed into beauty. It is well that these things should be impressed upon us, and that we should lay them to heart.

In fulfilling this portion of her task, which occupies exactly the first half of the novel, the author has very cleverly helped herself out of a difficulty. It is difficult to describe adults leading a purely bestial life of vulgar respectability without rendering the picture simply repulsive. But the life of children is essentially an animal life,—a life, therefore, that to a certain extent accords with the brutish habits of maturer personages; with this great difference, however,—that what is repulsive in the mature is amusing in the young. We do not expect boys and girls to have a strong sense of invisible things,—to be very spiritual in their aims—to make any striking display of poetry, sentiment, or religion. We wink at their enormities in sweets, we laugh at their savage tyrannies, and we take them for what they are—dear little animals, and nothing more. "George Eliot" relieves the repulsiveness of the insect life which she has exhibited in the Dodson family by making her bigger insects all revolve around these two little creatures, Maggie and Tom Tulliver. Her description of the child-life is unique. No one has yet ventured to paint the child-life in all its prosaic reality. It is true that we have long since got out of the Mrs. Barbauld and Miss Edgworth groove, in which we had contrasted pictures of the good boy and the bad boy, the girl who was lazy and the girl who was active. Then succeeded more careful studies of the child nature, and we do not know that in this respect the productions of Mr. Disraeli, both in *Venetia*, where he gives the youth of Lord Byron, and in *Coningsby*, have ever been surpassed. But in his writings and those of other novelists there is not a little of that poetical colouring which is natural to us in looking back on our childhood. "George Eliot," in approaching the subject, determined, as best agreeing with the general scope of her novel, to paint reality; and she has pictured the boy and girl life with the most amusing fidelity. We see all the little squabbling and domineering that goes on among children; we see them disgracefully intent on raspberry tart; we see the boy, after he has eaten up his share, mysteriously surveying his sister's, and wondering whether she will spare him a bit; we see the pleasure which they take in first tickling a toad, and then smashing it with a stone; we see all the envies, and cruelties, and gluttonies that in men would be revolting, but are only grotesque in these funny little animals.

—E.S. DALLAS,
"The Mill on the Floss,"
The Times, May 19, 1860, p. 10.

ALGERNON CHARLES SWINBURNE (1877)

The English poet and reviewer Algernon Charles Swinburne (1837–1909) associated with the pre-Raphaelite artists and writers. His works, often filled with sadomasochistic, lesbian, and blasphemous imagery, together with his excessive drinking and excitable temperament, attracted controversy throughout his life.

In her journal for December 1872, the writer Elizabeth Sewell quotes Swinburne as declaring that Eliot was "the woman of the most wonderful intellect the world had ever known." Paradoxically, this respect exacerbated his displeasure with *The Mill on the Floss*. Like many critics, Swinburne's disappointment focuses on the final volume of the novel and, more specifically, the love Maggie feels for Stephen Guest, "a cur so far beneath the chance of promotion to the notice of his horsewhip."

Swinburne's attack is hysterical and surprisingly bitter. It provides an interesting sense, however, of the strong reactions provoked by the novel—more extreme than any other written by Eliot.

And now we must regretfully and respectfully consider of what quality and what kind may be the faults which deform the best and ripest work of Charlotte Brontë's chosen rival. Few or none, I should suppose, of her most passionate and intelligent admirers would refuse to accept *The Mill on the Floss* as on the whole at once the highest and the purest and the fullest example of her magnificent and matchless powers—for matchless altogether, as I have already insisted, they undoubtedly are in their own wide and fruitful field of work. The first two-thirds of the book suffice to compose perhaps the very noblest of tragic as well as of humorous prose idyls in the language; comprising, as they likewise do, one of the sweetest as well as saddest and tenderest as well as subtlest examples of dramatic analysis—a study in that kind as soft and true as Rousseau's, as keen and true as Browning's, as full as either's of the fine and bitter sweetness of a pungent and fiery fidelity. But who can forget the horror of inward collapse, the sickness of spiritual reaction, the reluctant incredulous rage of disenchantment and disgust, with which he first came upon the thrice unhappy third part? The two first volumes have all the intensity and all the perfection of George Sand's best work, tempered by all the simple purity and interfused with all the stainless pathos of Mrs. Gaskell's; they carry such affluent weight of thought and shine with such warm radiance of humour as invigorates and illuminates the work of no other famous woman; they have the fiery clarity of crystal or of lightning; they go near to prove a higher claim and attest a clearer right on the part of their author than that of George Sand herself to the crowning crown of praise conferred on her by the hand of a woman even greater and more glorious than either in her sovereign gift of lyric genius, to the salutation given as by an angel indeed from heaven, of 'large-brained woman and large-hearted man.' And the fuller and deeper tone of colour combined with greater sharpness and precision of outline may be allowed to excuse the apparent amount of obligation—though we may hardly see how this can be admitted to explain the remarkable reticence which reserves all acknowledgment and dissembles all consciousness of that sufficiently palpable and weighty and direct obligation—to Mrs. Gaskell's beautiful story of "The Moorland Cottage"; in which not the identity of name alone, nor only their common singleness of heart and simplicity of spirit, must naturally recall the gentler memory of the less high-thoughted and high-reaching heroine to the warmest and the worthiest admirers of the later-born and loftier-minded Maggie; though the hardness and brutality of the baser brother through whom she suffers be the outcome in manhood as in childhood of mere greedy instinct and vulgar egotism, while the full eventual efflorescence of the same gracious qualities in Tom Tulliver is tracked with incomparable skill and unquestionable certitude of touch to the far other root of sharp narrow self-devotion and honest harsh self-reliance.

"So far, all honour," as Phraxanor says of Joseph in the noble poem of Mr. Wells. But what shall any one say of the upshot? If we are really to take it on trust, to confront it as a contingent or conceivable possibility, resting our reluctant faith on the authority of so great a female writer, that a woman of Maggie Tulliver's kind can be moved to any sense but that of bitter disgust and sickening disdain by a thing—I will not write, a man—of Stephen Guest's; if we are to accept as truth and fact, however astonishing and revolting, so shameful an avowal, so vile a revelation as this; in that ugly and lamentable case, our only remark, as our only comfort, must be that now at least the last word of realism has surely been spoken, the last abyss of cynicism has surely been sounded and laid bare. The three master cynics of French romance are eclipsed and distanced and extinguished, passed over and run down and snuffed out on their own boards. To the rosy innocence of Laclos, to the cordial optimism of Stendhal, to the trustful tenderness of Mérimée, no such degradation of female character seems ever to have suggested itself as imaginable. Iago never flung such an imputation on all womanhood; Madame de Merteuil would never have believed it. For a higher view and a more cheering aspect of the sex, we must turn back to these gentler teachers, these more flattering painters of our own; we must take up *La Double Méprise*—or *Le Rouge et le Noir*—or *Les Liaisons Dangereuses*.

But I for one am not prepared or willing to embrace a belief so much too degrading and depressing for the conception of those pure and childlike souls. My faith will not digest at once the first two volumes and the third volume of *The Mill on the Floss*; my conscience or credulity has not gorge enough for such a gulp. Whatever capacity for belief is in me I find here impaled once more as on the horns of that old divine's dilemma between the irreconcilable attributes of goodness and omnipotence in the supposed Creator of suffering and of sin. If the one quality be predicable, the other quality cannot be predicate of the same subject. As between κοινη and ποινη, we must choose. Lady Percy on the lap of Falstaff, bidding him patch up his old body for heaven; Miranda nestling in the arms of Trinculo; Virgilia seeking consolation for her husband's exile in the rival devotion of Brutus and Sicinius; Desdemona finding refuge from her troubles on the bosom of Roderigo—could no longer pretend to be the widow of Hotspur, the bride of Ferdinand, the wife of the noblest Roman, the fellow-martyr of the nobler

Moor. No higher tribute can be claimed and no deeper condemnation can be incurred by perverse or intermittent genius than is conveyed or implied in such comparisons as these. The hideous transformation by which Maggie is debased—were it but for an hour—into the willing or yielding companion of Stephen's flight would probably and deservedly have been resented as a brutal and vulgar outrage on the part of a male novelist. But the man never lived, I do believe, who could have done such a thing as this: as the man, I should suppose, does not exist who could make for the first time the acquaintance of Mr. Stephen Guest with no incipient sense of a twitching in his fingers and a tingling in his toes at the notion of any contact between Maggie Tulliver and a cur so far beneath the chance of promotion to the notice of his horsewhip, or elevation to the level of his boot.

Here then is the patent flaw, here too plainly is the flagrant blemish, which defaces and degrades the very crown and flower of George Eliot's wonderful and most noble work; no rent or splash on the raiment, no speck or scar on the skin of it, but a cancer in the very bosom, a gangrene in the very flesh. It is a radical and mortal plague-spot, corrosive and incurable; in the apt and accurate phrase of Rabelais, "an enormous solution of continuity". The book is not the same before it and after. No washing or trimming, no pruning or purging, could eradicate or efface it; it could only be removable by amputation and remediable by cautery.

—ALGERNON CHARLES SWINBURNE,
A Note on Charlotte Brontë,
1877, pp. 28–38

JOHN RUSKIN "FICTION—FAIR AND FOUL" (1881)

John Ruskin (1819–1900) was an influential English art and social critic. His works, which include *Modern Painters* (1843–60), combine art criticism with sociopolitical reflections. Though his private life caused controversy, Ruskin was revered, together with Thomas Carlyle, as one of the Victorian "sages." About him, George Eliot wrote to Barbara Leigh Smith in 1856: "He is the finest writer living" (*GE Letters*, II: 255).

Ruskin's description of *The Mill on the Floss* is noteworthy above all for its curious characterization of the novel's characters as the "sweepings out of a Pentonville omnibus." Like Dallas, Ruskin objects to the sordid nature of Eliot's characters; unlike him, he denies that portraying such individuals serves a valid artistic purpose. Ruskin does not argue that the characters are unconvincing—on the contrary, he suggests that similar individuals can be found across the nation—but that art should be preoccupied with the "beautiful." This is to a certain extent a curious position for Ruskin to take. In April 1856, Eliot had reviewed the third volume of Ruskin's *Modern Painters* and approved his defence of realism devolving from a "humble and faithful study of nature." Ruskin's attack on "Cockney literature" echoes John Gibson Lockhart's famous 1817 dismissal of the "Cockney school" of poetry represented by John Keats and Leigh Hunt. Where Lockhart railed at the low birth of the poets, Ruskin finds fault with the lowly nature of Eliot's characters. The association of Eliot, whose novels up until then had been uniquely concerned with rural matters, with such urban terminology, is curious.

All healthy and helpful literature sets simple bars between right and wrong; assumes the possibility, in men and women, of having healthy minds in healthy bodies, and loses no time in the diagnosis of fever or dyspepsia in either; least of all in the particular kind of fever which signifies the ungoverned excess of any appetite or passion. The 'dulness' which many modern readers inevitably feel, and some modern blockheads think it creditable to allege, in Scott, consists not a little in his absolute purity from every loathsome element or excitement of the lower passions; so that people who live habitually in Satyric or hircine conditions of thought find him as insipid as they would a picture of Angelico's. The accurate and trenchant separation between him and the common railroad-station novelist is that, in his total method of conception, only lofty character is worth describing at all; and it becomes interesting, not by its faults, but by the difficulties and accidents of the fortune through which it passes, while, in the railway novel, interest is obtained with the vulgar reader for the vilest character, because the author describes carefully to his recognition the blotches, burrs and pimples in which the paltry nature resembles his own. *The Mill on the Floss* is perhaps the most striking instance extant of this study of cutaneous disease. There is not a single person in the book of the smallest importance to anybody in the world but themselves, or whose qualities deserved so much as a line of printer's type in their description. There is no girl alive, fairly clever, half educated, and unluckily related, whose life has not at least as much in it as Maggie's, to be described and to be pitied. Tom is a clumsy and cruel lout, with the making of better things in him (and the same may be said of nearly every English-man at present smoking and elbowing his way through the ugly world his blunders have contributed to the making of); while the rest of the characters are simply the sweepings out of a Pentonville omnibus.

And it is very necessary that we should distinguish this essentially Cockney literature,—developed only in the London suburbs, and feeding the demands of the rows of similar brick houses, which branch in devouring cancer round every manufacturing town,—from the really romantic literature of France. Georges Sand is often immoral; but she is always beautiful. . . . But in the English Cockney school, which consummates itself in George Eliot, the personages are picked up from behind the counter and out of the gutter; and the landscape, by excursion train to Gravesend, with return ticket for the City-road.

—John Ruskin, "Fiction—Fair and Foul,"
Nineteenth Century, vol. 10,
October 1881, pp. 520–521

Leslie Stephen (1902)

Stephen emphasizes the autobiographical element of *The Mill on the Floss*. Though it is going too far to call Maggie the author's "double," of all Eliot's works, this novel draws most extensively from Eliot's personal experiences. Despite this insight, Stephen finds Tom Tulliver improbably stern. Tom's moral rigidity actually reflects that of Eliot's brother Isaac, who reacted strongly to her refusal to attend church and ceased contact with her altogether while she maintained her relationship with Lewes. Stephen's lively attack on the hapless Stephen Guest is rather more successful, as he tears into the young man, pronouncing him both a "typical provincial coxcomb" and, most memorably, a "hair-dresser's block." Leslie Stephen frequently commented in his criticism on Eliot's weakness in depicting young men, with more or less justice, and he was by no means the only critic to do so. Will Ladislaw and Daniel Deronda would later follow Stephen Guest as similar targets of criticism and not a little mockery.

Maggie is one example of the feminine type which occurs with important modifications in most of the other stories. But George Eliot throws herself so frankly into Maggie's position, gives her "double" such reality by the wayward foibles associated with her nobler impulses, and dwells so lovingly upon all her joys and sorrows, that the character glows with a more tender and poetic charm than any of her other heroines. I suppose that Dinah Morris would be placed higher in the scale of morality; but if the test of a heroine's merits be the reader's disposition to fall in love with her (and that, I confess, is my own), I hold that Maggie is worth a wilderness of Dinahs. . . .

The true difficulty is again, as I take it, that she was too thoroughly feminine to be quite at home in the psychology of the male animal. Her women are—so far as a man can judge—unerringly drawn. We are convinced at every point of the insight and fidelity of the analysis; but when she draws a man, she has not the same certainty of touch. She is, I have suggested, a little too contemptuous when the Samson yields to the Delilah; and when he asserts his privileges, his strength is apt to be too like brutality. Many rustic Tom Tullivers would, no doubt, ride roughshod over sisterly sensibilities; but if we are to retain sympathy for their better nature, they should show more twinges of conscience. Tom's profound conviction that whatever he does is therefore right, is no doubt characteristic; but he might at least feel that he is doing a painful duty, and not be represented as utterly insensible to the claims of the old childish affections.

The comparative weakness, however, of masculine portraits has a more unpleasant result. She admits that the tragedy which follows is "not adequately prepared." She will "always regret" the want of fulness in the treatment of the third volume, due, as she says, to the epische Breite [epic broadness] into which she was beguiled by love of her subject in its predecessors. But she defends the position itself, which many readers have condemned. "Maggie's position towards Stephen Guest—upon which the tragedy turns—is," she says, "too vital a part of my whole conception and purpose for me to be converted to the condemnation of it. If I am wrong there—if I did not really know what my heroine would feel and do under the circumstances in which I deliberately placed her—I ought not to have written this book at all, but quite a different work, if any. If the ethics of art do not admit the truthful presentation of a character essentially noble, but liable to great error—error that is anguish to its own nobleness—then it seems to me the ethics of art are too narrow, and must be widened to correspond with a widening psychology." Without discussing the "ethics of art," we may, I should think, fully agree that the critical canon thus abjured is erroneous. I am not aware, however, that any professor of aesthetics has laid down the rule that it is wrong to represent a noble character led into fatal error, and consequent remorse, by its weaknesses. I should have supposed that nothing could be a more legitimate topic. George Eliot is unintentionally changing the issue upon which a defence is really required. . . .

With Tom Tulliver in the background, we have now abundant material for tragedy. But, at the opening of the third volume, we are abruptly introduced to a new character. Maggie has become a young lady, visiting her cousin. The "fine young man," snapping a pair of scissors in the face of the "King Charles" spaniel on Miss Lucy Deane's feet, "is no other than Mr. Stephen Guest, whose diamond ring, attar of roses, and air of nonchalant leisure at twelve o'clock in the day are the graceful and odoriferous result of the largest oil-mill and the most extensive wharf in St. Ogg's." In other words, Mr. Guest is a typical provincial coxcomb, with a certain taste for music, fitted no doubt to excite the admiration of young ladies at St. Ogg's. No attempt is made to suggest that he is anything but a self-satisfied commonplace young gentleman, who has condescended to accept the hand of Miss Deane. There is no difficulty in understanding him and his manners. When he dances with Maggie at a ball soon afterwards, and takes her into a conservatory, she looks very lovely as she stretches her arm to a rose. "Who has not felt the beauty of a woman's arm? the unspeakable suggestions of tenderness that lie in the dimpled elbow, and all the varied gently lessening curves, down to the delicate wrist with its tiniest almost imperceptible nicks in the firm softness. A woman's arm touched the soul of a great sculptor two thousand years ago, so that he wrought an image of it for the Parthenon which moves us still as it clasps lovingly the timeworn marble of a headless trunk. Maggie's was such an arm as that, and it had the warm tints of life. A mad impulse seized on Stephen; he darted towards the arm and showered kisses on it, clasping the wrist. It is curious that a little later (1864) George Eliot describes a "divine picture" by Sir F. Burton, in which a mailed knight is kissing the arm of a woman "by an uncontrollable movement." The subject, she says, is from a "Norse Legend." It "might have been made the most vulgar thing in the world—the artist has raised it to the highest pitch of refined emotion. The kiss is on the fur-lined sleeve that covers the arm, and the face of the knight is the face of a man to whom the kiss is a sacrament." Mr. Stephen Guest's performance does not strike one in the sacramental light. Maggie is properly angry and astonished at the time, but she soon becomes more amenable; and though she has scruples, and goes through a "fierce battle of emotions," she presently finds herself drifting to sea with him in a boat, and is only arrested by her conscience at the last moment when she is some way towards Gretna Green. Renunciation gets the better of the longing for happiness. "We can only choose," she says, "whether we will indulge ourselves in the present moment, or whether we will renounce that for the sake of obeying the divine voice within us, for the sake of being true to all the motives that sanctify our lives." To let this belief go would be to lose the only light in the darkness of life. She returns; but the knot is insoluble, and has to be finally cut by the waves of the Floss. George Eliot herself, admitting the need for more development, maintained, as we have seen, that the conclusion was right, and it has been defended upon the same ground. It is right, because the "psychology" is right. Given the character and the circumstances, that is, this was the inevitable outcome. It is, no doubt, painful and disagreeable that a young woman of so many noble qualities should be guilty of such a step; but noble young women do make slips—that, I fear, is undeniable—and Maggie behaves as might be expected from her previous history. That is where I presume to doubt. Nobody, indeed, can deny that the passion of love is apt to generate illusions. Most men would probably be able to give examples from their own experience of the truth that young women who fall in love with somebody else have a singular inability for forming a correct judgment of the truly valuable qualities of masculine character. The fact has often been noticed, and is frequently turned to account by novelists. I will not deny that even Maggie's love for Stephen is conceivable. A young woman brought up in Dorlcote Mill was no doubt liable to be imposed upon by a false appearance of gentlemanlike character. But, one thing seems to be obvious. The whole theme of the book is surely the contrast between the "beautiful soul" and the commonplace surroundings. It is the awakening of the spiritual and imaginative nature and the need of finding some room for the play of the higher faculties, whether in the direction of religious mysticism or of human affection. That such a character, with little experience of life and with narrow education, should fall into error is natural, if not inevitable. But then the error should surely correspond to some impulse which we can feel to be noble. Maggie may be wrong in attributing high qualities to her hero; but we should feel that, in her eyes, he has high qualities, and that the passion, if misdirected, is itself congenial to her better impulses. Miss Brontë's heroines fall in love with men whom the reader may dislike; but it is because they take the men to be embodiments of great masculine qualities—energy, honour, and real generosity—under rather crusty outsides. Therefore, though we may doubt the perspicacity of the hero-worship, we do not feel that the sentiment is in itself degrading. But there is this difficulty with poor Maggie. Her admiration for Mr. Guest would be natural enough in the average miller's daughter suddenly brought into a rather superior social scale and introduced to a well-dressed young man scented with "attar of roses." But as Maggie, by her very definition, as one may say, is a highly exceptional young woman, she should surely have something exceptional in her love. We can understand her sympathy with Philip Wakem, who is a man of heart, and whose physical infirmity is an appeal for pity; we could have understood it if she had fallen in love with the excellent vicar of St. Ogg's, who would have been able to talk about a Kempis and religious sentimentalism; and we might even have forgiven her if, after being a little overpowered by the dandified Stephen, she had shown some power of perceiving what a very poor animal he was. The affair jars upon us, because it is not a development of her previous aspirations, but suddenly throws a fresh and unpleasant light upon her character. No one will say that the catastrophe is impossible; he, at least, who would pronounce dogmatically upon such matters must be a bolder man than I am; but neither, I think, can any one say that it was inevitable, or could have been expected, given the circumstances and the characters. The truth is, I think, different.

George Eliot did not herself understand what a mere hair-dresser's block she was describing in Mr. Stephen Guest. He is another instance of her incapacity for pourtraying the opposite sex. No man could have introduced such a character without perceiving what an impression must be made upon his readers. We cannot help regretting Maggie's fate; she is touching and attractive to the last; but I, at least, cannot help wishing that the third volume could have been suppressed. I am inclined to sympathise with the readers of Clarissa Earlowe when they entreated Richardson to save Lovelace's soul. Do, I mentally exclaim, save this charming Maggie from damning herself by this irrelevant and discordant degradation.

—LESLIE STEPHEN, *George Eliot*, 1902, pp. 88–104

SILAS MARNER

UNSIGNED "SILAS MARNER" (1861)

The following piece from the *Saturday Review* confirmed that Eliot was continuing to make an indelible mark on English literature. Because critics such as this writer felt that Eliot's principal contribution to literature lay in her realistic representations of the poor, they often expressed disappointment when she moved away from that particular subject. The article echoes the common nineteenth-century idea that the poor and rich were divided into "two nations" with the image of the novelist as someone venturing into "virgin soil." The review offers some insightful comparisons with the novels of Edward Bulwer-Lytton and Charles Dickens who (along with many other contemporary novelists) had also attempted to explore the hidden country of the poor but, as the reviewer remarks, in very different ways. Reviewers agreed that Eliot's art had reached its highest point with the scenes in the Rainbow Inn. The comparison to Shakespeare was not unique—Richard Holt Hutton similarly wrote in his review for the novel, published in the *Economist*, that these scenes reminded him of the tavern scenes in the *Henry IV* plays.

The highest tribute that can be paid to this book may be paid it very readily. It is as good as *Adam Bede*, except that it is shorter. And that an author should be able to produce a series of works so good in so very peculiar a style, is as remarkable as anything that has occurred in the history of English literature in this century. The plot of *Silas Marner* is good, and the delineation of character is excellent. But other writers who have the power of story-telling compose plots as interesting, and perhaps sketch characters as well. It is in the portraiture of the poor, and of what it is now fashionable to call 'the lower middle class,' that this writer is without a rival, and no phase of life could be harder to draw. A person with observation and humour might give a sketch of one or two sets of poor people, and of village farmers and carpenters, but the sketches he could give would be limited by his personal observation. George Eliot alone moves among this unknown, and to most people unknowable, section of society as if quite at home there, and can let imagination run loose and disport itself in a field that, we think, has been only very partially opened even to the best writers. Sir Walter Scott drew a few pictures of humble Scott life, and none of his creations won him more deserved reputation than the characters of Andrew Fairservice and Caleb Balderstone, and the scenes among the poor fishing population in the *Antiquary*. But, good as these sketches were, they were very limited. We soon got to an end of them; but in *Silas Marner*, the whole book, or nearly the whole book, is made up of such scenes. The writer can picture what uneducated villagers think and say, and can reproduce on paper the picture which imagination has suggested. The gift is so special, the difficulty is so great, the success is so complete, that the works of George Eliot come on us as a new revelation of what society in quiet English parishes really is and has been. How hard is it to draw the poor may easily be seen if we turn to the ordinary tales of country life that are written in such abundance by ladies. There the poor are always looked at from the point of view of the rich. They are so many subjects for experimenting on, for reclaiming, improving, being anxious about, and relieving. They have no existence apart from the presence of a curate and a district visitor. They live in order to take tracts and broth. This is a very natural, and in some degree a very proper view for the well-intentioned rich to take of the poor. It is right that those who have spiritual and temporal blessings should care for the souls and bodies of those around them. But the poor remain, during the process and in its description, as a distinct race. What they think of and do when they are not being improved and helped, remains a blank. Those, too, who are above the reach of occasional destitution are entirely omitted from these portraitures of village life. Every one is agreed that it would be impertinent to improve a man who gets anything like a pound a week. When, therefore, George Eliot describes the whole of a village, from the simple squire down to the wheelwright and his wife, the ground thus occupied is virgin soil.

There are two chapters in *Silas Marner* describing the conversation of a coterie at a public-house, and what they did and said on a man appearing before them to announce a robbery, which are perfectly wonderful. It is not, perhaps, saying much to say that an intelligent reader who knew beforehand that such a scene was to be described would be utterly puzzled to think of any one thing that such people could satisfactorily be represented as remarking or doing. But some notion of what George Eliot can do may be obtained by comparing what the best writers of the day are in the habit of doing when they attempt scenes of this sort. Sir Edward Lytton and Mr. Dickens would venture to try such a scene if it came in their way. Sir Edward Lytton would only go so far as to put some very marked character or some very important personage of the story in the centre of the group, and put everything into relation and connexion with him. This is really the good ladies' novel view of the poor in another shape. The poor cluster round some one superior to them, and the only reason of the superiority which Sir Edward Lytton can claim, so far as he can claim any at all, arises from the poor being supposed to be in a position of greater naturalness and simplicity. They are represented as taking their ease in their inn, and not as being talked to by their anxious-minded betters. Mr. Dickens sets himself to draw the poor and the uneducated much more thoroughly, but his mode is to invest each person with one distinguishing peculiarity. This gives a distinctness to each picture, but it makes the whole group artificial and mechanical. He always, or almost always, keeps us in the region of external peculiarities. We are made to notice the teeth, the hair, the noses, the buttons of the people described, or some oddity of manner that marks them. The sentiment of the poor if often caught in Mr. Dickens's works with great happiness, and the chance observations that they might make under particular circumstances are well conceived; but George Eliot goes far beyond this. The people in the public-house in *Silas Marner* proclaim in a few words each a distinct and probable character, and sustain it. The things they say are perfectly natural, and yet show at once what the sayers are like. We know that these poor are like real poor people, just as we know that the characters in Shakspeare are like real men and women. The humour of the author, of course, pervades the representation, just as it does in the comic parts of Shakspeare. Our enjoyment in a large measure depends on the enjoyment of the writer; nor is it probable that any group at a pothouse would really say so many things on any one evening that, if recorded, would amuse us so much. But this is one of the exigencies of art. In order not to waste space, that which is characteristic must be placed closely together. Were it not for this absence of dilution, the history of the village group of Raveloe, the village in which the scenes of *Silas Marner* are laid, might be a mere record of an actual evening passed at a country public. It is a kind of unpermissible audacity in England to say that anything is as good as Shakspeare, and we will not therefore say that this public-house scene is worthy of the hand that drew Falstaff and Poins; but we may safely say that, however much less in degree, the humour of George Eliot in such passages is of the same kind as that displayed in the comic passages of Shakspeare's historical plays.

—UNSIGNED, "Silas Marner," *Saturday Review*, vol. 11, April 13, 1861, p. 369

HENRY JAMES "THE NOVELS OF GEORGE ELIOT" (1866)

Henry James reacted positively to the greater artistic and moral simplicity of *Silas Marner* in comparison with Eliot's previous novels. The manner in which he outlines the characters highlights the talelike quality of the novel. The words *mildly rich* and *mellow* mirror the terms with which many readers upheld it as the most wholesome of her novels—a work that indulged in none of the dramatic or narrative excesses of *The Mill on the Floss*.

To a certain extent, I think *Silas Marner* holds a higher place than any of the author's works. It is more nearly a masterpiece; it has more of that simple, rounded, consummate aspect, that absence of loose ends and gaping issues, which marks a classical work. What was attempted in it, indeed, was within more immediate reach than the heart-trials of Adam Bede and Maggie Tulliver. A poor, dull-witted, disappointed Methodist cloth-weaver; a little golden-haired foundling child; a well-meaning, irresolute country squire, and his patient, childless wife;—these, with a chorus of simple, beer-loving villagers, make up the *dramatis persona*. More than any of its brother-works, *Silas Marner*, I think, leaves upon the mind a deep impression of the grossly material life of agricultural England in the last days of the old *regime*,—the days of full-orbed Toryism, of Trafalgar and of Waterloo, when the invasive spirit of French domination threw England back upon a sense of her own insular solidity, and made her for the time doubly, brutally, morbidly English. Perhaps the best pages in the work are the first thirty, telling the story of poor Marner's disappointments in friendship and in love, his unmerited disgrace, and his long, lonely twilight-life at Raveloe, with the sole companionship of his loom, in which his muscles moved "with such even repetition, that their pause seemed almost as much a constraint as the holding of his breath." Here, as in all George Eliot's books, there is a middle life and a low life; and here, as usual, I prefer the low life. In *Silas Marner,* in my opinion, she has come nearest the mildly rich tints of brown and gray, the mellow lights and the undreadful corner-shadows of the Dutch masters whom she emulates.

—HENRY JAMES, "The Novels of George Eliot," *The Atlantic Monthly*, vol. 18, October 1866, p. 482

FREDERIC HARRISON "GEORGE ELIOT" (1895)

Frederic Harrison (1831–1923) was an English author and positivist. Harrison became interested in Auguste Comte through the works of G.H. Lewes and John Stuart Mill. His efforts to publicize positivist ideas led him to resign from the London Working Men's College at which he taught and to cofound the first English positivist center in 1870. Eliot enlisted Harrison's help in verifying the accuracy of the legal entanglements within the plot of *Felix Holt*. Harrison also encouraged Eliot to pen a poem or drama, which led to *The Spanish Gypsy*.

Harrison is a careful reader who picks up on the Wordsworthian echoes in *Silas Marner*. Harrison's use of words such as *gem* and *crystalline* is appropriate for a story centrally concerned with gold and jewels. His reflections on the work further demonstrate how few critical disagreements the work caused. After *The Mill on the Floss*, readers were relieved to find "few ethical problems in it from beginning to end." It is reassuringly "quaint," a simple "tale." Unlike the morally ambiguous events in the final volume of Eliot's previous work, here the story is "healthy" and the moral "noble." There is a hint that, though the perfection claimed for the work lies in its smoothness, the work holds none of the passionate interest produced by other novelists. The impression that Eliot prefers "a lofty lesson" to "life, energy, jollity, or passion" contributes to the idea that Eliot was primarily a didactic novelist—a notion used by later critics to diminish her achievements.

I have no doubt myself that *Silas Marner* comes nearer to being a great success than any of the more elaborate books. Yet *Silas Marner* is about one-fifth part of the length of *Middlemarch*; and its plot, *mise-en-scene*, and incidents are simplicity itself. There is no science, no book-learning, and but few ethical problems in it from beginning to end; and it all goes in one small volume, for the tale concerns but the neighbours of one quiet village. Yet the quaint and idyllic charm of the piece, the perfection of tone and keeping, the harmony of the landscape, the pure, deep humanity of it, all make it a true and exquisite work of high art.

Modern English (and I am one of those who hold that the best modern English is as good as any in our literature) has few pieces of description more gem-like in its crystalline facets than the opening chapter that tells of the pale, uncanny weaver of Raveloe in his stone cottage by the deserted pit. Some of us can remember such house weavers in such lonesome cottages on the Northern moors, and have heard the unfamiliar rattle of the loom in a half-ruinous homestead. How perfect is that vignette of Raveloe—"a village where many of the old echoes lingered, undrowned by new voices"—with its "strange lingering echoes of the old demon-worship among the grey-haired peasantry!" The entire picture of the village and its village life a hundred years ago, is finished with the musical and reserved note of poetry, such as we are taught to love in Wordsworth and Tennyson. And for quiet humour modern literature has few happier scenes than the fireside at the "Rainbow," with Macey and Winthrop, the butcher and the farrier, over their pipes and their hot potations, and the quarrel about "seeing ghos'es," about smelling them!

Within this most graceful and refined picture of rural life there is a dominant ethical motive which she herself describes as its aim, "to set in a strong light the remedial influences of pure, natural, human relations." This aim is perfectly worked out: it is a right and healthy conception, not too subtle, not too common:—to put it in simpler words than hers, it is how a lonely, crabbed, ill-used old man is humanised by the love of a faithful and affectionate child. The form is poetic: the moral is both just and noble: the characters are living, and the story is original, natural, and dramatic. The only thing, indeed, which *Silas Marner* wants to make it a really great romance is more ease, more rapidity, more "go." The melody runs so uniformly in minor keys, the sense of care, meditation, and introspection is so apparent in every line, the amount of serious thought lavished by the writer and required of the reader is so continuous, that we are not carried away, we are not excited, inspired, and thrilled as we are by *Jane Eyre* or *Esmond*. We enjoy a beautiful book with a fine moral, set in exquisite prose, with consummate literary resources, full of fine thoughts, true, ennobling thoughts, and with no weak side at all, unless it be the sense of being over-wrought, like a picture which has been stippled over in every surface.

A clever French woman said of George Eliot's conversation—*elle s'écoute quand elle parle!* Just so, as we read on we seem to see how she held up each sentence into the light as it fell from her pen, scrutinised it to see if some rarer phrase might not be compacted, some subtler thought excogitated. Of all the more important tales, *Silas Marner* is that wherein we least feel this excessive thoughtfulness. And thus it is the best. Perhaps other born romancers would have thrown into it more life, energy, jollity, or passion. Thackeray would have made the weaver a serio-comic hermit: Dickens would have made Eppie a sentimental angel; Charlotte Brontë would have curdled our blood; Trollope might have made more of Nancy's courting. But no one of them could have given us a more lofty lesson "of the remedial influences of pure, natural, human relations." The only doubt is, whether a novel is the medium for such lessons. On this, opinions are, and will remain, divided. The lesson and the art ought both to be faultless.

—FREDERIC HARRISON, "George Eliot,"
Studies in Early Victorian Literature,
1895, pp. 211–213

ROMOLA

R.H. HUTTON "ROMOLA" (1863)

Richard Holt Hutton (1826–97) was an English journalist and theologian. Hutton worked as the vice principal, chaplain, and later principal of the dissenting London institution University Hall. Hutton's faith was challenged by F.D. Maurice, and he wavered throughout his life between different religious movements. Hutton gained a reputation as one of the leading contributors to contemporary periodicals on matters theological and literary.

Hutton's qualms about the serial publication of the novel reflect Eliot's own feelings. The slow manner in which Eliot lays the foundations of the novel appears, as Hutton suggests, ill suited to the serial form. Though many of Eliot's works were set in the past, *Romola* was her only genuine historical novel and grew out of months of research. Hutton is by no means the only critic to object to the manner in which this research found itself into the novel: like many readers, he found that the novel demonstrated "intellectual grasp" but did not "carry her readers *away.*" *Romola* would later mark the turning point many readers felt between Eliot's more emotional, nostalgic Midlands novels and her later, more intellectual period. Though Hutton's review anticipates this, he goes on to praise the novel in extremely generous terms. Hutton interestingly sums up the novel as "the conflict between liberal culture and the more passionate form of the Christian faith." Expressed in such terms, the reasons that may have attracted Eliot to the story are made clearer.

Throughout most of the reviews of *Romola* that appeared, greatest praise was reserved for the depiction of Savonarola, and the ensuing response to that character is representative. Eliot read Hutton's review and, uncharacteristically, responded to it, thanking him for his insightful reading and agreeing with many of his comments.

It was easy to be mistaken in the first chapters of this book, and it is pleasant to acknowledge that we were mistaken, and had not the insight to see the first faint signs of one of the greatest works of modern fiction. It is from no desire to vindicate that mistake that we regret that *Romola* should have been published in fragments. That it was not in any way affected by this mode of publication,—that it was not written in fragments, but was created by a continuous artistic effort, is clear enough. Still, perhaps, that is one reason for the inadequacy of the first impression. George Eliot's drawings all require a certain space, like Raffael's Cartoons, and are not of that kind which produce their effect by the reiteration of scenes each complete in itself. You have to unroll a large surface of the picture before even the smallest *unit* of its effect is attained. And this is far more true of this, probably the author's greatest work, than of her English tales. In the latter, the constant and striking delineation of social features with which we are all familiar, satisfies the mind in the detail almost as much as in the complete whole. It takes a considerable space to get a full view of Hetty or Dinah in *Adam Bede*, and a still greater space to understand the characters of Adam, or of Arthur Donnithorne. But, in the meantime, the vivid detail, the dry humour, the English pictures with which we are all so familiar, fascinate and satisfy us even before we have gained this clear view of the whole characters. This cannot be so when even greater power is shown in mastering the life of a foreign nation in a past age. We do not care about the light Florentine buzz with which so great a part of the first volume is filled. Its allusions are half riddles, and its liveliness a blank to us. Small local colours depend for their charm on the familiarity of small local knowledge. Then, again, George Eliot is—we will not say much greater as an imaginative painter of characters than as an imaginative painter of action, for action, also she paints with marvelous power,—but much more inclined for the one than the other. What her characters *do* is always subordinate with her to what they *are*. This is the highest artistic power, but it carries its inconveniences with it. She does not carry her readers *away*, as it is called; it is generally easy to stop reading her; she satisfies you for the moment, and does not make you look forward to the end. She has Sir Walter Scott's art for revivifying the past,—but not Scott's dynamical force in making you plunge into it with as headlong an interest as into the present. For this she compensates by a deeper and wider intellectual grasp,—but still it is easy enough to understand why half-developed characters, sketched in with unfamiliar local colours on a background of history that has long melted away, should have looked strange and uninviting, especially when not carried off by any exciting current of event, to the ordinary reader's eyes. It is marvellous that, in spite of these disadvantages, the wide and calm imaginative power of the writer should have produced a work which is likely to be permanently identified with English literature,—in which Italy and England may feel a common pride.

The great artistic purpose of the story is to trace out the conflict between liberal culture and the more passionate form of the Christian faith in that strange era, which has so many points of resemblance with the present, when the two in their most characteristic forms struggled for pre-eminence over Florentines who had been educated into the half-pedantic and half-idealistic scholarship of Lorenzo de Medici, who faintly shared the new scientific impulses of the age of Columbus and Copernicus, and whose hearts and consciences were stirred by the preaching, political as well as spiritual, of one of the very greatest as well as earliest of the reformers—the Dominican friar Savonarola. No period could be found when mingling faith and culture effervesced with more curious result. In some great and noble minds the new Learning, cleared away the petty rubbish of Romanist superstition, and revealing the mighty simplicities of the great age of Greece, grew into a feeling that supplied all the stimulus of fever, if not the rest of faith, and of these the author has drawn a very fine picture of the blind Florentine scholar, Romola's father, Bardo, who, with a restless fire in his heart, 'hung over the books and lived with the shadows' all his life. Nothing is more striking and masterly in the story than the subtle skill with which the dominant influence of this scholarship over the imagination of the elder generation of that time,—the generation which saw the first revival of learning, is delineated in the pictures of Bardo and Baldassarre. . . .

Of Romola it is less easy to say whether one is absolutely satisfied or not. The *soupçon* of hardness of which one is conscious as somewhat detracting from her power, the skill with which the author has prepared us for a mental struggle exactly similar, even in its minutest features, to what might occur today between the claims of a sublime faith appealing to the conscience, and a distate for miracle or vision in its prophet, the striking contrast with Tessa, the ignorant 'pretty little pigeon,' who thinks every one who is kind to her a saint,—all render it a little difficult to say whether we know her intimately, or whether we have only a very artistic idea of what she is *not*, and what she *is* only by inference and contrast. Our own feeling is that Romola is the least perfect figure in the book, though a fine one,—that she is a shade more modernized than the others, several shades less individual, and, after all, though the pivot of her character turns, as it were, on faith, that she does not distinctly show any faith except the faith in rigid honour, in human pity, and partially also in Savonarola's personal greatness and power. We do not say the character is not natural,—we only say it is half-revealed and more suggested than fully painted, though these harder feminine characters always seem to ask to be outlined more strongly than any others.

But the great and concentrated interest of the book—at least, after the wonderful development of Tito's character—is the portrait of Savonarola, which it is almost impossible not to feel as faithful as history, as it is great as romance. You see the same large human-hearted Italian Luther, narrower than Luther on the some sides, owing to the thin Medicean culture against which he led the reaction, but with a far more statesmanlike and political purpose, and far more fiery imagination, the same, in fact, whom Mr. Maurice has delineated intellectually with so much delicate fidelity in his history of modern philosophy, and who impresses himself upon us in almost everything he wrote, but yet never before presented clearly to the eye. His portrait evinces almost as great a graphic power, and far more scrupulous care than Sir Walter Scott used in those pictures of the various Stewarts which will certainly outlive the very different originals. Nothing can be finer and more impressive—nothing more difficult to make fine and impressive—than Savonarola's exhortation to Romola to return to the home from which she was flying. You see in every word the man's profound trust in God as the author of all human ties, and of all social and political ties, breaking through the fetters of his Dominican order, and asserting the divine order *in* nature rather than the divine order *out of* nature. This, however, is not the finest picture given of him. The finest is contained in the profoundly pathetic scene in which Savonarola, having in the fervour of his eloquence committed God to working him a miracle at the right moment, is brought to book both by his enemies and friends on the question of the trial by fire, and kneels in prayer that in fact refuses to be prayer, but rises into a political debate within himself as to the policy of seeming to take a step which he knows he must somehow evade. 'While his lips were uttering audibly *cor mundum crea in me*, his mind was still filled with the images of the snare his enemies had prepared for him, still busy with the arguments by which he could justify himself against their taunts and accusations.' But the scene is too long and too fine for us to spoil it by snatching it from the context, and is, indeed, closely bound up with the noble picture of the encounter with Tito which follows. Our author rejects apparently the authenticity of the last great words attributed to Savonarola as he is dying on the scaffold, which Mr. Maurice accepts. "'The voice of the Papal emissary,' says the historian of philosophy, 'was heard proclaiming that Savonarola was cut off from the Church militant and triumphant, they cannot shut me out of that.'" It is a pity that George Eliot rejects, as we suppose she does, the evidence for these words. They would have formed a far higher artistic ending to her story than the somewhat feeble and womanish chapter with which it concludes,—the only blot on the book. Large and genial as is the sympathy with Savonarola, there is, perhaps, no wish to represent his faith altogether as a triumphant faith. Yet Romola's faith in goodness and self-sacrifice, and in little children and 'the eternal marriage of love and duty,' and so forth, which the poem tells us is ever to last, would be an idle dream for the world, without a Christ in whose eternal nature all these realities live and grow.

But the defects, if they are defects, in this book, and the certainly somewhat unfortunate amplification of Florentine gossip in the first volume, before the reader is drawn into that rushing tide of Savonarola's revolution round the skirts of which Tito's treacherous destiny hovers, like a bird of prey over a raging battle, are blemishes too slight to do more than distinguish still more vividly the high purpose and calm imaginative serenity of this great romance. It will never be George Eliot's most popular book,—it seems to us, however, much the greatest she has yet produced.

—R.H. HUTTON, "Romola," *Spectator*,
vol. 36, July 18, 1863, pp. 2265–2267

MATHILDE BLIND (1883)

Mathilde Blind (1841–96) was a poet and biographer who moved from Germany to England with her family after the 1848 revolutions. Blind's political interests grew through contact with the foreign refugees, including Garibaldi and Mazzini, who gathered around her family. A staunch feminist, she eventually left her family home to live on her own and moved among a circle of artists and intellectuals that included Swinburne and the pre-Raphaelites. Blind's publications included volumes of poetry, the most significant of which was *The Ascent of Man* (1889), an epic on Darwinian theories of evolution. In 1883, Mathilde Blind published the first full-length biography of George Eliot. Throughout the work, Blind hesitates between judging Eliot as part of a female literary tradition and demanding that she be acknowledged as one of the greatest authors of the time, male or female.

Here, Blind adds to the ongoing debate about the division between Eliot's earlier and later works. Eliot herself objected to this schematic analysis and, with some justification, insisted that similar concerns can be traced throughout all her novels. Blind admires *Romola* but rehearses the common opinion that the work displayed too much learning. Eliot herself, Blind records, emerged exhausted from the effort. The sheer erudition and "architectural dignity" of the work, however, gave Eliot an added respectability in the literary world and it was around this time that visitors to the Priory became more numerous.

Romola marks a new departure in George Eliot's literary career. From the present she turned to the past, from the native to the foreign, from the domestic to the historical. Yet in thus shifting her subject-matter, she did not alter the strongly-pronounced tendencies underlying her earlier novels; there was more of spontaneous, humorous description of life in the latter, whereas in 'Romola' the ethical teaching which forms so prominent a feature of George Eliot's art, though the same in essence, was more distinctly wrought out. Touching on this very point, she observes in a letter to an American correspondent: "It is perhaps less irrelevant to say, apropos of a distinction you seem to make between my earlier and later works, that though I trust there is some growth in my appreciation of others and in my self-distrust, there has been no change in the point of view from which I regard our life since I wrote my first fiction, the *Scenes of Clerical Life*. Any apparent change of spirit must be due to something of which I am unconscious. The principles which are at the root of my effort to paint Dinah Morris are equally at the root of my effort to paint Mordecai." . . .

It is a majestic book, however: the most grandly planned of George Eliot's novels. It has a certain architectural dignity of structure, quite in keeping with its Italian nationality, a quality, by the way, entirely absent from the three later novels. The impressive historical background is not unlike one of Mr. Irving's magnificently wrought Italian stage-effects, rich in movement and colour, yet helping to throw the chief figures into greater relief. The erudition shown in this work; the vast yet minute acquaintance with the habits of thought, the manners, the very talk of the Florentines of that day are truly surprising; but perhaps the very fact of that erudition being so perceptible shows that the material has not been absolutely vitalised. The amount of labour George Eliot expended on *Romola* was so great, that it was the book which, she remarked to a friend, "she began a young woman and ended an old one." The deep impression her works had made upon the public mind heightened her natural conscientiousness, and her gratitude for the confidence with which each fresh contribution from her pen was received, increased her anxiety to wield her influence for the highest ends.

—MATHILDE BLIND, *George Eliot*,
1883, pp. 148–151

LESLIE STEPHEN (1902)

Stephen sums up what has now become the standard view on *Romola* in his characteristically lively language. For Henry James, the novel "smells of the lamp" (1885); for Stephen, it "suggests the professor's chair." The idea that Eliot's fifteenth-century Florence never fully comes alive is the accepted view of the novel. Stephen is, however, a little unfair in his evaluation of Lewes's responsibility in the novel's comparative failure. Lewes saw the effect that uncertainty and extensive research were having on Eliot, and wrote of his concerns to John Blackwood (though it was George Smith who would eventually publish the work). Lewes felt that the work seemed weakened by the encyclopedic knowledge behind it, but knew that to share this view with the sensitive Eliot could have devastating consequences, not only for the novel but also for her future literary career.

Romola is to me one of the most provoking of books. I am alternately seduced into admiration and repelled by what seems to me a most lamentable misapplication of first-rate powers. . . .

The criticism would be summed up by calling the book "academic"; meaning, I take it, that it suggests the professor's chair; and implies the belief that a careful study of authorities, and scrupulous attention to aesthetic canons, will be a sufficient outfit for a journey into the regions of romance. George Eliot was not blind to such considerations; and George Lewes, in his capacity of critic, could put them very keenly in writing of other people. His enthusiastic admiration for George Eliot perhaps obscured to him what he would have been the first to see elsewhere; and, anyhow, he encouraged her tendencies to a questionable direction of her genius.

Yet I do not deny that there was much to be said for the judgment of the contemporary critics who held that Romola would be one of the permanent masterpieces of English literature. Before I can adjust my own impressions to theirs, I must be allowed to remove from my mind any lingering impression that Romola and Tito lived at Florence in the fifteenth century. They were only masquerading there, and getting the necessary "properties" from the history-shops at which such things are provided for the diligent student.

—Leslie Stephen, George Eliot,
1902, pp. 126–136

FELIX HOLT

John Morley "Felix Holt" (1866)

John Morley (1838–1923) was an English politician and writer. He became friends with a number of people such as Leslie Stephen and Frederic Harrison who, like him, had experienced a similar crisis in religious faith. This spiritual crisis led to his temporary interest in positivism. Morley published literary criticism and biographies and made a name for himself by his editorial work for a number of periodicals. He succeeded G.H. Lewes as the editor of the *Fortnightly Review* in 1867 and helped to develop it as an organ of radical thought. He also edited the *Pall Mall Gazette* (1880–83) and *Macmillan's Magazine* (1883–85). Morley supplemented his literary career with a political one, as part of Gladstone's government.

Here, Morley breathes a sigh of relief that Eliot has left behind the foreign, erudite concerns of her previous novel and returned to the "Midland homesteads." Morley provides an accurate summary of how each of Eliot's novels made their impression on the reading public and critics. He indicates how Eliot's Victorian readers enjoyed the "quaint-speaking souls" who peopled her novels and their epigrammatic wit to such an extent that appreciation for these characters prevented a proper estimation of the more serious elements of her works.

Morley also pays attention to the question of how women are treated at the hands of men in Eliot's novels. Eliot did not take up the feminist cause through political engagement and campaigning but expressed her interest in women's rights more quietly by contributing financially to a number of progressive institutions. Her novels, however, vigorously portray the limitations experienced by women and dwell with particular insight on unhappy marriages. Many reviewers passed over the more feminist elements of Eliot's novels when they first appeared; the extract below provides an interesting example of a reviewer who brings the matter to the fore.

The opening lines of *Felix Holt* affect the reader like the first notes of the prelude to an old familiar melody. We find ourselves once more among the Midland homesteads, the hedgerows, 'liberal homes of unmarketable beauty,' and the great corn-stacks in the rick-yard, while here too, as in the old Loamshire of *Adam Bede*, 'the busy scenes of the shuttle and the wheel, of the roaring furnace, of the shaft and the pulley' lie 'in the midst of the large-spaced, slow-moving life of homesteads and far-away cottages and oak-sheltered parks.' Everybody recognizes the charm of the old touch in the picture of 'the neat or handsome parsonage and grey church set in the midst; there was the pleasant tinkle of the blacksmith's anvil, the patient cart-horses waiting at his door; the basket-maker peeling his willow wands in the sunshine; the wheelwright putting the last touch to a blue cart with red wheels; here and there a cottage with bright transparent windows showing pots full of blooming balsams or geraniums, and little gardens in front all double daisies or dark wall-flowers; at the well clean and comely women carrying yoked buckets, and towards the free school small Britons dawdling on and handling their marbles in the pockets of unpatched corduroys adorned with brass buttons.' And in contrast with these are the dirty children and languid mothers of the grimy towns—'pious Dissenting women, perhaps, who took life patiently and thought that salvation depended chiefly on predestination and not at all on cleanliness.' There was a great deal of nonsense talked about *Romola*, and foolish persons kept on cavilling at that wonderful book, because the authoress had left what they styled her own ground. As if she had not made Florence in the fifteenth century as much her own ground as Loamshire in the nineteenth, and as if, moreover, a writer of genius could always be ready to give the public just what it happens to want, instead of what she happens to be able to give. The authoress of *Felix Holt* probably had her eyes half turned upon these too captious admirers when she says of the parson who benefited his curate by pointing out how he could best defeat a Dissenting controversialist, that he had all 'those sensibilities to the odour of authorship which belong to almost everybody who is not expected to be a writer—and especially to that form of authorship which is called suggestion, and consists in telling another man that he might do a great deal with a given subject by bringing a sufficient amount of knowledge, reasoning and wit to bear upon it.' But though it was extremely absurd to persist in disliking Romola because she was not a Warwickshire dairymaid, and still more absurd to persist that the authoress had no business to shift her scenes or change her characters, we may still rejoice that she has again come back to those studies of English life, so humorous, so picturesque, and so philosophical, which at once raised her into the very first rank among English novelists.

The popular notion about the excellence and brilliancy of the style of George Eliot's novels is that it is simply the excellence of a painter like Teniers.

People talk of *Silas Marner* as if there were nothing in it except Nancy Lammeter and the famous meeting in the parlour of the inn; of the *Mill on the Floss*, as if it were only a rural chronicle of Gleigs and Dodsons and Tullivers; of *Adam Bede*, as if it contained no more than a photographic reproduction of the life of midland dairies and farm-houses and apple-orchards. No doubt the same kind of remarks will be made about the latest, and in some points the best, of the writer's stories. And there is no lack of material even for the limited appreciation involved in such criticism as this. The talk of the miners over their ale; of the respectable farmers and shopkeepers over their three-and-sixpenny ordinary in the country market-town; of the upper servants in the butler's pantry of an old manor-house, is as witty and as truthful, and in its own way as artistically admirable, as anything that the writer has ever done. And the variety is much greater among these quaint-speaking souls, with narrow slow-moving lives, and only the dimmest and haziest outlook, and the most heavily-clogged sensibilities. Instead of the one or two who have hitherto sufficed to furnish a background for the graver and more tragic action of the story, in *Felix Holt* there are a dozen. There is the Dissenting minister's old servant who is always being severely 'exercised' in spirit, who, if remonstrated with for boiling the eggs too hard, would sigh that 'there's hearts as are harder,' and who, in reply to anything like a joke, would exclaim, 'Dear me, don't you be so light, Miss; we may all be dead before night;' and the good-humoured pitman who says that he's 'been aforced to give my wife a black eye to hinder her from going to the preaching'; 'Lords-a-massy, she thinks she knows better nor me.' There is the little old waiting-woman who looks on life as she looks on her evening game of whist, 'I don't enjoy the game much, but I like to play my cards well, and see what will be the end of it.' And there is Mrs. Holt, the groaning member of the church assembled in Malthouse Yard, who, though full of humble professions, avows 'I've done *my* duty and more if anybody comes to that; for I've gone without my bit of meat to make broth for a sick neighbour; and if there's any of the church members say they've done the same, I'd ask them if they had the sinking at the stomach as I have.' These are only three or four out of a much greater number of similar characters, all fully and clearly drawn, and each thoroughly different from the other, except in the one point of leading a dull uncultured life. For though they all say good things, what they say is not all good in the same way, but because it is in each case the natural style of a distinct character which has been keenly observed and full conceived. But to see nothing in this or any other novel by the same writer but these droll, stupid, quaint beings, with their odd humours and rude conceits, is as bad as to see nothing in *Hamlet* except the gravediggers, nothing in *Romeo and Juliet* except the nurse and the friar and the apothecary, nothing in the *Midsummer's Night's Dream* but Bottom and Snug, Snout and Quince. It is natural that George Eliot's brilliant comedy should be most talked about, because everybody in the world feels bound to like humour, and no man does not think he understands it. And, besides, the authoress's view of life is always brought out with so much mellowness, with such artistic delicacy and finish, with an air of such even tranquility, that the incautious reader commonly overlooks the profound pathos which lies under the surface of nearly every book she has written. . . .

One of the puzzles, which runs pathetically through *Felix Holt* as through *Romola* and the *Mill on the Floss*, is the evil usage which women receive at the hands of men. Mrs. Transome, in the novel before us, is perhaps a stronger illustration than either Maggie Tulliver or Romola of the curse which a man can be to a woman. And it is not designed for a mere outburst of impotent anger and misery when she exclaims, partly crushed, partly defiant, that 'God was cruel when he made women.' She gives a reason for her seemingly impious accusation, and her own history and position supplied an extenuating condition, or else an argument in its support. 'A woman's love,' she said, 'is always freezing into fear; she wants everything, she is secure of nothing. . . . What is the use of a woman's will? if she tries, she doesn't get it, and she ceases to be loved.' Fate had been unkind to the unhappy woman. 'After sharing the common dream that when a beautiful man-child was born to her, her cup of happiness would be full, she had traveled through long years apart from that child to find herself at last in the presence of a son of whom she was afraid, and to whose sentiment in any given case she possessed no key.' This is a picture of which men would have seen more, and thought more, if they had been less ready to avoid pitying women in the right place by a willingness to pity them in the wrong place, where they don't either merit or want pity. Mrs. Transome has other causes than a rather cold and self-reliant son to exclaim, 'I would not lose the misery of being a woman, now I see what can be the baseness of a man.' 'One must be a man first to tell a woman that her love has made her your debtor, and then ask her to pay you by breaking the last poor threads between her and her son.' The whole chapter descriptive of the interview in which a man tries to save himself from disagreeable things by inducing a woman whom he has once loved to confess her past degradation to her own son, is a painful though unsurpassedly vigorous delineation of the ugliness to which anybody can stoop when 'led on through years by the gradual demands of a selfishness which has spread its fibres far and wide through the intricate vanities and sordid cares of an everyday existence.' This is the old strain of *Romola* taken up again. Mr. Jermyn, like Tito, is guilty of a hateful baseness, not because he is a wicked ravening fiend, but because he is weak and mean, and has got to think honour and pity and affection and every other virtue in his relations to another cheaply sacrificed at the price of some gain to himself. 'To such uses may tender relations come when they have ceased to be tender.'

Yet this strong and repeated conviction of how hard or mean or cruel men are to women has not prevented the authoress, here as in other books, from making a man the effective stirrer-up of a pure and lofty enthusiasim in the mind of her heroine. What Savanarola was to Romola, Felix Holt is to Esther. Only the first had the simpler and stronger level of religion, while Felix elevates Esther to a height as lofty as his own by the subtle force of his own character.

—John Morley, "Felix Holt," *Saturday Review*, vol. 21, June 16, 1866, pp. 722–724

Arthur Sedgwick
"Felix Holt, the Radical" (1866)

Arthur George Sedgwick (1844–1915) was an American literary critic encouraged to explore his literary interests by his brother-in-law, the critic Charles Eliot Norton. Sedgwick, who counted Henry James among his friends, authored numerous articles and held editorial positions at *The Nation, American Law Review,* and the *New York Evening Post*.

Even though by the time *Felix Holt* was published Eliot was considered one the greatest authors of the age, the notion that a woman could have undertaken such novels could still occasion curiosity. Sedgwick begins by expressing his interest that a woman should have left the "seclusion" of her sex and wished "to travel among men and cities." This leads to the claim that Eliot received a "boy's education," when in fact, though Eliot's parents sent her to both a day school and, later, a boarding school, there was nothing unusually masculine about her schooling. Much of the learning she gained as an adolescent and young adult was the result of her own endeavors. Sedgwick blames what he views as too much learning in the novel on this transgression of conventional female boundaries. Many critics, however, were too relieved to see that Eliot had not written another *Romola* to complain about laboriousness in *Felix Holt*. Segdwick also provides telling commentary on Eliot's politics. She is, he suggests, a radical but does not fanatically profess to be so. Indeed, she was no revolutionary but a meliorist who believed that progress would come through gradual social improvements. Sedgwick is right to note that, in accordance with her ideas, Felix Holt is no incendiary hero.

From the time when the interesting *Scenes of Clerical Life* were published down to the issue of *Felix Holt*, George Eliot has the great merit of being true to herself. Her last novel shows the distinctive marks of the first,—the vigor of style, the incisiveness of thought, the truth to nature. The corruption which a life of fiction-writing, like a life of politics, is apt to produce, has not been able to dull her moral sense, nor to rust the keenness of her sympathy for the sorrows and joys of men and women. She has neither become a cynic, nor a humorist, nor coarse, but still keeps in the path of realistic art, studying the roadside nature, and satisfied with it. She continues to receive the great reward which every true realist longs for, that she is true to nature without degenerating to the commonplace, and the old blame, that they have not enough of the ideal, which they covet too. And this classification among the realists, which is easy to make, and gives an author a hold on sympathy at once in England or America, means more in this case than if George Eliot had been the name of the author's actual, not literary, baptism. For a man to go on a voyage of discovery is not surprising; but for a woman to dare to leave the Abyssinian seclusion in which we are wont to place her, and to wish to travel among men and cities, to desire to see not only the things we are content to tell her about life, but life itself, to look into the dark corners and crannies and find what goes on there, shows an ambition which cannot but be interesting to any one who perceives in woman some higher sense than hearing and some deeper right than that of credulity.

Felix Holt is a picture of radicalism in England thirty-five years ago, quite as much as a picture of Felix himself. The introduction draws with a few bold strokes the prominent features of the landscape, at the time when Apollo, or whatever god had charge of stage-coaches, was driving them down the western horizon, while the whistle of steam was heard in the East. In America we know little of the England of thirty-five years ago, but we see enough of the fidelity of the author to nature to know that we may trust her. There is no danger of her writing one of the old-fashioned historical novels which seemed to be called so because only the greatest familiarity with history would account for such great contempt of it as was shown by the authors of them. George Eliot is a believer in radicalism, in the Reform Bill of 1832, and in the Reform Bill of 186-; but the noble ideality of her hopes does not prevent her from seeing facts as they actually are. The radical is with her no thunder-clad god, striding from mountain-top to mountain-top of reform, shouting "Tally-ho!" to the crusading multitudes in the valleys beneath. The radical is one of that multitude, a hungry and thirsty and angry man, creeping foot-sore through a doubtful land, hoping, and sometimes believing, that he may leave the world a little better for his children than he found it for himself.

. . .

But it must be confessed that the plot of *Felix Holt*, like that of *Romola*, marches a little slowly. We feel that the omission of a good deal would do no injury to the interest of the story. The boy's education which the author has been said to have received, acting upon a mind naturally turned toward learning and research, has made her fond of many things which the novels of women are not apt to show familiarity with. In this one there is enough of law and politics, as in *Romola* of history, to show great study and care; but in both cases they are made too prominent. These studies of the past, which no novelist of the past can make too careful, are valuable as a means; the public, which only care for a novel as a novel, is willing to justify the laboriousness of such means only if it is kept out of sight. It is a pleasure-loving public, the novel-reading one, and turns from law and history and politics and trade to hear the story of life. When it is so generous, it is nearly a shame to thrust it back into the ruts. This learning and research, too, appear to have their effect on a style which at the beginning was simple and direct, but has by the least alteration in the world become slightly indirect and tortuous. Ideas which in the *Scenes of Clerical Life* would have been expressed with perfect clearness are in *Felix Holt* now and then enveloped in syllables that coil themselves about the thought with dangerous, snake-like facility. It is seldom that this tendency shows clearly; but there is just enough to make us regret its presence, and to excuse a suggestion that, wherever an author goes, her style should sun itself in the warm light of human nature, and not shiver in the cold chambers of law and metaphysics.

—Arthur Sedgwick, "Felix Holt, the Radical," *North American Review*, vol. 103, October 1866, pp. 557–562

John Hutton Balfour Browne (1907)

John Hutton Balfour Browne (1845–1921) was a Scottish lawyer and writer. Browne's interests and activities were multiple: he published poetry, contributed articles to the *Times*, and established a successful career as a lawyer. His *Essays, Critical and Political* includes passages on Charlotte Brontë, Walter Savage Landor, and Dickens along with essays on British colonies. Browne's early-twentieth-century assessment of *Felix Holt* accurately sums up the popular opinion of the novel, which largely endures today: "The book retains no hold upon our heart and memory as her earlier works do".

The novel is, he and others suggested, full of interest but somehow has a lesser impact.

Her politics in *Felix Holt the Radical* earned her small praise. Here, as in all her novels, there were many things that no one else could have written. The first chapter is as full of beautiful description as any similar number of pages in any book. Some of the Sproxton collier's talk is excellent overhearing. But although there are many beauties there are grave faults. Her theories concerning the animal basis of all the moral virtues might have been interesting elsewhere. Her opinions on many matters might have deserved the prominence they attain in these pages—in pages of their own. The book retains no hold upon our heart and memory as her earlier works do.

—John Hutton Balfour Browne,
Essays, Critical and Political, 1907, p. 64

MIDDLEMARCH

Edith Simcox "Middlemarch" (1873)

Simcox's review provides a strong sense of the degree to which critics recognized *Middlemarch* as one of the most important novels published in the nineteenth century. The passage anticipates Richard Burton's view, included previously in this volume, that Eliot's fiction was essentially modern in the manner in which it gave unprecedented importance to the inner workings of the mind. Simcox also pays tribute to the "artistic harmony of construction" in *Middlemarch*, which appears all the more impressive as the stories of Lydgate and Dorothea were initially conceived quite separately.

Middlemarch marks an epoch in the history of fiction in so far as its incidents are taken from the inner life, as the action is developed by the direct influence of mind on mind and character on character, as the material circumstances of the outer world are made subordinate and accessory to the artistic presentation of a definite passage of mental experience, but chiefly as giving a background of perfect realistic truth to a profoundly imaginative psychological study. The effect is as new as if we could suppose a *Wilhelm Meister* written by Balzac. In *Silas Marner, Romola*, and the author's other works there is the same power, but it does not so completely and exclusively determine the form in which the conception is placed before us. In *Silas Marner* there is a natural and obvious unity in the life of the weaver, but in *Romola*—where alone the interest is at once as varied and as profound as in *Middlemarch*—though the historic glories of Florence, the passions belonging to what, as compared with the nineteenth century, is an heroic age, are in perfect harmony with the grand manner of treating spiritual problems, yet the realism, the positive background of fact, which we can scarcely better bear to miss, has necessarily some of the character of an hypothesis, and does not inspire us with the same confidence as truths we can verify for ourselves. For that reason alone, on the mere point of artistic harmony of construction, we should rate the last work as the greatest; and to say that *Middlemarch* is George Eliot's greatest work is to say that it has scarcely a superior and very few equals in the whole wide range of English fiction.

—EDITH SIMCOX, "Middlemarch,"
Academy, vol. 4, Jan. 1, 1873, p. 1

SIDNEY COLVIN "MIDDLEMARCH" (1873)

Sidney Colvin (1845–1927) was an English critic and museum administrator. Colvin contributed essays and reviews, principally on fine art, to periodicals such as the *Pall Mall Gazette* and the *Fortnightly Review*. He contributed biographies of Landor and Keats to the English Men of Letters series. Colvin also worked as a professor of fine art at Cambridge, director of the Fitzwilliam Museum, and supervisor of the prints and drawings held in the British Museum.

Like Simcox, Colvin acknowledges the importance of *Middlemarch* and seeks to convey a sense of the excitement generated by its publication. Colvin stresses the success of Eliot's depiction of the past: *Middlemarch* is a historical novel, though tackled in a very different way than *Romola*. Colvin further echoes Simcox in paying attention to Eliot's "psychological instrument." Critics had always paid tribute to Eliot's talent for portraiture, but it is a sign of the fresh impact made by *Middlemarch* that they began to use the emerging language of psychology and science ("physiognomical study," a "symptomatic" imagination) rather than the old comparisons to Dutch realism to express their admiration, reflecting Eliot's own increasing use of such language. This contributed to a sense of the novel's modernity though critics also found it difficult to see much charm in something as intellectually impressive.

Fifteen months of pausing and recurring literary excitement are at an end; and *Middlemarch*, the chief English book of the immediate present, lies complete before us. Now that we have the book as a whole, what place does it take among the rest with which its illustrious writer has enriched, I will not say posterity, because for posterity every present is apt in turn to prove itself a shallow judge, but her own generation and us who delight to honour her?

In the sense in which anything is called ripe because of fullness and strength, I think the last of George Eliot's novels is also the ripest. *Middlemarch* is extraordinarily full and strong, even among the company to which it belongs. And though I am not sure that it is the property of George Eliot's writing to satisfy, its property certainly is to rouse and attach, in proportion to its fullness and strength. There is nothing in the literature of the day so rousing—to the mind of the day there is scarcely anything so rousing in all literature—as her writing is. What she writes is so full of her time. It is observation, imagination, pathos, wit and humour, all of a high class in themselves; but what is more, all saturated with modern ideas, and poured into a language of which every word bites home with peculiar sharpness to the contemporary consciousness. That is what makes it less safe than it might seem at first to speak for posterity in such a case. We are afraid of exaggerating the meaning such work will have for those who come after us, for the very reason that we feel its meaning so pregnant for ourselves. If, indeed, the ideas of to-day are certain to be the ideas of to-morrow and the day after, if scientific thought and the positive synthesis are indubitably to rule the world, then any one, it should seem, might speak boldly enough to George Eliot's place. For the general definition of her work, I should say, is precisely this—that, among writers of the imagination, she has taken the lead in expressing and discussing the lives and ways of common folks—*votum, timor, ira, voluptas*—in terms of scientific thought and the positive synthesis. She has walked between two epochs, upon the confines of two worlds, and has described the old in terms of the new. To the old world belongs the elements of her experience, to the new world the elements of her reflection on experience. The elements of her experience are the 'English Provincial Life' before the Reform Bill—the desires and alarms, indignations and satisfactions, of the human breast in county towns and villages, farms and parsonages, manor-houses, counting-houses, surgeries, streets and lanes, shops and fields, of midlands unshaken in their prejudices and unvisited by the steam-engine. To the new world belongs the elements of her reflection; the many-sided culture which looks back upon prejudice with analytical amusement; the philosophy which declares the human family deluded in its higher dreams, dependent upon itself, and bound thereby to a closer if a sadder brotherhood; the habit in regarding and meditating physical laws, and the facts of sense and life, which leads up to that philosophy and belongs to it; the mingled depth of bitterness and tenderness in the human temper of which the philosophy becomes the spring.

Thus there is the most pointed contrast between the matter of these English tales and the manner of their telling. The matter is antiquated in our recollections, the manner seems to anticipate the future of our thoughts. Plenty of other writers have taken humdrum and narrow aspects of English life with which they were familiar, and by delicacy of perception and justness of rendering have put them together into pleasant works of literary art, without running the matter into a manner out of direct correspondence with it. But this procedure of George Eliot's is a newer thing in literature, and infinitely harder to judge of, than the gray and tranquil harmonies of that other mode of art. For no writer uses so many instruments in riveting the interest of the cultivated reader about the characters, and springs of character, which she is exhibiting. First, I say, she has the perpetual application of her own intelligence to the broad problems and conclusions of modern thought. That, for instance, when Fred Vincy, having brought losses upon the Garth family, feels his own dishonour more than their suffering, brings the reflection how '*we are most of us brought up in the notion that the highest motive for not doing a wrong is something irrespective of the beings who would suffer the wrong.*' That again, a few pages later, brings the humorous allusions to Caleb Garth's classification of human employments, into business, politics, preaching, learning, and amusement, as one which '*like the categories of more celebrated men, would not be acceptable in these more advanced times.*' And that makes it impossible to describe the roguery of a horse-dealer without suggesting that he '*regarded horse-dealing as the finest of the arts, and might have argued plausibly that it had nothing to do with morality.*'

Next, this writer possesses, in her own sympathetic insight into the working of human nature, a psychological instrument which will be perpetually displaying its power, its subtlety and trenchancy, in passages like this which lays bare the working of poor Mrs. Bulstrode's faithful mind upon the revelation of her husband's guilt: 'Along with her brother's looks and words, there darted into her mind the idea of some guilt in her husband. Then, under the working of terror, came the image of her husband exposed to disgrace; *and then, after an instant of scorching shame in which she only felt the eyes of the world, with one leap of her heart she was at his side in mournful but unreproaching fellowship with shame and isolation.*' Of the same trenchancy and potency, equally subtle and equally sure of themselves, are a hundred and other processes of analysis, whether applied to serious crises—like that prolonged one during which Bulstrode wavers before the passive murder which shall rid him of his one obstacle as an efficient servant of God—or to such trivial crises as occur in the experiences of a Mrs. Dollop or a Mrs. Taft, or others who, being their betters, still belong to the class of 'well-meaning women knowing very little of their own motives.' And this powerful knowledge of human nature is still only one of many instruments for exposing a character and turning it about. What the character itself thinks and feels, exposed by this, will receive a simultaneous commentary in what the modern analytic mind has to remark upon such thoughts and feelings: see a good instance in the account . . . of Mr. Casaubon's motives before marriage and experiences after it.

Then, the writer's studies in science and psychology will constantly come in to suggest for the spiritual processes of her personages an explanation here or an illustration there. For a stroke of overwhelming power in this kind, take what is said in one place of Bulstrode—that 'he shrank from a direct lie with an intensity disproportionate to the number of his more indirect misdeeds. *But many of these misdeeds were like the subtle muscular movements which are not taken account of in the consciousness; though they bring about the end that we fix in our minds and desire. And it is only what we are vividly conscious of what we can vividly imagine to be seen by Omniscience.*'

And it is yet another instrument which the writer handles when she seizes on critical points of physical look and gesture in her personages, in a way which is scientific and her own. True, there are many descriptions, and especially of the beauty and gestures of Dorothea—and these are written with a peculiarly loving and as it were watchful exquisiteness—which may be put down as belonging to the ordinary resources of art. But look at Caleb Garth; he is a complete physiognomical study in the sense of Mr. Darwin, with the 'deepend depression in the outer angle of his bushy eyebrows, which gave his face a peculiar mildness;' with his trick of 'broadening himself by putting his thumbs into his arm-holes,' and the rest. Such are Rosamond's ways of turning her neck aside and patting her hair when she is going to be obstinate. So, we are not allowed to forget 'a certain massiveness in Lydgate's manner and tone, corresponding with his physique;' nor indeed, any point of figure and physiognomy which strike the author's imagination as symptomatic. Symptomatic is the best word. There is a medical strain in the tissue of the story. There is a profound sense of the importance of physiological conditions in human life. But further still, I think, there is something like a medical habit in the writer, of examining her own creations for their symptoms, which runs through her descriptive and narrative art and gives it some of its peculiar manner.

So that, apart from the presence of rousing thought in general maxims and allusions, we know now what we mean when we speak of the fulness and strength derived, in the dramatic and narrative part of the work, from the use of so many instruments as we have seen. Then comes the question, do these qualities satisfy us as thoroughly as they rouse and interest? Sometimes I think they do, and sometimes not. Nothing evidently can be more satisfying, more illuminating, than that sentence which explained, by a primitive fact in the experimental relations of mind and body, a peculiar kind of bluntness in the conscience of the religious Bulstrode. And generally, wherever the novelist applies her philosophy or science to serious purposes, even if it may be applied too often, its effect seems to me good. But in lighter applications I doubt if the same kind of thing is not sometimes mistaken. The wit and humour of this writer every one of us knows and has revelled in; I do not think these want to gain body from an elaborate or semi-scientific language. In the expression of fun or common observation, is not such language apt to read a little technical and heavy, like a kind of intellectual slang? I do not think the delightful fun about Mrs. Garth and Mary and the children gains by it. I doubt if it is in place when it is applied to the mental processes of Mrs. Dollop or Mr. Bambridge. And when, for example, we are asked to consider what would have happened if Fred Vincy's 'prophetic soul had been urged to particularize,' that is what I mean by something like a kind of intellectual slang.

—Sidney Colvin, "Middlemarch,"
Fortnightly Review, vol. 13,
January 19, 1873, pp. 142–144

Henry James "Current Literature" (1873)

Henry James's ambivalent review of *Middlemarch* shows him trying to work through his own aesthetic ideas by tackling what was ostensibly one of the greatest novels of the century. James admits as much: it is "one of the strongest" of English novels, and Eliot seems to him "among English romancers to stand alone." When James states that the novel "sets a limit, we think, to the development of the old-fashioned English novel," he acknowledges both the artistic ambition of Eliot and his own desire to change the direction of contemporary fiction. One way in which he sought to do this was by challenging conceptions of fictional form, which in turn helps to explain his preoccupation with structure in the review. The piece contains the famous phrase that "*Middlemarch* is a treasure-house of details, but it is an indifferent whole." James's assessment is supported by numerous examples of powerful characters and evocative scenes that, he feels, do not amount to an entirely satisfactory whole. The review is also significant in the way that it sets forth the view, which would become a critical commonplace, that Eliot's novels, or at least the later ones, were more "intelligent" and "philosophic" than creative. Complaints about "obscure" passages and discursive paragraphs "too clever by half," together with the opinion that Eliot's fiction had lost its "simplicity" (which are amusing given the responses to James's own late fiction) were to become increasingly numerous.

Middlemarch is at once one of the strongest and one of the weakest of English novels. Its predecessors as they appeared might have been described in the same terms; *Romola,* is especially a rare masterpiece, but the least *entrainant* of masterpieces. *Romola* sins by excess of analysis; there is too much description and too little drama; too much reflection (all certainly of a highly imaginative sort) and too little creation. Movement lingers in the story, and with it attention stands still in the reader. The error in *Middlemarch* is not precisely of a similar kind, but it is equally detrimental to the total aspect of the work. We can well remember how keenly we wondered, while its earlier chapters unfolded themselves, what turn in the way of form the story would take—that of an organized, moulded, balanced composition, gratifying the reader with a sense of design and construction, or a mere chain of episodes, broken into accidental lengths and unconscious of the influence of a plan. We expected the actual result, but for the sake of English imaginative literature which, in this line is rarely in need of examples, we hoped for the other. If it had come we should have had the pleasure of reading, what certainly would have seemed to us in the immediate glow of attention, the first of English novels. But that pleasure has still to hover between prospect and retrospect. *Middlemarch* is a treasure-house of details, but it is an indifferent whole.

Our objection may seem shallow and pedantic, and may even be represented as a complaint that we have had the less given us rather than the more. Certainly the greatest minds have the defects of their qualities, and as George Eliot's mind is preeminently contemplative and analytic, nothing is more natural than that her manner should be discursive and expansive. "Concentration" would doubtless have deprived us of many of the best things in the book—of Peter Featherstone's grotesquely expectant legatees, of Lydgate's medical rivals, and of Mary Garth's delightful family. The author's purpose was to be a generous rural historian, and this very redundancy of touch, born of abundant reminiscence, is one of the greatest charms of her work. It is as if her memory was crowded with antique figures, to whom for very tenderness she must grant an appearance. Her novel is a picture—vast, swarming, deep-colored, crowded with episodes, with vivid images, with lurking master-strokes, with brilliant passages of expression; and as such we may freely accept it and enjoy it. It is not compact, doubtless; but when was a panorama compact? And yet, nominally, *Middlemarch* has a definite subject—the subject indicated in the eloquent preface. An ardent young girl was to have been the central figure, a young girl framed for a larger moral life than circumstance often affords, yearning for a motive for sustained spiritual effort and only wasting her ardor and soiling her wings against the meanness of opportunity. The author, in other words, proposed to depict the career of an obscure St. Theresa. Her success has been great, in spite of serious drawbacks. Dorothea Brooks is a genuine creation, and a most remarkable one when we consider the delicate material in which she is wrought. George Eliot's men are generally so much better than the usual trowsered offspring of the female fancy, that their merits have perhaps overshadowed those of her women. Yet her heroines have always been of an exquisite quality, and Dorothea is only that perfect flower of conception of which her predecessors were the less unfolded blossoms. An indefinable moral elevation is the sign of these admirable creatures; and of the representation of this quality in its superior degrees the author seems to have in English fiction a monopoly. To render the expression of a soul requires a cunning hand; but we seem to look straight into the unfathomable eyes of the beautiful spirit of Dorothea Brooks. She exhales a sort of aroma of spiritual sweetness, and we believe in her as in a woman we might providentially meet some fine day when we should find ourselves doubting of the immortality of the soul. By what unerring mechanism this effect is produced—whether by fine strokes or broad ones, by description or by narration, we can hardly say; it is certainly the great achievement of the book. Dorothea's career is, however, but an episode, and though doubtless in intention, not distinctly enough in fact, the central one. The history of Lydgate's *menage,* which shares honors with it, seems rather to the reader to carry off the lion's share. This is certainly a very interesting story, but on the whole it yields in dignity to the record of Dorothea's unresonant woes. The "love-problem," as the author calls it, of Mary Garth, is placed on a rather higher level than the reader willingly grants it. To the end we care less about Fred Vincy than appears to be expected of us. In so far as the writer's design has been to reproduce the total sum of life in an English village forty years ago, this common-place young gentleman, with his somewhat meagre tribulations and his rather neutral egotism, has his proper place in the picture; but the author narrates his fortunes with a fulness of detail which the reader often finds irritating. The reader indeed is sometimes tempted to complain of a tendency which we are at loss exactly to express—a tendency to make light of the serious elements of the story and to sacrifice them to the more trivial ones. Is it an unconscious instinct or is it a deliberate plan? With its abundant and massive ingredients *Middlemarch* ought somehow to have depicted a weightier drama. Dorothea was altogether too superb a heroine to be wasted; yet she plays a narrower part than the imagination of the reader demands. She is of more consequence than the action of which she is the nominal centre. She marries enthusiastically a man whom she fancies a great thinker, and who turns out to be but an arid pedant. Here, indeed, is a disappointment with much of the dignity of tragedy; but the situation seems to us never to expand to its full capacity. It is analyzed with extraordinary penetration, but one may say of it, as of most of the situations in the book, that it is treated with too much refinement and too little breadth. It revolves too constantly on the same pivot; it abounds in fine shades, but it lacks, we think, the great dramatic *chiaroscuro*. Mr. Casaubon, Dorothea's husband (of whom more anon) embittered, on his side, by matrimonial disappointment, takes refuge in vain jealousy of his wife's relations with an interesting young cousin of his own and registers this sentiment in a codicil to his will, making the forfeiture of his property the penalty of his widow's marriage with this gentleman. Mr. Casaubon's death befalls about the middle of the story, and from this point to the close our interest in Dorothea is restricted to the question, will she or will she not marry Will Ladislaw? The question is relatively trivial and the implied struggle slightly factitious. The author has depicted the struggle with a sort of elaborate solemnity which in the interviews related in the last two books tends to become almost ludicrously excessive.

The dramatic current stagnates; it runs between hero and heroine almost a game of hair-splitting. Our dissatisfaction here is provoked in great measure by the insubstantial character of the hero. The figure of Will Ladislaw is a beautiful attempt, with many finely-completed points; but on the whole it seems to us a failure. It is the only eminent failure in the book, and its defects are therefore the more striking. It lacks sharpness of outline and depth of color; we have not found ourselves believing in Ladislaw as we believe in Dorothea, in Mary Garth, in Rosamond, in Lydgate, in Mr. Brooke and Mr. Casaubon. He is meant, indeed, to be a light creature (with a large capacity for gravity, for he finally gets into Parliament), and a light creature certainly should not be heavily drawn. The author, who is evidently very fond of him, has found for him here and there some charming and eloquent touches; but in spite of these he remains vague and impalpable to the end. He is, we may say, the one figure which a masculine intellect of the same power as George Eliot's would not have conceived with the same complacency; he is, in short, roughly speaking, a woman's man. It strikes us as an oddity in the author's scheme that she should have chosen just this figure of Ladislaw as the creature in whom Dorothea was to find her spiritual compensations. He is really, after all, not the ideal foil to Mr. Casaubon which her soul must have imperiously demanded, and if the author of the "Key to all Mythologies" sinned by lack of order, Ladislaw too has not the concentrated fervor essential in the man chosen by so nobly strenuous a heroine. The impression once given that he is a *dilettante* is never properly removed, and there is slender poetic justice in Dorothea's marrying a *dilettante*. We are doubtless less content with Ladislaw, on account of the noble, almost sculptural, relief of the neighboring figure of Lydgate, the real hero of the story. It is an illustration of the generous scale of the author's picture and of the conscious power of her imagination that she has given us a hero and heroine of broadly distinct interests—erected, as it were, two suns in her firmament, each with its independent solar system. Lydgate is so richly successful a figure that we have regretted strongly at moments, for immediate interests' sake, that the current of his fortunes should not mingle more freely with the occasionally thin-flowing stream of Dorothea's. Toward the close, these two fine characters are brought into momentary contact so effectively as to suggest a wealth of dramatic possibility between them; but if this train had been followed we should have lost Rosamond Vincy—a rare psychological study. Lydgate is a really complete portrait of a *man,* which seems to us high praise. It is striking evidence of the altogether superior quality of George Eliot's imagination that, though elaborately represented, Lydgate should be treated so little from what we may roughly (and we trust without offence) call the sexual point of view. Perception charged with feeling has constantly guided the author's hand, and yet her strokes remain as firm, her curves as free, her whole manner as serenely impersonal, as if, on a small scale, she were emulating the creative wisdom itself. Several English romancers—notably Fielding, Thackeray, and Charles Reade—have won great praise for their figures of women: but they owe it, in reversed conditions, to a meaner sort of art, it seems to us, than George Eliot has used in the case of Lydgate; to an indefinable appeal to masculine prejudice—to a sort of titillation of the masculine sense of difference. George Eliot's manner is more philosophic—more broadly intelligent, and yet her result is as concrete or, if you please, as picturesque. We have no space to dwell on Lydgate's character; we can but repeat that he is a vividly consistent, manly figure—powerful, ambitious, sagacious, with the maximum rather than the minimum of egotism, strenuous, generous, fallible, and altogether human. A work of the liberal scope of *Middlemarch* contains a multitude of artistic intentions, some of the finest of which became clear only in the meditative after-taste of perusal. This is the case with the balanced contrast between the two histories of Lydgate and Dorothea. Each is a tale of matrimonial infelicity, but the conditions in each are so different and the circumstances so broadly opposed that the mind passes from one to the other with that supreme sense of the vastness and variety of human life, under aspects apparently similar, which it belongs only to the greatest novels to produce. The most perfectly successful passages in the book are perhaps those painful fireside scenes between Lydgate and his miserable little wife. The author's rare psychological penetration is lavished upon this veritably mulish domestic flower. There is nothing more powerfully real than these scenes in all English fiction, and nothing certainly more *intelligent*. Their impressiveness, and (as regards Lydgate) their pathos, is deepened by the constantly low key in which they are pitched. It is a tragedy based on unpaid butchers' bills, and the urgent need for small economies. The author has desired to be strictly real and to adhere to the facts of the common lot, and she has given us a powerful version of that typical human drama, the struggles of an ambitious soul with sordid disappointments and vulgar embarrassments. As to her catastrophe we hesitate to pronounce (for Lydgate's ultimate assent to his wife's worldly programme is nothing less than a catastrophe). We almost believe that some terrific explosion would have been more probable than his twenty years of smothered aspiration. Rosamond deserves almost to rank with Tito in *Romola* as a study of a gracefully vicious, or at least of a practically baleful nature. There is one point, however, of which we question the consistency. The author insists on her instincts of coquetry, which seems to us a discordant note. They would have made her better or worse—more generous or more reckless; in either case more manageable. As it is, Rosamond represents, in a measure, the fatality of British decorum.

In reading, we have marked innumerable passages for quotation and comment; but we lack space and the work is so ample that half a dozen extracts would be an ineffective illustration. There would be a great deal to say on the broad array of secondary figures, Mr. Casaubon, Mr. Brooke, Mr. Bulstrode, Mr. Farebrother, Caleb Garth, Mrs. Cadwallader, Celia Brooke. Mr. Casaubon is an excellent invention; as a dusky *repoussoir* to the luminous figure of his wife he could not have been better imagined. There is indeed something very noble in the way in which the author has apprehended his character. To depict hollow pretentiousness and mouldy egotism with so little of narrow sarcasm and so much of philosophic sympathy, is to be a rare moralist as well as a rare story-teller. The whole portrait of Mr. Casaubon has an admirably sustained greyness of tone in which the shadows are never carried to the vulgar black of coarser artists. Every stroke contributes to the unwholesome, helplessly sinister expression. Here and there perhaps (as in his habitual diction), there is a hint of exaggeration; but we confess we like fancy to be fanciful. Mr. Brooke and Mr. Garth are in their different lines supremely genial creations; they are drawn with the touch of a Dickens chastened and intellectualized. Mrs. Cadwallader is, in another walk of life, a match for Mrs. Poyser, and Celia Brooke is as pretty a fool as any of Miss Austen's. Mr. Farebrother and his delightful "womankind" belong to a large group of figures begotten of the superabundance of the author's creative instinct. At times they seem to encumber the stage and to produce a rather ponderous mass of dialogue; but they add to the reader's impression of having walked in the Middlemarch lanes and listened to the Middlemarch accent. To but one of these accessory episodes—that of Mr. Bulstrode, with its multiplex ramifications—do we take exception. It has a slightly artificial cast, a melodramatic tinge, unfriendly to the richly natural coloring of the whole. Bulstrode himself—with the history of whose troubled conscience the author has taken great pains—is, to our sense, too diffusely treated; he never grasps the reader's attention. But the touch of genius is never idle or vain. The obscure figure of Bulstrode's comely wife emerges at the needful moment, under a few light strokes, into the happiest reality.

All these people, solid and vivid in their varying degrees, are members of a deeply human little world, the full reflection of whose antique image is the great merit of these volumes. How bravely rounded a little world the author has made it—with how dense an atmosphere of interests and passions and loves and enmities and strivings and failings, and how motley a group of great folk and small, all after their kind, she has filled it, the reader must learn for himself. No writer seems to us to have drawn from a richer stock of those long-cherished memories which one's later philosophy makes doubly tender. There are few figures in the book which do not seem to have grown mellow in the author's mind. English readers may fancy they enjoy the "atmosphere" of *Middlemarch;* but we maintain that to relish its inner essence we must—for reasons too numerous to detail—be an American. The author has commissioned herself to be real, her native tendency being that of an idealist, and the intellectual result is a very fertilizing mixture. The constant presence of thought, of generalizing instinct, of *brain,* in a word, behind her observation, gives the latter its great value and her whole manner its high superiority. It denotes a mind in which imagination is illumined by faculties rarely found in fellowship with it. In this respect—in that broad reach of vision which would make the worthy historian of solemn fact as well as wanton fiction—George Eliot seems to us among English romancers to stand alone. Fielding approaches her, but to our mind, she surpasses Fielding. Fielding was didactic—the author *of Middlemarch* is really philosophic. These great qualities imply corresponding perils. The first is the loss of simplicity. George Eliot lost hers some time since: it lies buried (in a splendid mausoleum) in *Romola*. Many of the discursive portions of *Middlemarch* are, as we may say, too clever by half. The author wishes to say too many things, and to say them too well; to recommend herself to a scientific audience. Her style, rich and flexible as it is, is apt to betray her on these transcendental flights; we find, in our copy, a dozen passages marked "obscure." *Silas Marner* has a delightful tinge of Goldsmith—we may almost call it: *Middlemarch* is too often an echo of Messrs. Darwin and Huxley. In spite of these faults—which it seems graceless to indicate with this crude rapidity—it remains a very splendid performance. It sets a limit, we think, to the development of the old-fashioned English novel. Its diffuseness, on which we have touched, makes it too copious a dose of pure fiction. If we write novels so, how shall we write History? But it is nevertheless a contribution of the first importance to the rich imaginative department of our literature.

—HENRY JAMES, "Current Literature," *Galaxy*, vol. 15, March 1873, pp. 424–428

GEORGE PARSONS LATHROP "GROWTH OF THE NOVEL" (1874)

George Parsons Lathrop (1815–98) was an American writer who worked in a law office before turning to literature. Lathrop married Nathaniel Hawthorne's daughter Rose in 1871. The connection helped to stimulate his literary career, and some of his notable works were studies and editions of Hawthorne. Lathrop served as associate editor of the *Atlantic Monthly* from 1875 to 1877, after which he edited the *Boston Courier*. In 1891, the conversion of Lathrop and his wife to Catholicism was a widely publicized event.

Lathrop's response to *Middlemarch* echoes some of the more negative responses to the novel. Many who admitted that it had altered the literary landscape nevertheless expressed some reservations: as with *Romola*, though to a lesser extent, they complained that the work displayed too much effort—more intellect than passion. A number of critics similarly complained that Eliot displayed excessive harshness toward Middlemarch and its inhabitants. The criticism that readers approach Eliot's work for her powers of analysis rather than for a "sympathetic rendition of human nature" would have greatly disappointed the novelist, considering that she never ceased to hold the belief that art should generate sympathy.

Not less injurious, in its way, to dramatic perfection is the system of minute and deliberate analysis pursued by George Eliot. It makes us look to her books rather for instances of her remarkable acumen, and the terse statement of her perceptions, than for a sympathetic rendition of human nature that shall charm and soothe us, at the same time that it instructs or educates. Her writing does not soothe, because she keeps so constantly before us the stern effort she is making, not to swerve from strict analysis. The authoress presides too watchfully over the progress of our acquaintance with the imaginary beings to whom she has introduced us; and we should be more at ease, if she would omit some of the more wordy of her examinations into their mental status at each new turn of the story. . . .

As an effort of clear intellectual penetration into life, we could hardly demand anything better than *Middlemarch*. But it is still too much an effort, and not enough an accomplished insight; it remains, as the author has called it, a study, rather than a finished dramatic representation.

—GEORGE PARSONS LATHROP,
"Growth of the Novel," *Atlantic Monthly*,
vol. 33, June 1874, pp. 688–689

VIDA D. SCUDDER "GEORGE ELIOT AND THE SOCIAL CONSCIENCE" (1898)

Looking back at the range of literature produced by the Victorian age, Scudder reaffirms the importance of *Middlemarch*. The extract is particularly helpful for the manner in which it places Eliot in the context of her contemporaries. Many of Scudder's statements are discerning, such as the suggestion that Dickens would have felt more at ease dealing with the sensational events surrounding Bulstrode. Most importantly, Scudder's approach sheds light on the character of Dorothea, "a new type of heroine" who in turn anticipates the idea of the "modern heroine as a social force," which appeared in turn-of-the century literature. It is appropriate for the feminist social reformer Scudder to take this stance; her depiction of Eliot's "impassioned protest against modern society" would find little sympathy in the criticism of the next thirty years (with the notable exception of Virginia Woolf's 1919 essay) but is much closer to late-twentieth-century discussions of *Middlemarch*.

In social significance, *Middlemarch* is probably the most important novel of the central Victorian period. It is certainly the most comprehensive. The social environment of the book, sketched with remarkable breadth and power, is really a summary of that which we have learned to know in essay and novel. Here is the gentry,—a country gentry, this time,—Mr. Brooke and the Chethams, with their mild dilettanteism, their lack of purpose or ideals. Here is the bourgeois society of the town, divided from the country by a seemingly impassable gulf: the Bulstrodes and Vincys, painfully devoid of sweetness and light. In the intrigue centring around old Featherstone, George Eliot has tried her hand at types that the offhand melodrama of Dickens would have treated more successfully. But Arnold himself never drew a better Philistine than Bulstrode, with his "double Hell, of not making money and not saving his soul," nor is any one of Thackeray's women more selfish, bewitching, and trivially clever than Rosamund. George Eliot's studies of clergy are in all her books a new feature, unparalleled in fiction unless we return to the capital work of Miss Austen. *Middlemarch* gives none of her favorite and sympathetic pictures of dissent; but the Established Church is represented by admirable if rather depressing types, in Mr. Cadwallader, Mr. Farebrother, and Mr. Casaubon. Certainly, wherever the force for social salvation may reside, it is not in these gentlemen.

All these minor characters, whom Thackeray would have treated with contempt and Dickens with jest, George Eliot touches with unfailing pathos and redeems to human dignity; yet her obvious intention is to furnish through them a typical social background. Against this conventional society, she places in clear, warm relief two figures: Lydgate, the representative of intellectual force; Dorothea, the representative of moral force. Both rebel against convention, both in their different ways are routed by the world.

In Dorothea, that sweet and bewildered person, a new type of heroine appears upon the stage. Dickens' liking went out to fragile, emotional, and kittenish young ladies. In Louisa Bounderby *of Hard Times,* we may perhaps catch, as she visits Stephen Blackpool, her husband's "hand," a hint of wider compassion; but the hint is of the faintest. Thackeray, in Ethel Newcome, showed a restless, spirited, brilliant creature, ill at ease in the only life open to her. But Dorothea is run in another mould from these. That curious sense of the organic whole, that modern craving for untrammeled fellowship, for which the term altruism is degrading and no other term exists, gathers intensely in her person, and is the source of the warm glow that streams through the dreary book. Dorothea is the first example noted in English fiction of that new personal type which suffers with atoning pain for the sorrows of the world. Her life fails. Wholly unguided, differing from the modern woman by her lack of any adequate training, or indeed of any training at all, she finds no cause for which to live, and had she found one, is too solely a creature of noble instincts to serve it effectively. Her marriage with Ladislaw can hardly be held more reassuring than that with Casaubon: for the brilliant young Bohemian—"a sort of a Shelley, you know," says Mr. Brooke—surely illustrates the frivolity of the forces of revolt, as conceived by George Eliot, against the solid background of English respectability, the Cadwalladers and Chethams and Bulstrodes and Brookes. Poor Dorothea! Her power has not yet changed from impulse to purpose. She represents only the second stage in the evolution of the modern heroine as a social force. The first is shown in the domestic and soft-hearted ladies of Thackeray and Dickens; the last, so far, appears in such characters as Besant's Valentine and Mrs. Ward's Marcella,—women strong to achieve in their activities and influence that large cooperation with the forces making for righteousness which earlier heroines never imagined nor desired, and which Dorothea only dreamed.

How George Eliot herself construed the significance of her Dorothea is evident from the Prelude to *Middlemarch*. She reminds us in a lovely passage of the great life of St. Theresa, and continues: "That Spanish woman who lived three hundred years ago was certainly not the last of her kind. Many Theresas have been born who found for themselves no epic life wherein there was a constant unfolding of far-resonant action: perhaps only a life of mistakes, the offspring of a certain spiritual grandeur ill-matched with the meanness of opportunity; perhaps a tragic failure which found no sacred poet, and sank unwept into oblivion. With dim lights and tangled circumstance, they tried to shape their thought and deed in noble agreement; but after all, to common eyes their struggle seemed mere inconsistency and formlessness: for these later-born Theresas were helped by no coherent social faith and order which could perform the function of knowledge for the ardently willing soul."

Middlemarch, to the author, was doubtless the epos of failure. It expressed her impassioned protest against modern society, with its lack of a "coherent social faith and order," its mammonism and dilettanteism, its conventional class-divisions, its utter inability to present to young, large, eager natures a cause to live and die for, an atmosphere in which they could expand. But to us, the book, with all its sadness, is full of hope. It marks the turn of the tide in modern fiction; for it shows characters in whom a new social idealism is stirring, and their very failure implies the promise of social salvation.

—Vida D. Scudder, "George Eliot and the Social Conscience," *Social Ideals in English Letters*, 1898, pp. 185–188

DANIEL DERONDA

George Saintsbury "Daniel Deronda" (1876)

George Saintsbury approaches his review with the assumption that through the years the reading public had gained a sound understanding of the nature of Eliot's art. Once again, the idea that Eliot depicted characters with great power, wit, and sympathy, but did so through intellectual rather than more obvious narrative skills, is reiterated. Saintsbury agreed with many contemporary critics that *Daniel Deronda* carried both these virtues and faults to the extreme: the portrayal of Gwendolen and Grandcourt was almost unanimously praised as an "overwhelming success." Deronda, who is made to express rather more abstract ideas, found little favor.

Saintsbury expressed disappointment with the "Jewish episode": not, he vigorously states, because of any latent anti-Semitism but because of its artistic treatment. It is hard to assess how much of these objections to the Jewish portions of the novel—and there were numerous objections—can be attributed to an instinctive dislike of the subject matter and how much to genuine artistic weaknesses. Eliot tried hard to integrate the Jewish episodes into the rest of the work, interweaving similar motifs and imagery. As Saintsbury stresses, Eliot tackles the same theme in *Daniel Deronda* as she does in her previous novels: "the excellence of obeying the instigations of kinship and duty rather than the opposing instinct." Yet it is hard to disagree with the critics who found the long, serious, visionary speeches of Mordecai unsatisfactory.

Independently of its interest as a mere story and as a vehicle for reflections, *Daniel Deronda* is eminently interesting, because it presents in a fresh and brilliant light the merits as well as the faults of its writer—merits and faults which are here sharply accentuated, and are not, as is too frequently the case, blurred and confused by the wearing of the plate. Both classes of peculiarities should be by this time pretty well known to the student of English letters. One the one hand, we are prepared to find, and we do find, an extraordinarily sustained and competent grasp of certain phases of character; a capacity of rendering minute effects of light and shade, attitudes, transient moods of mind, complex feelings and the like, which is simply unparalleled in any other prose writer; an aptitude for minting sharply ethical maxims; and a wonderful sympathy with humanity, so far, at least, as is congenial to the writer. On the wrong side of the account must be placed a tendency to talk about personages instead of allowing them to develop themselves, a somewhat lavish profusion of sententious utterance, a preference for technical terms in lieu of the common dialect which is the fitter language of the novelist, and a proneness to rank certain debateable positions and one-sided points of view among the truths to which it is safe to demand universal assent. To this black list must be added some decided faults in style. In discussing a book which is in everybody's hands, it will be well to show how the above points are brought out, and how they affect the general merit of the book, rather than to indulge in superfluous description of the plot.

In the matter of character, then, we find two signal triumphs of portraiture. The part of Gwendolen Harleth is throughout an over-whelming success: and the minutest and least friendly examination will hardly discover a false note or a dropped stitch. Her self-willed youth; the curious counterfeit of superiority in intellect and character, which her self-confidence and her ignorance of control temporarily give her; her instant surrender at the touch of material discomfort; the collapse of her confidence in the presence of a stronger spirit; the helpless outbursts of self-pity, of rage, of supplication, which follow that collapse; the struggle between blind hatred and almost equally blind glimmerings of conscience; the torrent of remorse and final prostration of will—are all imagined with a firmness, and succeed each other with an undoubted right of sequence, which cannot but command admiration. The husband is almost equally admirable; indeed, one's admiration is here increased by the perception that the hand which is so faithful is distinctly unfriendly, and that the author would like us to detest Grandcourt. Yet there is not the slightest exaggeration in the portrait, as he appears before us, acting with strict politeness to his wife, in no way violent towards her (if we except the occasional use of somewhat forcible language), and employing, for the purposes of his refined tyranny, nothing stronger than the methods of 'awful rule and right supremacy.' If he should appear to anyone all the more detestable, it may be suggested that it is difficult for any husband to extricate himself handsomely from the position of being hated by his wife and having that hatred confided to a bewitching rival.

The more study we give to these wonderful creations the better we like them, and an additional interest is imparted by the discovery that Gwendolen is at heart a counterfoil of Dorothea, animated by an undisciplined egotism instead of the fanaticism of sympathy. It might even suggest itself to a symmetrical imagination that the soul might of Casaubon clothed with the circumstances and temperament of a fine gentleman would animate just such a personage as Grandcourt. But these are fancies. The point of present importance is that the interest of the story undoubtedly tends to centre in these two admirable characters and is unfortunately not allowed to do so. Of the third (according to the author's design, the first) personage we cannot speak as we have just spoken. The blameless young man of faultless feature who clutches his coat-collor continually; who at the age of some twenty years wished 'to get rid of a merely English attitude in studies;' who, in the words of his best friend, was disposed 'to take an antediluvian point of view lest he should do injustice to the megatherium;' of whom it was impossible to believe, in the still more graphic words of the friend's sister, 'that he had a tailor's bill and used boot-hooks:' who never does a wicked thing, and never says one that is not priggish—is a person so intolerably dreadful that we not only dislike, but refuse to admit him as possible. Only once, perhaps, is he human—when he persuades himself on all sorts of ethico-physico-historical grounds that he should like to be a Jew, solely because (as that very sensible woman his mother, the Princess, discovers at once) he wishes to marry a fascinating Jewess. We cannot except as an excuse for the selection of this 'faultless monster' as hero the pleas put forward in the book that it is only the 'average man' and the 'dull man' that will not understand him, and that the average man is not very clear about the 'structure of his own retina,' and the dull man's 'dulness subsists, notwithstanding his lack of belief in it.' In the first place, the cases are not parallel: for, though the average man may know very little about the structure of his retina, he can tell a real eye from a glass one well enough. And, in the second place, the dull man may fairly retort, 'If you are a great novelist, *make* me believe in your characters.'

In this dearth, or rather distortion, of central interest, the minor characters do not help us much. They are far less individual, and far less elaborate than is usual in George Eliot. *Daniel Deronda* does not supply a fifth to join the noble quartette of Mdmes. Holt and Cadwallader, Poyser and Glegg. Sir Hugo Mallinger, with Hans Meyrick and his sister Mab, makes a shift to fill up the gap, but it is but a shift. Lapidoth, the unwelcome father, is chiefly welcome to us, the readers, because of the happy boldness of the incident which finally unites the lovers. Mordecai we must not, we suppose, call a minor character, but of him more hereafter.

There is no lack in these volumes of the exquisite cabinet pictures to which George Eliot has accustomed us. The account of Gwendolen's 'grounds of confidence;' the charming etching of the wagon passing Pennicote Rectory; the scene of the first ride with Grandcourt; Gwendolen, after Klesmer has crushed her hopes of artistic success, and again immediately before she at last accepts her lover; the wonderful sketch of Grandcourt 'sitting meditatively on a sofa and abstaining from literature;' Deronda in the synagogue; the stables at the Abbey; the waiting at Genoa for the Princess; and lastly, Gwendolen's retrospect of Offendene—are all effects of the finest in this kind. But this good gift and other good gifts have been somewhat repressed, as it seems to us, in order that certain tendencies not so excellent in themselves, and very much the reverse of excellent when unordinately indulged, might have freer play. No one can read *Daniel Deronda* without perceiving and regretting the singular way in which the characters are incessantly pushed back in order that the author may talk about them and about everything in heaven and earth while the action stands still. Very sparingly used this practice is not ineffective, but the unsparing use of it is certainly bad, especially when we consider in what kind of language these parabases or excursus are expressed. We cannot away (in a novel) with 'emotive memory' and 'dynamic quality,' with 'hymning of cancerous vices' and 'keenly perceptive sympathetic emotiveness,' with 'coercive types' and 'spiritual perpetuation,' still less with hundreds of phrases less quotable because bulkier. No doubt many of these expressions are appropriate enough, and they are all more or less intelligible to decently-educated people. No doubt the truths of science, mental and physical, are here, as elsewhere in our author's works, rendered with astonishing correctness and facility. But it appears to us that the technical language of psychology is as much out of place in prose fiction as illustration of its facts is appropriate. In philosophy, in politics, in religion, in art, a novelist, when he speaks in his own person, should have no opinion, should be of no sect, should indulge in no *argot*.

If we are dissatisfied with the Jewish episode which is so remarkable in this book, it is not merely because it has supplied temptations to indulge in psychological disquisition. We do not in the slightest degree feel 'imperfect sympathy' with Jews, and we hold that Shylock had the best of the argument. But the question here is whether the phase of Judaism now exhibited, the mystical enthusiasm for race and nation, has sufficient connexion with broad human feeling to be stuff for prose fiction to handle. We think that it has not, and we are not to be converted by references to the 'average man.' The average man has never experienced the passion of Hamlet, of Othello, or of Lear; he is not capable of the chivalry of Esmond, of the devotion of Des Grieux, of the charity of the Vicar of Wakefield. But he has experienced, and he is capable of, something of which all these sublime instances are merely exalted forms. Now the 'Samothracian mysteries of bottled moonshine' (to borrow a phrase from *Alton Locke*) into which Mordecai initiates Deronda are not thus connected with anything broadly human. They are not only 'will-worship,' but they have a provincial character which excludes fellow feeling. Poetry could legitimately treat them; indeed, many of Mordecai's traits may be recognized,—as we think, more happily placed—in the Sephardo of *The Spanish Gypsy*. They are, no doubt, interesting historically;

they shrow light on the character and aspirations of a curious people, and supply an admirable subject for a scientific monograph. But for all thus they are not the stuff of which the main interest or even a prominent interest, or anything but a very carefully reduced side interest, or prose novels should be wrought. It is hardly necessary to say that this dissatisfaction with the manner and scale of his appearances does not blind us to the skill applied in the construction of Mordecai. Probably no other living writer is capable of the patient care with which these intricate and unfamiliar paths are followed; certainly no other is master of the pathos which half reconciles the reluctant critic. If the thing was to be done, it could hardly have been done better, assuredly it could not have been done with greater cunning of analysis or in a manner more suggestive.

We should have no right to complain that to the simplicity and passion which characterise the subjects of the author's earlier books there has succeeded something more complex and analytic in the present: it is a time-honoured transition, and one which has before now yielded excellent results. But in reality the transition is not in this case great, because the subject-matter really remains the same although there may be somewhat less directness of treatment. The book is little more than a fresh variation on the theme which has informed so much of George Eliot's work, which lurks even in the *Scenes of Clerical Life*, which is hardly in abeyance in *Adam Bede*, which is the professed motive of *The Mill on the Floss*, of *The Spanish Gypsy*, and of *Romola*, which gives charm to the slightness of *Silas Marner*—to wit, the excellence of obeying the instigations of kinship and duty rather than the opposing instinct, 'All for Love and the World well Lost.' Perhaps the motive has hardly depth and volume enough to bear such constant application. But this is matter of opinion. The matter of fact remains, that we have one more presented to us in the contrast between Gwendolen's misery and the prosperity of the sleek Deronda the same moral as we had in Hetty's catastrophe, in the fate which punished Maggie Tulliver's partial declension from the standard, in the ruin and disgrace that sprang from Duke Silva's passion, in the degradation and death of Tito Melema; the same theories which led to the sympathetic selection of Felix Holt for a hero and of Dorothea Brooke for a heroine. The moral, and the standard, and the theories are doubtless of a fine severity, and deal deserved rebuke to the lax pleasure-seeking which has been considered a vice at all times, and is not openly considered a virtue even yet. In the illustrations of these doctrines the author has again given us admirable portraits, and much exquisitely-drawn surrounding. But perhaps she has also once more illustrated the immutable law that no perfect novel can ever be written in designed illustration of a theory, whether moral or immoral, and that art, like Atticus and the Turk, will bear no rival near the throne.

—GEORGE SAINTSBURY, "Daniel Deronda," *The Academy*, vol. 10, September 9, 1876, pp. 253–254

R.E. FRANCILLON "GEORGE ELIOT'S FIRST ROMANCE" (1876)

Robert Edward Francillon (1841–1919) was an English writer. Though initially in pursuit of a legal career, his attention turned to journalism and fiction. Much of Francillon's fiction was published in popular magazines; his novels include *Olympia* (1874) and *King or Knave?* (1888).

Francillon's response to *Daniel Deronda* is a clear-sighted reflection on the changes of fortune of the novel's reception. Francillon is correct in emphasizing that readers felt disoriented by the work; he also accurately guesses that the time would come when the importance of *Daniel Deronda* would be reassessed, as the more generous criticism of the last few decades indicates. Francillon seeks to give a sense of George Eliot's literary ambitions when embarking on her final novel and her attempts to expand the boundaries of the novel. Perhaps even more so than with *Middlemarch*, Eliot was attempting something new, which, Francillon argues, "calls for more special criticism."

When a great artist, whose very name has become a sure note of excellence, produces a work that the great fame-giving majority refuses to accept on the sole ground that it is his, or hers, there is a matter for dull congratulation. Such an event shows that past triumphs have been neither decreed blindly on the one hand, nor on the other accepted as a dispensation from the duty of making every new work a new and original title to future laurels. And such an event is the production of *Daniel Deronda*.

The author herself can have looked for no immediate fortune but that of battle. The very merits of the book are precisely the reverse of those to which the wide part of her fame is due. Not a few critics have already said that *Daniel Deronda* is not likely to extend George Eliot's reputation. That is unquestionably true—the sympathies to which it appeals are not, as in the case of *Adam Bede*, the common sympathies of all the world. But whether *Daniel Deronda* is not likely to *heighten* her reputation is an entirely different question, and will, I firmly believe, meet with a very different answer when certain natural and perhaps inevitable feelings of disappointment have passed away, and her two generations of admirers have reconciled themselves to seeing in her not only the natural historian of real life, whom we know and have known for twenty years, but also a great adept in the larger and fuller truth of romance, whom as yet we have only just begun to know.

Daniel Deronda is essentially, both in conception and in form, a Romance: and George Eliot has not only never written a romance before, but is herself, by the uncompromising realism of her former works, a main cause for the disesteem into which romantic fiction has fallen—a disesteem that has even turned the tea-cup into a heroine and the tea-spoon into a hero. George Eliot should be the last to complain that the inimitable realism *of Middlemarch* has thrown a cold shade over the truth and wisdom that borrow the form of less probable fiction in *Daniel Deronda*. She is in the position of every great artist who having achieved glory in one field sets out to conquer another. The world is not prone to believe in many-sided genius: one supremacy is enough for one man.

In short, I cannot help thinking that George Eliot's new novel has caused some passing disappointment because it is not another *Adam Bede* or *Middlemarch,* and not because it is *Daniel Deronda.* The first criticism of a book is sure to be founded on a comparison with others. Fortunately, *Daniel Deronda* lies so far outside George Eliot's other works in every important respect as to make direct comparison impossible. It cannot be classed as first, or second, or third, or last—that favourite but feeble make-shift for criticism, as if any book, or picture, or song could be called worse in itself because another is better, or better because another is worse. I believe that *Daniel Deronda* is absolutely good—and the whole language of criticism contains no stronger form of literary creed. Not only so, but I believe that it promises to secure for its author a more slowly growing, perhaps less universal, but deeper and higher fame than the works with which it does not enter into rivalry. In any case it marks an era in the career of the greatest English novelist of our time. It is as much a first novel, from a fresh hand and mind, as if no scene of clerical life had ever been penned. And, as such, it calls for more special criticism even than *Middlemarch*—the crown and the climax of the series that began with the sad fortunes of the Reverend Amos Barton. It is not even to be compared with *Romola*—that was no romance in the sense that the term must be applied to *Daniel Deronda* as the key to its place and nature.

However we may divide and subdivide, there are in reality only two distinct orders of fiction. Unfortunately, while we have a distinctive name for the one, we have none for the other. Perhaps the difference between the fiction which deals with ordinary or actual things and people and that which deals with extraordinary things and people is so marked and obvious that no names are wanted to express it any more than a scientific term is needed to express the difference between an eagle and a phoenix. The important point is that *Daniel Deronda* is very broadly distinguishable from all its predecessors by not dealing with types—with the ordinary people who make up the actual world, and with the circumstances, events, characteristics, and passions that are common to us all. We have all been so accustomed to see ourselves and all our relations and friends mirrored and dissected that we naturally expected to find the same familiar looking-glass or microscope in *Daniel Deronda*. It is small consolation to a plain man, who looks forward to the ever-new pleasure of examining his own photograph, to be presented with the portrait of a stranger, though the stranger may be handsomer and less common than he. Nevertheless it may well be that he will prize the picture most when he is in the mood to remember that the world does not consist wholly of types, and that the artist who ignores the existence of even improbable exceptions gives a very inadequate, nay, a very false representation of the *comedie humaine*.

—R.E. Francillon, "George Eliot's First Romance," *Gentleman's Magazine*, vol. 17, October 1876, pp. 411–413

Henry James "Daniel Deronda: A Conversation." (1876)

Henry James's fanciful conversation about *Daniel Deronda* rehearses some of the principal arguments made both for and against the novel, and echoes his own previous objections to *Middlemarch*. James once again shows a strong concern for form. Constantius, who most closely echoes James's views, describes the novel as a "little baggy," anticipating James's description of the "baggy monsters" of nineteenth century fiction in his preface to *The Tragic Muse*. Pulcheria joins Constantius in objecting to the novel's lack of "current": for her, "it is a series of lakes," or a looking-glass "lying in fragments."

Most readers, however, were more preoccupied with the success of the characters and the Jewish episodes. Again, James allows his characters to give representative views. Gwendolen is by and large pronounced a success, while, despite Theodora's timid arguments in his defence, the group agrees on Deronda's "priggish" nature. The Jewish episode provides an opportunity for flippancy, as it did for later critics such as Oliver Elton. Theodora once again provides a case for the defence, and, as a comparatively small number of critics felt, she argues that the "Jewish element" displayed "a large conception of what one may do in a novel." However, there is a consensus that these passages and the characters within them fail to come alive. James returns to the idea that Eliot's weakness lay in her intelligence, and her addiction, as Pulcheria declares, to "moralizing and philosophizing *a tout bout de champ*" which can make her "protacted, pretentious, pedantic." Despite the influence of Eliot's novel on James's writings, the dialogue is, in the final analysis, somewhat harsh on *Daniel Deronda*, and Theodora's enthusiasm takes a battering from her more forthright companions.

Theodora, one day early in the autumn, sat on her verandah with a piece of embroidery, the design of which she made up as she proceeded, being careful, however, to have a Japanese screen before her, to keep her inspiration at the proper altitude. Pulcheria, who was paying her a visit, sat near her with a closed book, in a paper cover, in her lap. Pulcheria was playing with the pug-dog, rather idly, but Theodora was stitching, steadily and meditatively. 'Well', said Theodora at last, 'I wonder what he accomplished in the East'. Pulcheria took the little dog into her lap and made him sit on the book. 'Oh', she replied, 'they had tea-parties at Jerusalem—exclusively of ladies—and he sat in the midst and stirred his tea and made high-toned remarks. And then Mirah sang a little, just a little, on account of her voice being so weak. Sit still, Fido', she continued, addressing the little dog, 'and keep your nose out of my face.' 'But it's a nice little nose, all the same', she pursued, 'a nice little short snub nose and not a horrid big Jewish nose. Oh, my dear, when I think what a collection of noses there must have been at that wedding!' At this moment Constantius steps upon the verandah from within, hat and stick in hand and his shoes a trifle dusty. He has some distance to come before he reaches the place where the ladies are sitting, and this gives Pulcheria time to murmur, 'Talk of snub noses!' Constantius is presented by Theodora to Pulcheria, and he sits down and exclaims upon the admirable blueness of the sea, which lies in a straight band across the green of the little lawn; comments too upon the pleasure of having one side of one's verandah in the shade. Soon Fido, the little dog, still restless, jumps off Pulcheria's lap and reveals the book, which lies title upward. 'Oh', says Constantius, 'you have been finishing *Daniel Deronda*?' Then follows a conversation which it will be more convenient to present in another form.

Theodora. Yes, Pulcheria has been reading aloud the last chapters to me. They are wonderfully beautiful.
Constantius. (after a moment's hesitation). Yes, they are very beautiful. I am sure you read well, Pulcheria, to give the fine passages their full value.

Theodora. She reads well when she chooses, but I am sorry to say that in some of the fine passages of this last book she took quite a false tone. I couldn't have read them aloud myself; I should have broken down. But Pulcheria—would you really believe it?—when she couldn't go on it was not for tears, but for—the contrary.

Constantius. For smiles? Did you really find it comical? One of my objections to *Daniel Deronda* is the absence of those delightfully humorous passages which enlivened the author's former works.

Plucheria. Oh, I think there are some places as amusing as anything in *Adam Bede* or *The Mill on the Floss*: for instance where, at the last, Deronda wipes Gwendolen's tears and Gwendolen wipes his.

Constantius. Yes, I know what you mean. I can understand that situation presenting a slightly ridiculous image; that is, if the current of the story don't swiftly carry you past.

Pulcheria. What do you mean by the current of the story? I never read a story with less current. It is not a river; it is a series of lakes. I once read of a group of little uneven ponds resembling, from a bird's-eye view, a looking-glass which had fallen upon the floor and broken, and was lying in fragments. That is what *Daniel Deronda* would look like, on a bird's-eye view.

Theodora. Pulcheria found that comparison in a French novel. She is always reading French novels.

Constantius. Ah, there are some very good ones.

Pulcheria (perversely). I don't know; I think there are some very poor ones.

Constantius. The comparison is not bad, at any rate. I know what you mean by *Daniel Deronda* lacking current. It has almost as little as *Romola*.

Pulcheria. Oh, *Romola is* unpardonably slow; it is a kind of literary tortoise.

Constantius. Yes, I know what you mean by that. But I am afraid you are not friendly to our great novelist.

Theodora. She likes Balzac and George Sand and other impure writers.

Constantius. Well, I must say I understand that.

Pulcheria. My favourite novelist is Thackeray, and I am extremely fond of Miss Austen.

Constantius. I understand that too. You read over *The Newcomes* and *Pride and Prejudice.*

Pulcheria. No, I don't read them over now; I think them over. I have been making visits for a long time past to a series of friends, and I have spent the last six months in reading *Daniel Deronda* aloud. Fortune would have it that I should always arrive by the same train as the new number. I am accounted a frivolous, idle creature; I am not a disciple in the new school of embroidery, like Theodora; so I was immediately pushed into a chair and the book thrust into my hand, that I might lift up my voice and make peace between all the impatiences that were snatching at it. So I may claim at least that I have read every word of the work. I never skipped.

Theodora. I should hope not, indeed!

Constantius. And do you mean that you really didn't enjoy it?

Pulcheria. I found it protracted, pretentious, pedantic.

Constantius. I see; I can understand that.

Theodora. Oh, you understand too much! This is the twentieth time you have used that formula.

Constantius. What will you have? You know I must try to understand; it's my trade!

Theodora. He means he writes reviews. Trying *not* to understand is what I call that trade!

Constantius. Say then I take it the wrong way; that is why it has never made my fortune. But I do try to understand; it is my—my— (He pauses).

Theodora. I know what you want to say. Your strong side.

Pulcheria. And what is his weak side?

Theodora. He writes novels.

Constantius. I have written *one. You* can't call that a side. It's a little facet, at the most.

Pulcheria. You talk as if you were a diamond. I should like to read it—not aloud!

Constantius. You can't read it softly enough. But you, Theodora, you didn't find our book too 'protracted'?

Theodora. I should have liked it to continue indefinitely; to keep coming out always; to be one of the regular things of life.

Pulcheria. Oh, come here, little dog! To think that *Daniel Deronda* might be perpetual when you, little short-nosed darling, can't last at the most more than nine or ten years!

Theodora. A book like *Daniel Deronda* becomes part of one's life; one lives in it, or alongside of it. I don't hesitate to say that I have been living in this one for the last eight months. It is such a complete world George Eliot builds up; it is so vast, so much-embracing! It has such a firm earth and such an ethereal sky. You can turn into it and lose yourself in it.

Pulcheria. Oh, easily, and die of cold and starvation!

Theodora. I have been very near to poor Gwendolen and very near to that sweet Mirah. And the dear little Meyricks also; I know them intimately well.

Pulcheria. The Meyricks, I grant you, are the best thing in the book.

Theodora. They are a delicious family; I wish they lived in Boston. I consider Herr Klesmer almost Shakespearean, and his wife is almost as good. I have been near to poor, grand Mordecai—

Pulcheria. Oh, reflect, my dear; not too near!

Theodora. And as for Deronda himself I freely confess that I am consumed with a hopeless passion for him. He is the most irresistible man in the literature of fiction.

Pulcheria. He is not a man at all.

Theodora. I remember nothing more beautiful than the description of his childhood, and that picture of his lying on the grass in the abbey cloister, a beautiful seraph-faced boy, with a lovely voice, reading history and asking his Scotch tutor why the Popes had so many nephews. He must have been delightfully handsome.

Pulcheria. Never, my dear, with that nose! I am sure he had a nose, and I hold that the author has shown great pusillanimity in her treatment of it. She has quite shirked it. The picture you speak of is very pretty, but a picture is not a person. And why is he always grasping his coat-collar, as if he wished to hang himself up? The author had an uncomfortable feeling that she must make him do something real, something visible and sensible, and she hit upon that clumsy figure. I don't see what you mean by saying you have been *near* those people; that is just what one is not. They produce no illusion. They are described and analysed to death, but we don't see them nor hear them nor touch them. Deronda clutches his coat-collar, Mirah crosses her feet, Mordecai talks like the Bible; but that doesn't make real figures of them. They have no existence outside of the author's study.

Theodora. If you mean that they are nobly imaginative I quite agree with you; and if they say nothing to your own imagination the fault is yours, not theirs.

Pulcheria. Pray don't say they are Shakespearean again. Shakespeare went to work another way.

Constantius. I think you are both in a measure right; there is a distinction to be drawn. There are in *Daniel Deronda* the figures based upon observation and the figures based upon invention. This distinction, I know, is rather a rough one. There are no figures in any novel that are pure observation, and none that are pure invention. But either element may preponderate, and in those cases in which invention has preponderated George Eliot seems to me to have achieved at the best but so many brilliant failures.

Theodora. And are *you* turning severe? I thought you admired her so much.

Constantius. I defy any one to admire her more, but one must discriminate. Speaking brutally, I consider *Daniel Deronda* the weakest of her books. It strikes me as very sensibly inferior to *Middlemarch*. I have an immense opinion of *Middlemarch*.

Pulcheria. Not having been obliged by circumstances to read *Middlemarch* to other people, I didn't read it at all. I couldn't read it to myself. I tried, but I broke down. I appreciated Rosamond, but I couldn't believe in Dorothea.

Theodora (very gravely). So much the worse for you, Pulcheria. I have enjoyed *Daniel Deronda* because I had enjoyed *Middlemarch*. Why should you throw *Middlemarch* up against her? It seems to me that if a book is fine it is fine. I have enjoyed *Deronda* deeply, from beginning to end.

Constantius. I assure you, so have I. I can read nothing of George Eliot's without enjoyment. I even enjoy her poetry, though I don't approve of it. In whatever she writes I enjoy her intelligence; it has space and air like a fine landscape. The intellectual brilliancy of *Daniel Deronda* strikes me as very great, in excess of anything the author has done. In the first couple of numbers of the book this ravished me. I delighted in its deep, rich English tone, in which so many notes seemed melted together.

Pulcheria. The tone is not English, it is German.

Constantius. I understand that—if Theodora will allow me to say so. Little by little I began to feel that I cared less for certain notes than for others. I say it under my breath—I began to feel an occasional temptation to skip. Roughly speaking, all the Jewish burden of the story tended to weary me; it is this part that produces the poor illusion which I agree with Pulcheria in finding. Gwendolen and Grandcourt are admirable—Gwendolen is a masterpiece. She is known, felt and presented, psychologically, altogether in the grand manner. Beside her and beside her husband—a consummate picture of English brutality refined and distilled (for Grandcourt is before all things brutal), Deronda, Mordecai and Mirah are hardly more than shadows. They and their fortunes are all improvisation. I don't say anything against improvisation. When it succeeds it has a surpassing charm. But it must succeed. With George Eliot it seems to me to succeed, but a little less than one would expect of her talent. The story of Deronda's life, his mother's story, Mirah's story, are quite the sort of thing one finds in George Sand. But they are really not so good as they would be in George Sand. George Sand would have carried it off with a lighter hand.

Theodora. Oh, Constantius, how can you compare George Eliot's novels to that woman's? It is sunlight and moonshine.

Pulcheria. I really think the two writers are very much alike. They are both very voluble, both addicted to moralizing and philosophizing *a tout bout de champ*, both inartistic.

Constantius. I see what you mean. But George Eliot is solid, and George Sand is liquid. When occasionally George Eliot liquefies—as in the history of Deronda's birth, and in that of Mirah—it is not to so crystalline a clearness as the author of *Consuelo* and *Andre*. Take Mirah's long narrative of her adventures, when she unfolds them to Mrs. Meyrick. It is arranged, it is artificial, *ancien jeu,* quite in the George Sand manner. But George Sand would have done it better. The false tone would have remained, but it would have been more persuasive. It would have been a fib, but the fib would have been neater.

Theodora. I don't think fibbing neatly a merit, and I don't see what is to be gained by such comparisons. George Eliot is pure and George Sand is impure; how can you compare them? As for the Jewish element in Deronda, I think it a very fine idea; it's a noble subject. Wilkie Collins and Miss Braddon would not have thought of it, but that does not condemn it. It shows a large conception of what one may do in a novel. I heard you say, the other day, that most novels were so trivial—that they had no general ideas. Here is a general idea, the idea interpreted by Deronda. I have never disliked the Jews as some people do; I am not like Pulcheria, who sees a Jew in every bush. I wish there were one; I would cultivate shrubbery. I have known too many clever and charming Jews; I have known none that were not clever.

Pulcheria. Clever, but not charming.

Constantius. I quite agree with you as to Deronda's going in for the Jews and turning out a Jew himself being a fine subject, and this quite apart from the fact of whether such a thing as a Jewish revival be at all a possibility. If it be a possibility, so much the better—so much the better for the subject, I mean.

Pulcheria. A la bonne heure!

Constantius. I rather suspect it is not a possibility; that the Jews in general take themselves much less seriously than that. They have other fish to fry. George Eliot takes them as a person outside of Judaism—aesthetically. I don't believe that is the way they take themselves.

Pulcheria. They have the less excuse then for keeping themselves so dirty.

Theodora. George Eliot must have known some delightful Jews.

Constantius. Very likely; but I shouldn't wonder if the most delightful of them had smiled a trifle, here and there, over her book. But that makes nothing, as Herr Klesmer would say. The subject is a noble one. The idea of depicting a nature able to feel and worthy to feel the sort of inspiration that takes possession of Deronda, of depicting it sympathetically, minutely and intimately—such an idea has great elevation. There is something very fascinating in the mission that Deronda takes upon himself. I don't quite know what it means, I don't understand more than half of Mordecai's rhapsodies, and I don't perceive exactly what practical steps could be taken. Deronda could go about and talk with clever Jews—not an unpleasant life.

Pulcheria. All that seems to me so unreal that when at the end the author fords herself confronted with the necessity of making him start for the East by the train, and announces that Sir Hugo and Lady Mallinger have given his wife 'a complete Eastern outfit', I descend to the ground with a ludicrous jump.

Constantius. Unreal, if you please; that is no objection to it; it greatly tickles my imagination. I like extremely the idea of Mordecai believing, without ground of belief, that if he only wait, a young man on whom nature and society have centred all their gifts will come to him and receive from his hands the precious vessel of his hopes. It is romantic, but it is not vulgar romance; it is finely romantic. And there is something very fine in the author's own feeling about Deronda. He is a very liberal creation. He is, I think, a failure—a brilliant failure; if he had been a success I should call him a splendid creation. The author meant to do things very handsomely for him; she meant apparently to make a faultless human being.

Pulcheria. She made a dreadful prig.

Constantius. He *is* rather priggish, and one wonders that so clever a woman as George Eliot shouldn't see it.

Pulcheria. He has no blood in his body. His attitude at moments is like that of a high-priest in a *tableau vivant.*

Theodora. Pulcheria likes the little gentlemen in the French novels who take good care of their attitudes, which are always the same attitude, the attitude of 'conquest'—of a conquest that tickles their vanity. Deronda has a contour that cuts straight through the middle of all that. He is made of a stuff that isn't dreamt of in their philosophy.

Pulcheria. Pulcheria likes very much a novel which she read three or four years ago, but which she has not forgotten. It was by Ivan Turgenieff, and it was called *On the Eve.* Theodora has read it, I know, because she admires Turgenieff, and Constantius has read it, I suppose, because he had read everything.

Constantius. If I had no reason but that for my reading, it would be small. But Turgenieff is my man.

Pulcheria. You were just now praising George Eliot's general ideas. The tale of which I speak contains in the portrait of the hero very much such a general idea as you find in the portrait of Deronda. Don't you remember the young Bulgarian student, Inssaroff, who gives himself the mission of rescuing his country from its subjection to the Turks a Poor man, if he had foreseen the horrible summer of 1876! His character is the picture of a race-passion, of patriotic hopes and dreams. But what a difference in the vividness of the two figures. Inssaroff is a man; he stands up on his feet; we see him, hear him, touch him. And it has taken the author but a couple of hundred pages—not eight volumes—to do it.

Theodora. I don't remember Inssaroff at all, but I perfectly remember the heroine, Helena. She is certainly most remarkable; but remarkable as she is, I should never dream of calling her as wonderful as Gwendolen.

Constantius. Turgenieff is a magician, which I don't think I should call George Eliot. One is a poet, the other is a philosopher. One cares for the aspect of things and the other cares for the reason of things. George Eliot, in embarking with Deronda, took aboard, as it were, a far heavier cargo than Turgenieff with his Inssaroff: She proposed, consciously, to strike more notes.

Pulcheria. Oh, consciously, yes!

Constantius. George Eliot wished to show the possible picturesqueness—the romance, as it were—of a high moral tone. Deronda is a moralist—a moralist with a rich complexion.

Theodora. It is a most beautiful nature. I don't know anywhere a more complete, a more deeply analysed portrait of a great nature. We praise novelists for wandering and creeping so into the small corners of the mind. That is what we praise Balzac for when he gets down upon all fours to crawl through *Le Pere Goriot* or *Les Parents Pauvres*. But I must say I think it a finer thing to unlock with as firm a hand as George Eliot some of the greater chambers of human character. Deronda is in a manner an ideal character, if you will, but he seems to me triumphantly married to reality. There are some admirable things said about him; nothing can be finer than those pages of description of his moral temperament in the fourth book—his elevated way of looking at things, his impartiality, his universal sympathy, and at the same time his fear of their turning into mere irresponsible indifference. I remember some of it verbally: 'He was ceasing to care for knowledge—he had no ambition for practice—unless they could be gathered up into one current with his emotions.'

Pulcheria. Oh, there is plenty about his emotions. Everything about him is 'emotive'. That bad word occurs on every fifth page.

Theodora. I don't see that it is a bad word.

Pulcheria. It may be good German, but it is poor English.

Theodora. It is not German at all; it is Latin. So, my dear!

Pulcheria. As I say, then, it is not English.

Theodora. This is the first time I ever heard that George Eliot's style was bad!

Constantius. It is admirable; it has the most delightful and the most intellectually comfortable suggestions. But it is occasionally a little too long-sleeved, as I may say. It is sometimes too loose a fit for the thought, a little baggy.

Theodora. And the advice he gives Gwendolen, the things he says to her, they are the very essence of wisdom, of warm human wisdom, knowing life and feeling it. 'Keep your fear as a safeguard, it may make consequences passionately present to you.' What can be better than that?

Pulcheria. Nothing, perhaps. But what can be drearier than a novel in which the function of the hero—young, handsome and brilliant—is to give didactic advice, in a proverbial form, to the young, beautiful and brilliant heroine?

Constantius. That is not putting it quite fairly. The function of Deronda is to make Gwendolen fall in love with him, to say nothing of falling in love himself with Mirah.

Pulcheria. Yes, the less said about that the better. All we know about Mirah is that she has delicate rings of hair, sits with her feet crossed, and talks like an article in a new magazine.

Constantius. Deronda's function of adviser to Gwendolen does not strike me as so ridiculous. He is not nearly so ridiculous as if he were lovesick. It is a very interesting situation—that of a man with whom a beautiful woman in trouble falls in love and yet whose affections are so preoccupied that the most he can do for her in return is to enter kindly and sympathetically into her position, pity her and talk to her. George Eliot always gives us something that is strikingly and ironically characteristic of human life; and what savours more of the essential crookedness of our fate than the sad cross-purposes of these two young people? Poor Gwendolen's falling in love with Deronda is part of her own luckless history, not of his.

Theodora. I do think he takes it to himself rather too little. No man had ever so little vanity.

Pulcheria. It is very inconsistent, therefore, as well as being extremely impertinent and ill-mannered, his buying back and sending to her her necklace at Leubronn.

Constantius. Oh, you must concede that; without it there would have been no story. A man writing of him, however, would certainly have made him more peccable. As George Eliot lets herself go, in that quarter, she becomes delightfully, almost touchingly, feminine. It is like her making Romola go to housekeeping with Tessa, after Tito Melema's death; like her making Dorothea marry Will Ladislaw. If Dorothea had married any one after her misadventure with Casaubon, she would have married a trooper.

Theodora. Perhaps some day Gwendolen will marry Rex.

Pulcheria. Pray, who is Rex?

Theodora. Why, Pulcheria, how can you forget?

Pulcheria. Nay, how can I remember? But I recall such a name in the dim antiquity of the first or second book. Yes, and then he is pushed to the front again at the last, just in time not to miss the falling of the curtain. Gwendolen will certainly not have the audacity to marry any one we know so little about.

Constantius. I have been wanting to say that there seems to me to be two very distinct elements in George Eliot—a spontaneous one and an artificial one. There is what she is by inspiration and what she is because it is expected of her. These two heads have been very perceptible in her recent writings; they are much less noticeable in her early ones.

Theodora. You mean that she is too scientific? So long as she remains the great literary genius that she is, how can she be too scientific? She is simply permeated with the highest culture of the age.

Pulcheria. She talks too much about the 'dynamic quality' of people's eyes. When she uses such a phrase as that in the first sentence in her book she is not a great literary genius, because she shows a want of tact. There can't be a worse limitation.

Constantius. The 'dynamic quality' of Gwendolen's glance has made the tour of the world.

Theodora. It shows a very low level of culture on the world's part to be agitated by a term perfectly familiar to all decently educated people.

Pulcheria. I don't pretend to be decently educated; pray tell me what it means.

Constantius (promptly). I think Pulcheria has hit it in speaking of a want of tact. In the manner of the book, throughout, there is something that one may call a want of tact. The epigraphs in verse are a want of tact; they are sometimes, I think, a trifle more, pretentious than really pregnant; the importunity of the moral reflections is a want of tact; the very diffuseness is a want of tact. But it comes back to what I said just now about one's sense of the author writing under a sort of external pressure. I began to notice it in *Felix Holt*; I don't think I had before. She strikes me as a person who certainly has naturally a taste for general considerations, but who has fallen upon an age and a circle which have compelled her to give them an exaggerated attention. She does not strike me as naturally a critic, less still as naturally a sceptic; her spontaneous part is to observe life and to feel it—to feel it with admirable depth. Contemplation, sympathy and faith—something like that, I should say, would have been her natural scale. If she had fallen upon an age of enthusiastic assent to old articles of faith, it seems to me possible that she would have had a more perfect, a more consistent and graceful development than she has actually had. If she had cast herself into such a current—her genius being equal—it might have carried her to splendid distances. But she has chosen to go into criticism, and to the critics she addresses her work; I mean the critics of the universe. Instead of feeling life itself, it is 'views' upon life that she tries to feel.

Pulcheria. She is the victim of a first-class education. I am so glad!

Constantius. Thanks to her admirable intellect she philosophizes very sufficiently; but meanwhile she has given a chill to her genius. She has come near spoiling an artist.

Pulcheria. She has quite spoiled one. Or rather I shouldn't say that, because there was no artist to spoil. I maintain that she is not an artist. An artist could never have put a story together so monstrously ill. She has no sense of form.

Theodora. Pray, what could be more artistic than the way that Deronda's paternity is concealed till almost the end, and the way we are made to suppose Sir Hugo is his father?

Pulcheria. And Mirah his sister. How does that fit together? I was as little made to suppose he was not a Jew as I cared when I found out he was. And his mother popping up through a trap-door and popping down again, at the last, in that scrambling fashion! His mother is very bad.

Constantius. I think Deronda's mother is one of the unvivified characters; she belongs to the cold half of the book. All the Jewish part is at bottom cold; that is my only objection. I have enjoyed it because my fancy often warms cold things; but beside Gwendolen's history it is like the empty half of the lunar disk beside the full one. It is admirably studied, it is imagined, it is understood, but it is not embodied. One feels this strongly in just those scenes between Deronda and his mother; one feels that one has been appealed to on rather an artificial ground of interest. To make Deronda's reversion to his native faith more dramatic and profound, the author has given him a mother who on very arbitrary grounds, apparently, has separated herself from this same faith and who has been kept waiting in the wing, as it were, for many acts, to come on and make her speech and say so. This moral situation of hers we are invited retrospectively to appreciate. But we hardly care to do so.

Pulcheria. I don't *see* the princess, in spite of her flame-coloured robe. Why should an actress and prima-donna care so much about religious matters?

Theodora. It was not only that; it was the Jewish race she hated, Jewish manners and looks. You, my dear, ought to understand that.

Pulcheria. I do, but I am not a Jewish actress of genius; I am not what Rachel was. If I were I should have other things to think about.

Constantius. Think now a little about poor Gwendolen.

Pulcheria. I don't care to think about her. She was a second-rate English girl who got into a flutter about a lord.

Theodora. I don't see that she is worse than if she were a first-rate American girl who should get into exactly the same flutter.

Pulcheria. It wouldn't be the same flutter at all; it wouldn't be any flutter. She wouldn't be afraid of the lord, though she might be amused at him.

Theodora. I am sure I don't perceive whom Gwendolen was afraid of. She was afraid of her misdeed—her broken promise—after she had committed it, and through that fear she was afraid of her husband. Well she might be! I can imagine nothing more vivid than the sense we get of his absolutely clammy selfishness.

Pulcheria. She was not afraid of Deronda when, immediately after her marriage and without any but the most casual acquaintance with him, she begins to hover about him at the Mallingers' and to drop little confidences about her conjugal woes. That seems to me very indelicate; ask any woman.

Constantius. The very purpose of the author is to give us an idea of the sort of confidence that Deronda inspired—its irresistible potency.

Pulcheria. A lay father-confessor—horrid!

Constantius. And to give us an idea also of the acuteness of Gwendolen's depression, of her haunting sense of impending trouble.

Theodora. It must be remembered that Gwendolen was in love with Deronda from the first, long before she knew it. She didn't know it, poor girl, but that was it.

Pulcheria. That makes the matter worse. It is very disagreeable to see her hovering and rustling about a man who is indifferent to her.

Theodora. He was not indifferent to her, since he sent her back her necklace.

Pulcheria. Of all the delicate attention to a charming girl that I ever heard of, that little pecuniary transaction is the most felicitous.

Constantius. You must remember that he had been *en rapport* with her at the gaming-table. She had been playing in defiance of his observation, and he, continuing to observe her, had been in a measure responsible for her loss. There was a tacit consciousness of this between them. You may contest the possibility of tacit consciousness going so far, but that is not a serious objection. You may point out two or three weak spots in detail; the fact remains that Gwendolen's whole history is vividly told. And see how the girl is known, inside out, how thoroughly she is felt and understood. It is the most *intelligent* thing in all George Eliot's writing, and that is saying much. It is so deep, so true, so complete, it holds such a wealth of psychological detail, it is more than masterly.

Theodora. I don't know where the perception of character has sailed closer to the wind.

Pulcheria. The portrait may be admirable, but it has one little fault. You don't care a straw for the original. Gwendolen is not an interesting girl, and when the author tries to invest her with a deep tragic interest she does so at the expense of consistency. She has made her at the outset too light, too flimsy; tragedy has no hold on such a girl.

Theodora. You are hard to satisfy. You said this morning that Dorothea was too heavy, and now you find Gwendolen too light. George Eliot wished to give us the perfect counterpart of Dorothea. Having made one portrait she was worthy to make the other.

Pulcheria. She has committed the fatal error of making Gwendolen vulgarly, pettily, drily selfish. She was *personally* selfish.

Theodora. I know nothing more personal than selfishness.

Pulcheria. I am selfish, but I don't go about with my chin out like that; at least I hope I don't. She was an odious young woman, and one can't care what becomes of her. When her marriage turned out ill she would have become still more hard and positive; to make her soft and appealing is very bad logic. The second Gwendolen doesn't belong to the first.

Constantius. She is perhaps at the first a little childish for the weight of interest she has to carry, a little too much after the pattern of the unconscientious young ladies of Miss Yonge and Miss Sewell.

Theodora. Since when is it forbidden to make one's heroine young? Gwendolen is a perfect picture of youthfulness—its eagerness, its presumption, its preoccupation with itself, its vanity and silliness, its sense of its own absoluteness. But she is extremely intelligent and clever, and therefore tragedy *can* have a hold upon her. Her conscience doesn't make the tragedy; that is an old story and, I think, a secondary form of suffering. It is the tragedy that makes her conscience, which then reacts upon it; and I can think of nothing more powerful than the way in which the growth of her conscience is traced, nothing more touching than the picture of its helpless maturity.

Constantius. That is perfectly true. Gwendolen's history is admirably typical—as most things are with George Eliot: it is the very stuff that human life is made of. What is it made of but the discovery by each of us that we are at the best but a rather ridiculous fifth wheel to the coach, after we have sat cracking our whip and believing that we are at least the coachman in person? We think we are the main hoop to the barrel, and we turn out to be but a very incidental splinter in one of the staves. The universe forcing itself with a slow, inexorable pressure into a narrow, complacent, and yet after all extremely sensitive mind, and making it ache with the pain of the process—that is Gwendolen's story. And it becomes completely characteristic in that her supreme perception of the fact that the world is whirring past her is in the disappointment not of a base but of an exalted passion. The very chance to embrace what the author is so fond of calling a 'larger life' seems refused to her. She is punished for being narrow, and she is not allowed a chance to expand: Her finding Deronda pre-engaged to go to the East and stir up the race-feeling of the Jews strikes me as a wonderfully happy invention. The irony of the situation, for poor Gwendolen, is almost grotesque, and it makes one wonder whether the whole heavy structure of the Jewish question in the story was not built up by the author for the express purpose of giving its proper force to this particular stroke.

Theodora. George Eliot's intentions are extremely complex. The mass is for each detail and each detail is for the mass.

Pulcheria. She is very fond of deaths by drowning. Maggie Tulliver and her brother are drowned, Tito Melema is drowned, Mr. Grandcourt is drowned. It is extremely unlikely that Grandcourt should not have known how to swim.

Constantius. He did, of course, but he had a cramp. It served him right. I can't imagine a more consummate representation of the most detestable kind of Englishman—the Englishman who thinks it low to articulate. And in Grandcourt the type and the individual are so happily met: the type with its sense of the proprieties and the individual with his absence of all sense. He is the apotheosis of dryness, a human expression of the simple idea of the perpendicular.

Theodora. Mr. Casaubon, in *Middlemarch,* was very dry too; and yet what a genius it is that can give us two disagreeable husbands who are so utterly different!

Pulcheria. You must count the two disagreeable wives too—Rosamond Vincy and Gwendolen. They are very much alike. I know the author didn't mean it; it proves how common a type the worldly, *pincée*, selfish young woman seemed to her. They are both disagreeable; you can't get over that.

Constantius. There is something in that, perhaps, I think, at any rate, that the secondary people here are less delightful than in *Middlemarch*; there is nothing so good as Mary Garth and her father, or the little old lady who steals sugar, or the parson who is in love with Mary, or the country relatives of old Mr. Featherstone. Rex Gascoigne is not so good as Fred Vincy.

Theodora. Mr. Gascoigne is admirable, and Mrs. Davilow is charming.

Pulcheria. And you must not forget that you think Herr Klesmer 'Shakespearean'. Wouldn't 'Wagnerian' be high enough praise?

Constantius. Yes, one must make an exception with regard to the Klesmers and the Meyricks. They are delightful, and as for Klesmer himself, and Hans Meyrick, Theodora may maintain her epithet. Shakespearean characters are characters that are born of the *overflow* of observation—characters that make the drama seem multitudinous, like life. Klesmer comes in with a sort of Shakespearean 'value', as a painter would say, and so, in a different tone, does Hans Meyrick. They spring from a much-peopled mind.

Theodora. I think Gwendolen's confrontation with Klesmer one of the finest things in the book.

Constantius. It is like everything in George Eliot; it will bear thinking of.

Pulcheria. All that is very fine, but you cannot persuade me that *Deronda* is not a very ponderous and ill-made story. It has nothing that one can call a subject. A silly young girl and a solemn, sapient young man who doesn't fall in love with her! That is the *donnée* of eight monthly volumes. I call it very flat. Is that what the exquisite art of Thackeray and Miss Austen and Hawthorne has come to? I would as soon read a German novel outright.

Theodora. There is something higher than form—there is spirit.

Constantius. I am afraid Pulcheria is sadly aesthetic. She had better confine herself to Merimee.

Pulcheria. I shall certainly to-day read over *La Double Meprise*.

Theodora. Oh, my dear, *y pensez-vous*?

Constantius. Yes, I think there is little art in *Deronda*, but I think there is a vast amount of life. In life without art you can find your account; but art without life is a poor affair. The book is full of the world.

Theodora. It is full of beauty and knowledge, and that is quite art enough for me.

Pulcheria (to the little dog). We are silenced, darling, but we are not convinced, are we? (The pug begins to bark.) No, we are not even silenced. It's a young woman with two bandboxes.

Theodora. Oh, it must be our muslins!
Constantius (rising to go). I see what you mean!

—HENRY JAMES, "Daniel Deronda:
A Conversation," *The Atlantic Monthly*, vol. 38,
December 1876, pp. 684–694

JOSEPH JACOBS "MORDECAI: A PROTEST AGAINST THE CRITICS" (1877)

Joseph Jacobs (1854–1916) was an Australian historian and folklorist. After completing his education at Cambridge, Jacobs became acquainted with a circle of London Jewish intellectuals called the Wanderers and published a number of works on Jewish history and identity. Jacobs also achieved success as the editor of volumes of fairy tales and editor of *Folklore Magazine*. In 1900, Jacobs immigrated with his family to the United States to work on the *Jewish Encyclopaedia* and, later, as editor of *American Hebrew*.

Jacobs's passionate defense of the Jewish episodes of *Daniel Deronda* opens with an analysis of the novel that would have disheartened Eliot: for Jacobs, as for many readers, the novel is made of "two almost unconnected parts," despite Eliot's strenuous efforts to unite the work through both theme and language. However, Jacobs goes on to defend the most vulnerable part of the novel. Jacob twice expresses the "gratitude" of the Jewish community for Eliot's portrayal of them, something that is confirmed by the numerous letters of thanks received by the novelist. Jacobs recalls the negative portrayals of Jewish characters in contemporary fiction and laments the lack of interest displayed by critics and readers in the far more realistic portraits offered by Eliot. Jacobs's expression of gratitude is all the more poignant when juxtaposed with Oliver Elton's dismissal that Deronda "is not a Jew" because he does not fulfill certain stereotypes.

Jacobs does not simply defend the novel for its sympathetic portrayal but also in terms of artistic criteria. Lack of interest in the Jewish characters has led to a misunderstanding of the tragic effects for which Eliot was striving. In somewhat exaggerated terms, he argues that the meeting between Deronda and Mordecai on the bridge should be rehabilitated as "perhaps the most remarkable incident in English fiction," a moment of Wagnerian or Shakespearean intensity. Jacobs is rather too generous in his estimate of the artistic success of Mordecai's characterization. However, he makes a bold case for the importance of approaching these episodes with the sympathetic outlook that George Eliot had set out to defend and embody since her first work of fiction. Nevertheless, Jacobs did not convert many readers to his point of view.

The critics have had their say: the recording angels of literature, more sorrowful than angry, have written down *Daniel Deronda* a failure. And there seems to be at least this much of truth in their judgment, that one of the parts of which the book is composed has failed to interest or even to reach its audience. For the least observant reader must have noticed that *Daniel Deronda* is made up of two almost unconnected parts, either of which can be read without the other. Every "book" after the first is divided into two parts, whose only claim to be included under the same covers is the common action or inaction of the eponymous hero. One set of characters and interests centres round the fate and fortunes of Gwendolen Harleth, and of this part of the book we can surely say that it has excited as much interest and bitten as deeply into men's minds as any of the author's previous studies of female character. Indeed, we would submit that George Eliot's last portrait of female egoism is in many ways her best; her hand has become more tender, and, because more tender, more true than when she drew such narrow types as Hetty Sorrel and Rosamond Vincy, so unnaturally consistent in their selfishness. The story of Gwendolen Harleth's purification from egoism is, then, one might say, even a greater success than the former pictures of girlish struggles, and displays the author's distinguishing excellences in undiminished brilliancy. But there is another part of the book with which the English-speaking public and its literary "tasters" have failed to sympathise, and which they have mostly been tempted to omit on reperusal. The tragedy of Mordecai Cohen's missionary labours, on which the author has spent immense labour of invention and research, must be pronounced to have completely failed in reaching and exciting the interest and sympathy of the ordinary reader. Mr. Bagehot has told us that the greatest pain man can feel is the pain of a new idea, and the readers of *Daniel Deronda* have refused painfully to assimilate the new idea of the Mordecai part of the book. This idea we take to be that Judaism stands on the same level as Christianity, perhaps even on a higher level, in point of rationality and capacity to satisfy the wants of the religious consciousness, "the hitherto neglected reality," to use the author's own words (ii. 292), "that Judaism is something still throbbing in human lives, still making for them the only conceivable vesture of the world." The difficulty of accepting this new idea comes out most prominently in the jar most readers must have felt in the omission of any explanation of the easy transition of Deronda from the Christianity in which he was bred to the Judaism into which he had been born.

The present notice proposes to discuss the failure of this unsuccessful part, from the standpoint of one for whom this initial difficulty does not exist, and who has from his childhood seen the world habited in those Hebrew Old Clothes of which Mr. Carlyle and others have spoken so slightingly. And the first thing that it is natural for a Jew to say about *Daniel Deronda* is some expression of gratitude for the wonderful completeness and accuracy with which George Eliot has portrayed the Jewish nature. Hitherto the Jew in English fiction has fared unhappily, being always represented as a monstrosity, most frequently on the side of malevolence and greed, as in Marlowe's Barabas and Dickens's Fagin, or sometimes, as in Dickens's Riah, still more exasperatingly on the side of impossible benevolence. What we want is truth, not exaggeration, and truth George Eliot has given us with the large justice of the great artist. The gallery of Jewish portraits contained in *Daniel Deronda* gives in a marvellously full and accurate way all the many sides of our complex national character. The artistic element, with the proper omission of painting and sculpture, in which Jews, though eminent, have not been pre-eminent, is well represented by Klesmer, Mirah, and the Alcharisi. Ezra Cohen is a type of the commonplace Jew, the familiar figure of prosperous mercantile dealing, the best-known trait of Jews to Englishmen; while little Jacob exhibits in a very humorous form the well-known precocity of Jewish children. The affectionate relations of Ezra Cohen and his mother, and the tender respect of Mordecai and Mirah for the memory of theirs, point to the exceptional influence of the Mother and the Home in the inner life of Jews. Then in Kalonymos, whom we feel tempted to call the Wandering Jew, we get the nomadic spirit which has worked in Israel from times long previous to the Dispersion, while all must join in the scorn the author evidently feels for Pash, the Jew who is no Jew. Yet he is the representative of what might be called the Heine side of Jewry—the wit and cynicism that reached their greatest intensity in the poet of Young Germany. The more temperate Gideon represents, it is to be feared, a large proportion of English Jews, one not ashamed of his race, yet not proud of it, and willing to see the racial and religious distinctions we have fought for so valiantly die out and perish utterly among men. Perhaps the most successful of the minor portraits is that of the black sheep Lapidoth, the Jew with no redeeming love for family, race, or country to preserve him from that sordid egoism—the new name for wickedness—into which he has sunk. His utter unconsciousness of good and evil is powerfully depicted in the masterly analysis of his state of mind before purloining Deronda's ring. To some extent the weird figure of the Alcharisi serves as a sort of companion picture of female renunciation of racial claims, but the struggle between her rebellious will and what old-fashioned folk call the Will of God (Professor Clifford would perhaps name it the Tribal Will) raises her to a tragic height which makes Deronda's mother perhaps the most imposing figure in the book. Deronda himself, by the circumstance of his education, is prevented from typifying any of the social distinctions of a Jew, yet it is not unlikely that his gravity of manner and many-sided sympathy were meant by the author to be taken as hereditary traits.

These, with Ram the bookseller, the English Jew of the pre-emancipation era, and some minor characters, give to the reader a most complete picture of Jews and Jewesses in their habits as they live, of Jews and Jewesses as members of a peculiar people in relation to the Gentile world. To point the moral of human fallibility, besides some minor slips in ceremonial details, on which it were ungrateful to dwell, we cannot but think (a critic is nothing if not critical) that the author has failed to give in Mirah an adequate type of Jewish girlhood. Mirah is undoubtedly tame; and tameness, for those who know them, is the last infirmity of Jewish girls. Still, even here the sad experience of Mirah's youth may be held to have somewhat palliated any want of brightness, and the extra vivacity of Mrs. Cohen junior perhaps supplies the deficiency.

So much for the outer life of Judaism. The English reader will find here no idea so startlingly novel as to raise opposition to its admission, or to disturb his complacent feeling of superiority over Jews in all but a certain practical sagacity (he calls it sharpness or cunning), which must be postulated to explain the "differentia of success" characterising the Jewish species of commercial dealings. One new fact he may indeed profitably learn: from the large group of Jewish characters in *Daniel Deronda* he may perhaps gather that there are Jews and Jews, that they are not all Lapidoths, nor even all Ezra Cohens, as he has been accustomed to think.

But the new idea of which we have spoken is embodied in the person of Mordecai Cohen, the Jew *par excellence* of the book, the embodiment of the inner life of Judaism. The very fact of this recognition of an inner life, not to speak of the grand personality in which she has typified it, entitles George Eliot to the heart-deep gratitude of all Jews; the more so inasmuch as she has hazarded and, at least temporarily, lost success for her most elaborated production by endeavouring to battle with the commonplace and conventional ideas about Judaism. The present article aims at striking another blow to convince the English world of the existence in the present day, and for all past time, of a spiritual life in Judaism. And we can conceive of no better point of defence for the position than the historic probability of the character of Mordecai, which critics have found so mystic, vague, and impossible.

For those who know anything of the great leaders of spiritual Judaism will recognise in Mordecai all the traits that have characterised them. Saul of Tarsus, Ibn Gebirol (Avice-bron), Jehuda Halevi, Ibn Ezra, Maimonides, Abrabanel, Spinoza, Mendelssohn (not to mention other still more unfamiliar names) were all men like Mordecai—rich in inward wealth, yet content to earn a scanty livelihood by some handicraft; ardently spiritual, yet keenly alive to the claims of home affection; widely erudite, yet profoundly acquainted with human nature; mystics, yet with much method in their mysticism. The author seems even to have a bolder application of the historic continuity of the Hebraic spirit in view: she evidently wishes Mordecai to be regarded as a "survival" of the prophetic spirit, a kind of Isaiah Redivivus. Hence a somewhat unreal effect is produced by his use of a diction similar to what might be expected from a "Greater Prophet" stepping out of the pages of the Authorised Version. Still, it is to be remembered that we almost always see Mordecai in states of intense excitement, when his thought would naturally clothe itself in the forms in which all his literary efforts had been written. He speaks in a sufficiently prosaic and unbiblical style when the subject is prosaic, as to Daniel Deronda at their first meeting (ii. 336): "What are you disposed to give for it?" "I believe Mr. Ram will be satisfied with half-a-crown, sir," remarks sufficiently on the level of nineteenth-century conversation to give Mordecai some community with ordinary folk.

There is yet another quality which Mordecai shares with the sages and prophets of the past: he is a layman. The natural thing for a writer describing "a spiritual destiny embraced eagerly in youth," a representative of the religious life of a nation, would be to describe some young priest ardently striving for the spiritual enlightenment of his flock, some Mr. Tryan, some Savonarola; and it would have been right for all other religions. But in Judaism the inner development of the Spirit has been carried on almost entirely by laymen: the Jewish Summa Theologiae, *The Guide to the Perplexed (Morê Nebouchim)* of Maimonides, was written by a physician. We shall be using more familiar illustrations when we remind the reader that Moses and, above all, the prophets were men from the lay community, not members of an organised priesthood. This may account for that spirit of Compromise (writers of the New English call it "adaptation to environment"), which is as marked a characteristic of the religious history of Jews as of the political history of Englishmen. Other religions have had churches, bureaucracies; Judaism has had a synagogue, a representative assembly.

Mordecai shares yet another gift of his predecessors: he is a poet. The fragment in chapter xxxviii. commencing—

> Away from me the garment of forgetfulness,
> Withering the heart,

might well be a translation from a Piut of Ibn Gebirol or a Selicha of Jehuda Halevi, and makes him a fit *dramatis persona* of that "national tragedy lasting 1500 years, in which the actors have been also the heroes and the poets."

We do not speak without knowledge of the history of Jews, post-biblical as well as biblical, when we say that Mordecai Cohen is a lineal successor of those great leaders of spiritual Judaism who have fought in the van in that moral warfare which Judaism has waged and won against the whole world; a fitting companion of that valiant band which has guarded through the ages the ark of the Lord intrusted to Israel's keeping 4000 years ago; a noble representative of that spirit of resistance that has repulsed the most powerful disintegrating forces ever brought against a nation or a creed. A "nation of shopkeepers" has produced a Milton, a Shelley, a Newman; a "nation of pawnbrokers," if you will, has given birth to a Jehuda Halevi, a Spinoza, a Mordecai. . . .

We have laid so much stress upon the artistic truth of Mordecai's character because, if this be granted, it is inexplicable that the central incident of the Jewish part of *Daniel Deronda,* the meeting on the bridge between him and Deronda, should have failed to strike readers as perhaps the most remarkable incident in English fiction. If Mordecai has artistic reality, we contend that the meeting on the bridge in chapter xl. reaches a tragic intensity which almost transcends the power of the novel, and would perhaps require the manifold emotive inlets of the Wagnerian drama to do it justice—eye, ear, brain, and heart should all be responsive. We boldly deny greater tragic intensity to any incident in Shakespeare. Nor are there wanting signs that the author herself, no contemptible critic of her own productions, sets an equal value on the incident. In the motto prefixed to chapter xxxviii., describing Mordecai's yearnings, she tells us in Brownesque English—

> There be who hold that the deeper tragedy were a Prometheus bound, not *after,* but *before,* he had well got the celestial fire into the narthex, whereby it might be conveyed to mortals. Thrust by the Kratos and Bia of instituted methods into a solitude of despised ideas, fastened in throbbing helplessness by the fatal pressure of poverty and disease—a solitude where many pass by, but none regard.

In other words, George Eliot considers the circumstances of Mordecai's fate to surpass in tragic pathos the most colossal monument of Greek dramatic art. Notice, too, the care with which she leads up to the incident. In chapter xxxvii.

we have Deronda coming to the Meyricks at Chelsea to announce to Mirah the forthcoming visit of Klesmer, and the chapter finishes as he is leaving Chelsea. The next chapter (xxxviii.) is filled with a description of Mordecai's yearning for a spiritual successor, and give us *en passant* a fine picture of the scene of the meeting (iii. 137). We get here, in short, all we need to understand and sympathise with the final episode of the "book;" but lest we should come upon the fulfilment of the prophecy with too vivid a memory of the author's sublimation of the idea of prophecy, we have interposed, like a comic scene in an Elizabethan tragedy, the magnificent account of Klesmer's visit to the Meyricks in chap. xxxix., which clearly occurred *after* the events described in chapter xl., which takes up the stream of narrative from chapter xxxvii.

It seems to us clear that all this seemingly inartistic transposition of events is intended to make the incident of chapter xl. stand out more sharply into relief. We have the miracle explained away, it is true—the modern analytic spirit requires it—but the author wishes us to forget the explanation, or at least to relegate the intellectual element of chapter xxxviii. to the unconscious background, where it may be ready to assist, though not present to obstruct, emotion. All this care appears to show the importance attached by the author to the last chapter of Book v.

And in itself, apart from what the author may think of it, what a soul-moving incident is there contained! A representative of an ancient world-important people, whose royalty of wrongs makes the aristocracies of Europe appear petty, finds himself clutched by the gripping hands of want and death before he can move the world to that vision of the Phoenix-rise of Israel which the prophetic instincts of his race have brought up clear before him. Careless of his own comfort, careless of coming death, he desires only to live anew—as the quasi-Positivist doctrine of the Cabbala bids him live—in "minds made nobler by his presence." His prophetic vision pictures to him the very lineaments of his spiritual *alter ego,* whom he pathetically thinks of as differing from himself in all externals, and, as death draws nigh, the very scene of their meeting. And in this nineteenth century, in prosaic London, this inward vision of the poor consumptive Jew is fulfilled to the letter.

Would it be too bold a suggestion if we suspected the author of having typified in the meeting of Deronda and Mordecai that

One far-off divine event
To which the whole creation moves,

the meeting of Israel and its Redeemer? In personal characteristics, in majestic gravity (we cannot imagine Deronda laughing), in width of sympathy and depth of tenderness, even in outward appearance, Daniel resembles the great

Galilean Pharisee whom all Christendom has accepted as in very truth the Messiah that will restore Judaea to the Holy People. To say the least, the author suggests the audacity in her comparison of the two to the figures of Jesus and the Pharisee in Titian's "Tribute Money." . . .

Enough has perhaps been said to show that Mordecai's views about the future of Judaism and of Jews have all history and much reason on their side, and display those powers of intellectual intuition of the future which the psychological system of Maimonides assigns to the Prophet. And we have perhaps contributed somewhat to an explanation of Deronda's acceptance of his spiritual inheritance. Like Mordecai, Deronda protests against the "blasphemy of the time," that men should stand by as spectators of life instead of living. But before he meets with Mordecai, what noble work in life has this young and cultured Englishman with his thousands a year? This age of unfaith gives no outlet for his deep, spiritual yearnings, nor for those of thousands like him. The old beliefs are gone; the world is godless, and Deronda cannot, for all the critics have said, offer to Gwendolen Grandcourt any consolation in the higher order of things instead of the vague platitudes which alone remain to be offered. Yet there comes to this young ardent soul an angel of the Lord (albeit in the shape of a poor Jew watch-mender) with a burning message, giving a mission in life as grand as the most far-reaching ideal he could have formed. Is it strange that his thirsty soul should have swallowed up the soul of Mordecai, in the Cabbalistic way which the latter often refers to? Is it strange that Deronda should not have refused the heritage of his race when offered by the hands of Mirah's brother? But is it not strange that the literary leaders of England should have failed to see aught but unsatisfactory vagueness in all the parts of *Daniel Deronda* which treat of the relations of the hero with Mordecai Cohen? Is it possible that they have failed to see the grandeur and beauty of these incidents because of the lack of that force of imagination necessary to pierce to the pathos of a contemporary tragedy, however powerful their capacity might be to see the romance of a Rebecca of York, or the pathos of a Baruch Spinoza?

One possible source of misconception for English readers may be mentioned. Since the time of Moses Mendelssohn the home of spiritual Judaism has been in Germany, and George Eliot, whose pages are informed with the writings of German Jews like Zunz, Geiger, and Gratz, has, with true historic insight, attributed Mordecai's spiritual birth to the teachings of his German uncle. English Judaism is without signs of life: the only working of the spirit, the abortive reform agitation, was due to a similar movement in Germany. And English Jews have themselves much to blame for the neglect that English criticism has shown for Mordecai.

What we have attempted to show has been that the adverse criticism on the Mordecai part of *Daniel Deronda* has been due to lack of sympathy and want of knowledge on the part of the critics, and hence its failure is not (if we must use the word) objective. If a young lady refuses to see any pathos in Othello's fate because she dislikes dark complexions, we blame the young lady, not Shakespeare; and if the critics have refused to see the pathos of Mordecai's fate because he is a Jew of the present day, so much the worse for the critics.

—Joseph Jacobs, "Mordecai: A Protest Against the Critics," *Macmillan's Magazine*, 1877, reprinted in *Jewish Ideals and Other Essays*, 1896, pp. 61–83

OLIVER ELTON "GEORGE ELIOT AND ANTHONY TROLLOPE" (1920)

Oliver Elton (1861–1945) was an English literary scholar and translator. Elton worked as a private tutor, reviewer, and translator before his appointment as English lecturer at the University of Manchester in 1890 and, starting in 1901, at the University of Liverpool (then a college). Elton published three surveys of English literature, spanning the eighteenth and nineteenth centuries, and an account of English poetry: *The English Muse: A Sketch* (1933).

In the 1920s, *Daniel Deronda* did little to redress Eliot's lack of popularity. Elton's account of the novel provides a trivial summary of the status of the novel at a time when Eliot's reputation was at its lowest point. Elton agrees that it is too easy to undervalue the novel, but his description of the novel confirms the dissatisfaction with the novel far more than it challenges it. It remained common to praise Gwendolen, perceive Grandcourt as something of a theatrical villain, and dismiss Deronda as a prig. Elton pursues with a denigration of the Jewish portions of the novel that provides further evidence that anti-Semitism continued to add to the novel's poor reputation: Elton's condescending comments undermine a serious point about the problematic representation of Deronda's gradual identification as a Jewish man. Elton's dismissive stance continues with his amusement at Eliot's "philosophic talks with the author of *Social Statics*." Herbert Spencer, rather than Lewes, to whom Elton presumably aimed to refer, authored *Social Statics*. It would be left to later critics to give *Daniel Deronda* the attention it deserved.

Daniel Deronda (1876), which unsealed the lips of the scorner, shows misguidance rather than failure of power; but the book can easily be undervalued. It is duly blamed for its excess of dissertation and dissection; and, what is worse, there seems to be a wrong twist in the moral sympathies of the great moralist. Gwendolen Harleth is another victim of folly in marriage. Her pride and humbling, her agony of helpless hatred for her husband, are drawn with bitter strength; of all George Eliot's ladies she is the most alive. The authoress drops on her a load of brickbats, and seems to wish to leave the impression that Gwendolen deserves them. But then she does not deserve them. Her worst fault is to be handsome. She is young and rather hard, sprightly and rather domineering. We feel that she would have made better terms with the aristocratic boa-constrictor, Grandcourt. Some critics have hinted, with justice, that George Eliot's upbringing hardly qualified her to draw the Wicked Blasé Swell. But at all costs the young lady's moral nature must be awakened. She is almost as much tormented by her lay confessor, Deronda (who assures us that he is 'not a priest'), as by her husband. She explains how a sudden, paralysing impulse (all too human) had kept her from throwing a rope to the drowning Grandcourt. Deronda remarks that he would probably anyhow have sunk with the cramp; but he practically adds that Gwendolen must all the same treat herself as a murderess in heart and intention, and must flagellate her soul; which she duly does, and her life is broken for a time. As for the intent to murder, we know what the verdict of a French jury would have been; and it would be a more truly moral one than Deronda's. However, Grandcourt never really existed; how then, we may frivolously add, could he be murdered? One may yawn, laugh, or cry over the whole Judaic business in this novel; it has found few to praise it, in spite, as Sir Leslie Stephen pleasantly says, of 'the approval of learned Jews.' People have mocked at the enormous satisfaction shown by an English gentleman who finds out that he is a Jew:

> Feelings had lately been at work within him which had very much modified the reluctance he would formerly have had to think of himself as probably a Jew.

I would rather say that Deronda is not a Jew. He has no resemblance within or without, to a Jew good or bad. All Jews are salient; he is featureless. They love arguing, they are dialecticians even in the family circle; he preaches, no doubt with a certain taste for casuistry. His very ethics are occidental. The little boy Jacob and the thieving old sponger Lapidoth (*Schnorrer* is, I believe, the correct word) are much more satisfactory. George Eliot protested well against vulgar anti-Semitism; she studied, she appreciated, the loftier dreams of modern Israel; but she could not embody them. Yet it is not safe to leave the book unread. The old skill is there in the light sketches of the country gentry. The gambling scene at the outset makes us hope for an honest, full-blown romance; and some sound melodrama, some healthy violence, we do get in the scenes with Grandcourt's cast mistress and the fatal diamonds. It is singular to think of the inventress of these things enjoying walks and philosophic talks with the author of Social Statics.

—Oliver Elton, "George Eliot and
Anthony Trollope," *A Survey of English Literature,
1780–1880*, vol. 4 (1920), pp. 265–267

Chronology

1819   Mary Anne Evans born November 22 on the Arbury estate, Warwickshire, to Robert Evans, carpenter and estate agent, and his wife, Christiana Pearson Evans, daughter of a yeoman farmer.

1824–35   Educated first at a local dame school, then at boarding schools in Attleborough, Nuneaton, and Coventry. In 1832, she witnesses the election riot caused by the first Reform Bill.

1836   Death of mother. Evans and elder sister take over management of the household.

1837   Marriage of elder sister; Evan's runs the household herself. Studies Italian, German, and music under tutors.

1838   Visits London for the first time with her brother Isaac. Schooling has made Evans a zealous evangelical. Returns to father's house.

1841   Evans and her father move to Coventry. Reads Charles Hennell's *Inquiry into the Origins of Christianity* and Bray's *The Philosophy of Necessity*. Converted from evangelical Christianity to "a crude state of free-thinking."

1842   Refuses to attend church with her father; later returns to Coventry and to church (although not to her old beliefs).

1843–44   Stays with Dr. and Mrs. Brabant at Devizes. Works on a translation of Strauss's *Das Leben Jesu*. Leaves precipitously, probably at the insistence of Mrs. Brabant, because of her strong admiration for the elderly intellectual Dr. Brabant. Returns to Coventry and continues work on the translation, which is published in 1846.

1845   Rejects a marriage proposal from an artist friend. Teaches herself Hebrew.

1849   Death of father. Begins translation of Spinoza's *Tractatus Theologico-Politicus*. Travels to Geneva, where she remains until 1850.

1850–53	Returns to England, becomes assistant (acting) editor of *Westminster Review*. Friendship with Herbert Spencer and George Henry Lewes, critic and author.
1854	Publishes translation of Feuerbach's *The Essence of Christianity*. Takes up residence in Germany with Lewes. Meets Liszt. Beings a translation of Spinoza's *Ethics*.
1855	Returns to England, where she and Lewes take up residence in Richmond. Evans is not received by her family.
1856	Begins to write fiction.
1858	*Scenes of Clerical Life* is published under the name George Eliot. Dickens writes Eliot that he is sure she is a woman; her identity is made public after the book is attributed to a dissenting clergyman of Nuneaton.
1859	Publishes *Adam Bede*. Established as leading woman novelist of the day.
1860	Publishes *The Mill on the Floss*.
1861	Publishes *Silas Marner*. Begins writing *Romola*.
1862	Publishes *Romola* serially in *The Cornhill Magazine*, of which Lewes had recently become consulting editor.
1866	Publishes *Felix Holt, the Radical*.
1868	Publishes *The Spanish Gypsy*.
1869	Meets John Cross, a wealthy businessman.
1871–72	*Middlemarch* is published in parts.
1874	Publishes *The Legend of Jubal and Other Poems*.
1876	Publication of *Daniel Deronda* in parts.
1877	Eliot and Lewes received by Princess Louise and the Crown Princess of Germany, daughter of Queen Victoria.
1878	Meets Turgenev. Lewes toasts Turgenev's health, calling him the greatest living novelist. Turgenev insists the title belongs to Eliot. Lewes dies on November 30 of cancer.
1879	Works on preparing edition of essays, *Impressions of Theophrastus Such*, for press. John Blackwood, her publisher, dies on October 29.
1880	Eliot marries John Walter Cross (20 years her junior). Dies on December 22 at her home in Cheyne Walk.
1885	John Cross publishes *George Eliot's Life*.

Index

A

Adam (*Adam Bede*), 114
Adam Bede, 107–119
    aunt as source for, 114
    autobiographical element of, 62, 118
    characterization main strength of, 110
    confiscation of from child, 60
    critical acclaim for, 107–108, 119
    Dickens's praise of, 108–109
    Eliot on, 118, 119
    female authorship and, 119, 120
    life of Midland dairies, 149
    publication of, 25, 68
    sensation and frailty in, 112, 113
    style of, 27
    writing of, 113–114
agnosticism, 5–6, 7, 12, 15, 32, 53, 59, 100
Allen, Grant, 19
American Prose Masters (Brownell), 72
Arthur Donnitahorne (*Adam Bede*), 114, 118
Aurora Floyd (Braddon), 27
Austen, Jane, Eliot compared to, 120, 168
autobiographical elements in work
    Adam Bede, 43, 62, 118, 130
    Mill on the Floss, The 43
    Scenes of Clerical Life, 101–102
Autobiography of Mark Rutherford, The (White), 21–22

B

Biographical History of Philosophy (Lewes), 6
biography, 1–2
    birth of, 1
    burial at Highgate, 7
    Christian burial in Abby denied, 8
    death of, 2
    early life, 15, 83–84
    education, 151
    Poets' Corner memorial, 7
    See also Cross, John Walter; Lewes, George Henry
Blackwood, John, 100, 104, 118
Blackwood's Edinburgh Magazine, 1, 100
Blind, Mathilde, 12, 144–146
Bloom, Harold, xi–xii
Braddon, Mary Elizabeth, 26–27
Brontë, Charlotte, Eliot compared to, 119, 140
Browne, John Hutton Balfour, 153–154
Brownell, William Crary, 72–77
Browning, Oscar, 61–64, 101–105
Bulstrode (*Middlemarch*), 157–158, 159, 165, 168

Burton, Richard Eugene, 77–78
Byron, May Clarissa Gillington, 19

C

Caleb Garth (*Middlemarch*), 157
Carlyle, Jane Welsh, 107–108
Chapman, John, 21
Collins, Wilkie, 27
Colvin, Sidney, 155–159
Comte's Philosophy of the Sciences (Spencer), 7
Cooke, George Willis, 51–60
criticisms
    ascetic tone of work, 58
    asides and, 34–35, 39
    caricatural sound bites, 64–66
    characterization main strength, 42–43
    confessor's point of view, 41–42
    English country life in early work, 31, 41, 84–86, 97, 99–100, 137–138
    genius in first period, 35–36
    genius limited by philosophy, 54–55, 59–60
    grave faults in *Felix Holt*, 153–154
    of heroines, 86–88
    individualism suppressed in work, 56–58
    labeling as preacher, 123
    laboriousness of plots, 153
    of male heroes, 44, 65–66, 87, 131, 134, 161
    of *Middlemarch*, 45, 47
    on positivism, 55
    of poetry, 30, 62
    reputation fluctuation, 66–68
    of *Romala*, 45
    true to herself, 152
    as true woman, 40
    uniqueness of work, 37
    works "unreadable," 78, 79
    See also *specific titles*
Cross, John Walter Cross (husband), 2, 7, 12–13

D

Dallas, Eneas Sweetland, 109–111, 123–125
Daniel (*Daniel Deronda*), 41, 171–174
Daniel Deronda, 170–203
    book worth reading for promise of romance, 202–203
    critical difficulties with, 95
    criticisms of, 47, 63–64
    disappointment of, 175–176
    distinguishable from predecessors, 177
    faults of, 170–171, 174–175
    Jewish episodes and, 170, 173, 183–184, 188–189, 201, 202
    See also "Mordecai: A Protest Against the Critics"
    merits of, 170
    as nightmare, 68
    praise for, 12, 71
    reassessment prediction for, 175–176
    rehabilitation of, 61, 64
    as a romance novel, 176
    undervalued by critics, 201–202
    See also "Daniel Deronda: A Conversation"; *names of characters*
"*Daniel Deronda*: A Conversation" (James), 177–193
    book full of life and the world, 192
    conversation setting, 178
    Deronda as a "brilliant failure," 184
    Deronda as advisor to Gwendolen, 186–187
    Deronda defended as being ideal character, 185
    Deronda's relationship with Gwendolen, 189
    disagreement on Mordecai's manliness, 181
    discussion on characters as real, 181

elements in Eliot not in earlier work, 187
Eliot compared to George Sand, 182–183
Eliot compared to Turgenieff, 184–185
Eliot's style seen as "baggy," 186
Gwendolen's character, 190–191
Jewish episodes discussed, 183–184, 188–189
last chapter found comical by some, 179
Meyricks as good characters, 180, 192
pedantic and pretentious, 180, 192
slowness compared to *Romola*, 179
tactlessness throughout book, 187–188
Theodora wants book to never end, 180
weakest of Eliot's books (Constantius), 181–182
Dickens, Charles, 108–109
Dickinson, Emily, 12–13
Dinah Morris (*Adam Bede*), 114, 117, 130
Dorothea (*Middlemarch*), 161, 162, 163, 168–169
Dowden, Edward, 27–29

E
early versus later works
early works more successful, 41, 50–51, 84–86, 106–107
maturity in later work, 68, 69, 71
reputation fluctuation, 31
Scenes versus *Felix Holt*, 153–154
works divided in two groups, 25–28
See also reputation, fluctuation of
Elton, Oliver, 201–203
Esther (*Felix Holt*) Felix and, 151

Evans, Marian (Mary Ann) (George Eliot, pseud), 1–2
Ezra (*Daniel Deronda*), 195

F
Felix (*Felix Holt*), Esther and, 151
Felix Holt, 147–154
back to Midland homesteads, 147–148
characterization in, 149–150
evil usage of woman by men, 150
grave faults in, 153–154
minor work in 20th century, 94
radicalism and, 152
scenes from, 149
slowness of plot, 153
women at hands of men, 147, 150–151
See also *names of characters*
fiction, psychological, 72–73, 78
Ford, Ford Madox, 78–80
Francillon, Robert Edward, 175–177
Fred Vincy (*Middlemarch*), 157, 159, 161

G
gender stereotypes
author as ugly and humorless, 20–21
boldness of "modern female novelist," 119–120, 151–152
caricature of Eliot by Myers, 11–12
Dickenson on female artists, 12–13
female artists primarily autobiographical, 66–67
harsh criticism withheld for "male" author, 93
ideas "unbecoming in a woman," 34
Novel-with-a-Purpose, 65–66
woman limited by feminine concerns, 32, 43–44, 48, 63–64

"George Eliot as I Knew Her" (White), 21–22
George Eliot's Life as Related in Her Letters and Journals (Cross), 13–14
Grandcourt (*Daniel Deronda*), 171–172, 202
Great Tradition, The (Leavis), 26
Gwendolen Harleth (*Daniel Deronda*), 171, 172, 174, 202

H

Harrison, Frederic, 138–140
Heir of Redclyffe, The (Yonge), 60
Henley, William Ernest, 64–66
Hetty (*Adam Bede*), 62, 108, 113
"How Lisa Loved the King" (poem), 30
humor, 31, 38–39, 76, 86, 119, 125
Hutton, Richard Holt, 140–144
Huxley, Thomas Henry, 7–8

I

identity of Eliot
    adoption of pseudonym, 1
    clergyman suspected as author, 100–101
    discovery of, 118–119
    gender guessed by Dickens, 108, 109
    Liggins's claim to authorship, 105
    revelation of, 5, 119, 120
    speculation on after *Scenes*, 1, 93
    See also gender stereotypes
individualism, suppression of, 56–58

J

Jacobs, Joseph, 193–201
James, Henry, 15, 137–138, 159–166, 177–193

K

Kegan, Paul, 8–10
Kenyon, James Benjamin, 112–113

L

Lady Auden's Secret (Braddon), 27
Lapidoth (*Daniel Deronda*), 195
Lathrop, George Parsons, 166–167
Leavis, F.R., 26
legacy, 32–33
"Legend of Jubal, The" (poem), 30
Lewes, George Henry
    Adam Bede and, 113–114
    death of, 2
    Eliot and, 5–6, 10–11, 16, 84, 96–97
    public perception of relationship, 16–17, 19, 107
    Trollope and, 50–51
    unfounded rumor about, 61
Life of Goethe (Lewes), 10–11
lifestyle, irregular. *See* Lewes, George Henry
Liggins, Joseph, authorship claimed by, 100, 105
Lydgate (*Middlemarch*), 163–164, 168

M

Maggie (*Mill on the Floss*)
    Eliot on, 131
    as Eliot's "double," 130
    as heroine, 43
    pitiable character, 129
    Stephen and, 132–133
Mary Garth (*Middlemarch*), 160, 161
Maxwell, John, 27
Methodism, 93, 113, 117
Middlemarch, 154–169
    Bloom on, xii
    characterization in, 157–158, 160–165
    charm lost to intellectuality, 155, 159
    conclusion of, 49
    dignity of minor characters in, 168
    as Eliot's greatest work, 155
    great prose epic, 63
    harmony of construction in, 154

harshness against town, 166
imaginative psychological study, 154
Lewes's influence on, 10–11
limits set on old-fashioned English novel, 166
loss of simplicity in, 165–166
as painful book, 45–47
pathos in, 164
praise for, 71, 86, 94–95, 154–155
protest against modern society, 167, 169
social significance of, 167–168, 169
strengths vs. weaknesses of, 160–166
too much effort in, 166–167
warmth lacking in, 25, 48
See also *names of characters*
Mill on the Floss, 119–134
absence of religion in, 123
autobiographical element of, 43, 130
bleakness of, 123
characterization in, 121
childhood depicted in, 123, 124–125
as "Cockney literature," 129–130
criticisms of, 43, 44
echoes of Greek tragedy in, 123, 124
Eliot as preacher in, 123, 124
evil usage of woman by men, 150
humor in, 119, 125
mixed reception of, 93–94
passions objected to in, 119–120, 121–123
popularity of, 119, 120
publication of, 16, 25
realism offensive in depicting rural life, 123, 124
as rural chronicle of families, 149
sordid nature of characters, 128, 129

strong critical reactions to, 125–126
Swinburne's praise for, 126
third volume of, 126–128, 131–133, 134
use of dialogue in, 119
See also *names of characters*
Mirah (*Daniel Deronda*), 186, 196
modernism, 77–78, 155–157
Mordecai (*Daniel Deronda*), 170, 172, 173, 195
"Mordecai: A Protest Against the Critics" (Jacobs), 193–201
overview, 193–194
adverse criticism on the Jewish episodes due to lack of sympathy, 201
bridge meeting between Mordecai and Deronda, 198–199
Deronda's acceptance of spiritual inheritance, 200
Eliot's revelation of "Jews and Jews," 196
Gwendolen's purification from egoism, 194
Jews faithfully described by Eliot, 195–196
Judaism/Christianity part of book, 194
Mordecai as layman, 197
Mordecai as poet, 197–198
Mordecai as representative of Judaism, 197
Mordecai as successor of spiritual Judaism, 198
two unconnected parts of *Deronda*, 194
Morley, John, 146
Mr. Brooke (*Middlemarch*), 165
Mr. Cadwallader (*Middlemarch*), 168
Mr. Casaubon (*Middlemarch*), 162, 164, 168
Mr. Garth (*Middlemarch*), 165
Mr. Irwine (*Adam Bede*), 110–111, 117

Mrs. Bulstrode (*Middlemarch*), 157
Mrs. Cadwallader (*Middlemarch*), 165
Mrs. Poyser (*Adam Bede*)
    comparison with Mrs. Cadwallader, 165
    pithy sayings of, 109, 111, 117
    unequaled as character, 121
Myers, Frederic William Henry, 11–12

N
Novel-with-a-Purpose, 64–65

O
"O may I join the choir invisible" (poem), 30
Oliphant, Margaret, 16–17

P
personal characteristics
    overview, 5–7
    evolutionary ideas, 69, 70
    as hostess in the Heights in Witley, 9–10
    lack of self-confidence in writing, 96, 104
    physical appearance, 6, 11–12, 15, 18–19, 20, 82
    positivism, 8–9, 51–52
    respectability, 21–22
    speaking voice, 18–19
    poetry, 30, 62, 68
    positivism, 8–9, 51–52, 55, 138

R
radicalism of Eliot, 151–153
realist novelists, 27
reputation, fluctuation of
    overview, 25–26
    caricatural sound bites and, 64–65
    demise of popularity, 72–73
    as novelist of past, 78–80
    twentieth century reevaluation, 66–68, 81–82
    See also early vs later works
Romola, 140–147
    academic quality of, 146
    characterization in, 141
    criticisms of, 45, 47, 48
    Eliot exhausted by effort, 145
    evil usage of woman by men, 150
    flawed masterpiece, 160
    historical novel, 62–63, 140, 145
    Lewes not responsible for, 146
    loss of simplicity in, 166
    most grandly planned of writings, 145–146
    praise for, 71, 142, 144
    research on, 25, 30
    Savonarola and, 143–144
    seriousness of, 60
    sharp depreciation of, 94
    unsuited to serialization, 1, 141
Rosamond (*Middlemarch*), 158, 164, 168
Ruskin, John, 128–130

S
Saintsbury, George, 66–68, 170–175
Sala, George Augustus, 112
Salem Chapel (Oliphant), 16
Savonarola, Eliot compared to, 18, 143
Scenes of Clerical Life, 95–107
    "Amos Barton," 1, 106–107
    autobiographical element of, 101–102
    commonplace lives as topic of, 118
    critical success of, 118
    Eliot on writing of, 95–97
    Eliot thought to be Liggins, 100–101, 105
    first book, 84, 97
    "Janet's Repentance," 101, 104–105, 106, 107

"Mr. Gilfil's Love-Story," 102–104, 106
   review on publication, 97–100
   serialization of, 1, 100
   women at center of, 40–41
Scudder, Vida D., 69–71, 167–169
Sedgwick, Arthur, 151–153
sensation novelists, 27
Silas Marner, 134–140
   acclaimed in 20th century, 94
   affection for, 25
   exquisite workmanship of, 62
   as fairy tale, 60
   gem-like quality of, 61
   opening of, 65
   portraits of poor without rival, 135
   Rainbow Inn scenes and, 134, 135–136, 149
   Shakespeare and, 134, 137
   simplicity of plot, 138–139
   superiority of opening to sequel, 43
   superior to previous novels, 137
   unsigned review of, 134–137
Simcox, Edith, 10–11, 154–155
Simpson, Richard, 100–101
Spanish Gypsy, The, 2, 30, 173
Spencer, Herbert, 7
Stedman, Edmund Clarence, 30
Stephen, Leslie
   "George Eliot" (1881), 31–49
   George Eliot (1902), 113–119, 130–134, 146–147
   on Eliot's shift in style, 25
Stephen Guest (*Mill on the Floss*), 43, 131, 132–133, 134
St. Theresa, Eliot on, 169
style of Eliot
   absence of, 74–77
   didacticism criticized, 63–66
   intellectuality of, 50–51, 153
   obscurity of passages, 166
   as pedantic, 72, 76
   pedestrian, 79
   portraits from the past, 82–83
   realism and, 27, 77–78, 99, 123, 124, 152
   sensational plot devices, 27
   spiritual appeal of work, 69
   work crippled by philosophy, 59
   See also early vs later works
Swinburne, Algernon Charles, 125–128

T

Thackeray, Eliot and, 77–78
themes
   cheerlessness, 58
   conflict between private desires and duty, 27–29, 174
   obscure lives contribute to human happiness, 30
   organic social life, 52, 56
   outward beauty/inward ugliness, 27
   praise of feeling, 55, 56
   self-renunciation, 52
   sympathy, 109
   tradition vs. modernity, 52, 53–54
   woman in need of confessor, 41
Tito (*Romola*), 62–63, 164
Tom (*Mill on the Floss*), 43, 129, 130
Tomlinson, May, 106–107
Trollope, Thomas Adolphus, 17–19, 25, 50–51, 79–80, 140

U

unsigned reviews
   Mill on the Floss, 119–123
   Scenes of Clerical Life, 97–100
   Silas Marner, 134–137

V

Victoria, Queen, 25
Victorian Prose Masters (Brownell), 72

PR
4688
.G372
2009